Java EE 5
Development with NetBeans 6

Develop professional enterprise Java EE 5 applications
quickly and easily with this popular IDE

David R. Heffelfinger

PUBLISHING

BIRMINGHAM - MUMBAI

Java EE 5 Development with NetBeans 6

First published: October 2008

Production Reference: 2241008

Published by Packt Publishing Ltd.
32 Lincoln Road
Olton
Birmingham, B27 6PA, UK.

ISBN 978-1-847195-46-3

www.packtpub.com

Cover Image by Michelle O'Kane (michelle@kofe.ie)

Credits

Author

David R. Heffelfinger

Reviewers

David Salter

Mario Pérez Madueño

Senior Acquisition Editor

Douglas Paterson

Development Editor

Swapna V. Verlekar

Technical Editor

Bhupali Khule

Editorial Team Leader

Akshara Aware

Project Manager

Abhijeet Deobhakta

Project Coordinator

Neelkanth Mehta

Indexer

Monica Ajmera

Proofreader

Cathy Cumberlidge

Production Coordinator

Shantanu Zagade

Cover Work

Shantanu Zagade

About the Author

David Heffelfinger is the Chief Technology Officer of Ensode Technology, LLC, a software consulting firm based in the greater Washington DC area. He has been architecting, designing, and developing software professionally since 1995, and has been using Java as his primary programming language since 1996. He has worked on many large scale projects for several clients including the US Department of Homeland Security, Freddie Mac, Fannie Mae, and the US Department of Defense. He has a Masters degree in Software Engineering from Southern Methodist University. David is editor in chief of Ensode.net (`http://www.ensode.net`), a web site about Java, Linux, and other technology topics.

I would like to thank everyone at Packt Publishing for making this book a reality. Douglas, Swapna, Bhupali, Neelkanth, Shantanu, Abhijeet, Monica, Camilie, Akshara, without your help and direction, this book wouldn't have been possible.

I would also like to thank the technical reviewers, David Salter and Mario Pérez Madueño; your feedback certainly was essential, greatly improving the quality of the material presented in the book.

Last, and most certainly not least, I would like to thank my wife and daughter for enduring the long hours I spent working on the book, unable to spend time with my family.

About the Reviewers

David Salter is an enterprise software architect who has been developing software professionally since 1991. His relationship with Java goes right back to the beginning, using Java 1.0 for writing desktop applications and applets for interactive web sites. David has been developing Enterprise Java Applications using both the J2EE standards and open source solutions for the last five years. David runs the Java community web site, Develop In Java, a web site for all levels of Java developers. David co-authored the book *Building SOA-Based Composite Applications Using NetBeans IDE 6*.

Mario Pérez Madueño started developing applications for Zeus Sistemas in 1995 using Borland C++ Builder. He graduated in computer science in 2006 and is still studying to obtain a Master's degree in the EHEA, although what he actually would like is the Java programming with passion graduate.

Mario also works most recently as software engineer for Altra Software, helping to develop Java desktop and EE5 applications.

Nothing attracts as much enthusiasm as an IDE for the developer, so Mario is a NetBeans fan. His lastest contributions have been in the NetBeans 6 Spanish localization process and currently as NetCAT 6.5 backup team member.

As technical reviewer, Mario also worked for Packt Publishing on the title *Building SOA-Based Composite Applications Using NetBeans IDE 6*.

My warm acknowledgments always go to María for still supporting or being compatible with Martín, with me, and now also with the great thing she has in her paunch.

Table of Contents

Preface

In 1999, Sun Microsystems split the Java language into three editions, J2SE
(Java 2, Standard Edition), J2ME (Java 2, Micro Edition), and J2EE (Java 2, Enterprise
Edition). The reason for the split was that the Java language was covering a lot of
territory, and not all developers used all the features of the language. To make the
language more manageable, the decision was made to split the language into the
three editions.

Since then, the different editions of the language have been renamed to Java SE,
Java ME, and Java EE. The reason for renaming the different editions was that the
Java platform obtained brand recognition among consumers, and Sun Microsystems
wanted to make it obvious that Java SE, ME, and EE were recognized as part of the
Java platform.

All three editions share the core of the Java language, but additional APIs are
included in each edition that are not available in the others. In this book we will
cover Java EE, and how to use NetBeans to more effectively write applications
conforming to the Java EE specification.

What This Book Covers

Chapter 1 provides an introduction to NetBeans, giving time saving tips and tricks
that will result in more efficient development of Java applications.

Chapter 2 covers how NetBeans aids in the development of web applications using
the servlet API and JavaServer Pages.

Chapter 3 shows how NetBeans can help us create maintainable web applications by
taking advantage of JavaServer Pages Standard Tag Library (JSTL), and it also covers
how to write our own custom JSP tags.

Chapter 4 explains how NetBeans can help us easily develop web applications that take advantage of the JavaServer Faces framework.

Chapter 5 explains how NetBeans allows us to easily develop applications taking advantage of the Java Persistence API (JPA), including how to automatically generate JPA entities from existing schemas. This chapter also covers how complete web based applications can be generated with a few clicks from an existing database schema.

Chapter 6 covers the NetBeans visual web JSF designer, which allows us to visually build JSF applications by dragging and dropping components into our JSF pages.

Chapter 7 discusses how NetBeans simplifies EJB 3 session bean development.

Chapter 8 addresses Java EE messaging technologies such as the Java Messaging Service (JMS) and Message Driven Beans (MDB), covering NetBeans features that simplify application development taking advantage of these APIs.

Chapter 9 explains how NetBeans can help us easily develop web services based on the Java API for XML Web Services (JAX-WS) API.

Chapter 10 provides a sample application taking advantages of most of the material covered in the book, including Visual Web JSF, EJB 3, and JPA .

Appendix A provides an introduction to the NetBeans debugger, and how it can be used to discover defects in our application.

Appendix B covers the NetBeans profiler, explaining how it can be used to analyze performance issues in our applications.

Who is This Book For

The book is aimed at three different types of developers:

- Java developers (not necessarily familiar with NetBeans) wishing to become proficient in Java EE 5, and who wish to use NetBeans for Java EE development.

- NetBeans users wishing to find out how to use their IDE of choice to develop Java EE applications.

- Experienced Java EE 5 developers wishing to find out how NetBeans can make their Java EE 5 development easier.

Conventions

In this book, you will find a number of styles of text that distinguish between different kinds of information. Here are some examples of these styles, and an explanation of their meaning.

Code words in text are shown as follows: "Earlier in this chapter we discussed how the `required` attribute for JSF input fields allows us to easily make input fields mandatory."

A block of code will be set as follows:

```
<navigation-rule>
    <from-view-id>/welcomeJSF.jsp</from-view-id>
    <navigation-case>
        <from-outcome>submit</from-outcome>
        <to-view-id>/confirmation.jsp</to-view-id>
    </navigation-case>
</navigation-rule>
```

When we wish to draw your attention to a particular part of a code block, the relevant lines or items will be made bold:

```
<h:inputText id="email" label="Email Address"
        required="true" value="#{RegistrationBean.email}">
    <f:validator validatorId="emailValidator"/>
</h:inputText>
```

Any command-line input and output is written as follows:

```
chmod +x ./filename.sh
```

New terms and **important words** are introduced in a bold-type font. Words that you see on the screen, in menus or dialog boxes for example, appear in our text like this: " At this point JSF navigation "kicks-in", and we are taken to the **Confirmation Page**."

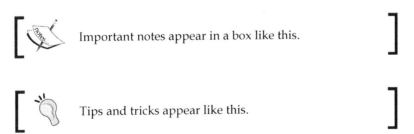

Important notes appear in a box like this.

Tips and tricks appear like this.

Reader Feedback

Feedback from our readers is always welcome. Let us know what you think about this book, what you liked or may have disliked. Reader feedback is important for us to develop titles that you really get the most out of.

To send us general feedback, simply drop an email to feedback@packtpub.com, making sure to mention the book title in the subject of your message.

If there is a book that you need and would like to see us publish, please send us a note in the **SUGGEST A TITLE** form on www.packtpub.com or email suggest@packtpub.com.

If there is a topic that you have expertise in and you are interested in either writing or contributing to a book, see our author guide on www.packtpub.com/authors.

Customer Support

Now that you are the proud owner of a Packt book, we have a number of things to help you to get the most from your purchase.

Downloading the Example Code for the Book

Visit http://www.packtpub.com/files/code/5463_Code.zip to directly download the example code.

The downloadable files contain instructions on how to use them.

Errata

Although we have taken every care to ensure the accuracy of our contents, mistakes do happen. If you find a mistake in one of our books—maybe a mistake in text or code—we would be grateful if you would report this to us. By doing this you can save other readers from frustration, and help to improve subsequent versions of this book. If you find any errata, report them by visiting http://www.packtpub.com/support, selecting your book, clicking on the **let us know** link, and entering the details of your errata. Once your errata are verified, your submission will be accepted and the errata added to the list of existing errata. The existing errata can be viewed by selecting your title from http://www.packtpub.com/support.

Piracy

Piracy of copyright material on the Internet is an ongoing problem across all media. At Packt, we take the protection of our copyright and licenses very seriously. If you come across any illegal copies of our works in any form on the Internet, please provide the location address or website name immediately so we can pursue a remedy.

Please contact us at copyright@packtpub.com with a link to the suspected pirated material.

We appreciate your help in protecting our authors, and our ability to bring you valuable content.

Questions

You can contact us at questions@packtpub.com if you are having a problem with some aspect of the book, and we will do our best to address it.

1

Getting Started with NetBeans

In this chapter, we will cover how to get started with NetBeans, topics covered in this chapter include:

- Introduction
- Downloading NetBeans
- Installing NetBeans
- Starting NetBeans for the first time
- Configuring NetBeans for Java EE development
- Deploying our first application
- NetBeans tips for effective development

Introduction

NetBeans is an **Integrated Development Environment** (IDE) and platform. Although initially the NetBeans IDE could only be used to develop Java applications, as of version 6 NetBeans supports several programming languages, either by built-in support or by installing additional plugins. Programming languages natively supported by NetBeans include Java, C, C++, Ruby, PHP, and Groovy. Developers can use NetBeans' API's to create both NetBeans plugins and standalone applications, taking advantage of NetBeans as a platform.

For a detailed history of NetBeans, see:
http://www.netbeans.org/download/books/definitive-guide/html/apis-c_history.html

The NetBeans IDE supports several programming languages, but because of its roots as Java-only IDE, it is a lot more popular with Java language. As a Java IDE, NetBeans has built-in support for Java SE (Standard Edition) applications, which typically run in the user's desktop or notebook computer; Java ME (Micro Edition), which typically run in small devices such as cell phones or PDAs; and for Java EE (Enterprise Edition) applications, which typically run on "big iron" servers and can support thousands of concurrent users.

In this book, we will be focusing on the Java EE development capabilities of NetBeans, and how to take advantage of NetBeans features to help us develop Java EE applications more efficiently.

Some of the features we will cover include how NetBeans can help us speed up web applications using the Servlet API and JSPs by providing a starting point for these kind of artifacts, and how we can use the NetBeans palette to drag-and-drop code snippets into our JSPs, including HTML and JSP markup. We will also see how NetBeans can help us generate JPA entities from an existing database schema (JPA is the Java Persistence API, the standard Object-Relational mapping tool included with Java EE). We will see how NetBeans allows us to visually create web applications using the JavaServer Faces framework via its visual web development tool.

In addition to web development, we will also see how NetBeans allows us to add business methods to a stateless or stateful session bean in one shot, without having to add the method both to the bean and to its business interface, and how to easily develop web services. We will also cover how to easily write both EJB and web service clients by taking advantage of some very nice NetBeans features.

Before taking advantage of all of the above NetBeans features, we of course need to have NetBeans installed, as covered in the next section.

Downloading NetBeans

NetBeans can be downloaded from `http://www.netbeans.org`.

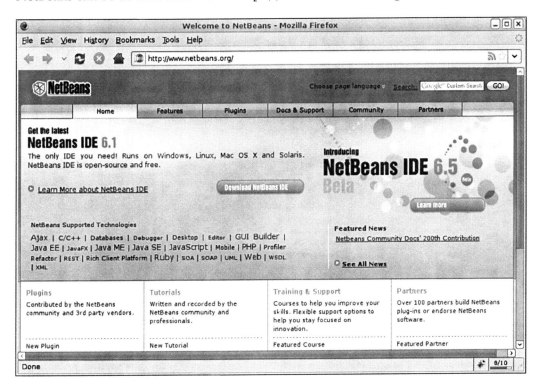

At the time of writing, NetBeans 6.5 is in beta, by publication time it should be the current version. To download NetBeans we need to click on the button labeled **Download NetBeans IDE**. Clicking on this button will take us to a page displaying all of NetBeans download bundles.

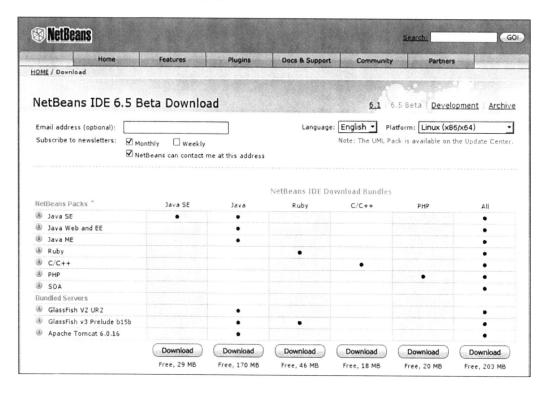

NetBeans download bundles contain different NetBeans Packs that provide different levels of functionality. The following table summarizes the different available NetBeans packs and describes the functionality they provide.

 These packs can also be installed at a later date into an existing NetBeans installation by installing the appropriate plugins.

NetBeans Pack	Description
Java	Includes features for development of Java Standard Edition applications, as well as web and Java Enterprise Edition and mobile applications.
Ruby	Includes features for development of applications written in the Ruby language.
C/C++	Includes features for development of applications written in the C or C++ languages.
PHP	Includes features for development of PHP applications.
All	Includes functionality of all NetBeans packs.

To follow the examples in this book, either the **Java** or the **All** Pack is needed.

 The screenshots in this book were taken with the **All** Pack. NetBeans may look slightly different if the **Java** Pack is used, particularly, some menu items might be missing.

The following platforms are officially supported:

- Windows 2000/XP/Vista
- Linux x86
- Linux x64
- Solaris x86
- Solaris x64
- Mac OS X

Additionally, NetBeans can be used under any platform containing JDK 5.0 or newer. To download a version of NetBeans to be used under one of these platforms, an OS independent version of NetBeans is available for download.

 Although the OS-independent version of NetBeans can be executed in all of the supported platforms, it is recommended to obtain the platform-specific version of NetBeans for your platform.

The NetBeans download page should detect the operating system being used to access it, and the appropriate platform should be selected by default. If this is not the case, or if you are downloading NetBeans with the intention of installing it in another workstation on another platform, the correct platform can be selected from the drop-down labeled, appropriately enough, **Platform**.

Once the correct platform has been selected, we need to click on the appropriate download button for the NetBeans pack we wish to install; for Java EE development, we need either the **Java** or the **All** Pack. NetBeans will then be downloaded to a directory of our choosing.

 Java EE applications need to be deployed to an application server. Several application servers exist in the market, both the **Java** and the **All** NetBeans Packs come with GlassFish bundled. GlassFish is a 100 percent Java EE compliant application server. We will be using the bundled GlassFish application server to deploy and execute our examples.

Installing NetBeans

NetBeans requires a **Java Development Kit** (JDK) version 5.0 or newer to be available before it can be installed.

 Since this book is aimed at experienced Java Developers, we will not spend much time explaining how to install and configure the JDK, since we can safely assume the target market for the book more than likely has a JDK installed. Installation instructions for JDK 6 Update 3 (the latest at the time of writing) can be found at http://java.sun.com/javase/6/webnotes/install/index.html.

Readers wishing to use Mac OS X can get installation instructions and the JDK download for their platform at http://developer.apple.com/java/, please note that Java 5 is supplied as standard with OS X 10.4 and above, as such Mac OS X developers should not need to download the JDK.

NetBeans installation varies slightly between the supported platforms. In the following few sections we'll look at how to install NetBeans on each supported platform.

Microsoft Windows

For Microsoft Windows platforms, NetBeans is downloaded as an executable file named something like **netbeans-6.5-windows.exe** (the exact name depends on the version of NetBeans and the NetBeans pack that was selected for download). To install NetBeans on Windows platforms, simply navigate to the folder where NetBeans was installed and double-click on the executable file that was downloaded.

Mac OS X

For Mac OS X, the downloaded file is called something like **netbeans-6.5-macosx. dmg** (the exact name depends on the NetBeans version and the NetBeans pack that was selected for download). In order to install NetBeans, navigate to the location where the file was downloaded and double-click on it.

The Mac OS X installer contains four packages: NetBeans, Glassfish, Tomcat, and OpenESB. These four packages need to be installed individually; they can be installed by simply double-clicking on each one of them. Please note that GlassFish must be installed before.

Linux and Solaris

For Linux and Solaris, NetBeans is downloaded in the form of a shell script. The name of the file will be something like **netbeans-6.5-linux.sh**, **netbeans-6.5-solaris-x86.sh**, and **netbeans-6.5-solaris-sparc.sh**, depending on the version of NetBeans, the selected platform, and the selected NetBeans pack.

Before NetBeans can be installed in these platforms, the downloaded file needs to be made executable, this can be done in the command line by navigating to the directory where the NetBeans installer was downloaded and executing the following command:

```
chmod +x ./filename.sh
```

Substitute `filename.sh` with the appropriate file name for the platform and NetBeans pack.

Once the file is executable it can be installed from the command line:

```
./filename.sh
```

Again, substitute `filename.sh` with the appropriate file name for the platform and NetBeans pack.

Other Platforms

For other platforms, NetBeans can be downloaded as a platform independent zip file. The name of the zip file will be something like **netbeans-6.5-200811261600.zip** (the exact file name may vary, depending on the version of NetBeans downloaded and the NetBeans pack that was selected).

To install NetBeans on one of these platforms, simply extract the zip file to any suitable directory.

Installation Procedure

Even though the way to execute the installer varies slightly between platforms, the installer behaves in a similar way between all of them.

One exception is the Mac OS X installer. Under Mac OS X, each individual component (NetBeans, GlassFish, Tomcat, and OpenESB) comes with its own installer and must be installed individually. GlassFish must be installed before OpenESB.

Another exception is the platform-independent zip file; in this case there is essentially no installer. Installing this version of NetBeans consists of extracting the zip file to any suitable directory.

After executing the NetBeans installation file for our platform, we should see a window similar to the one illustrated in the following screenshot:

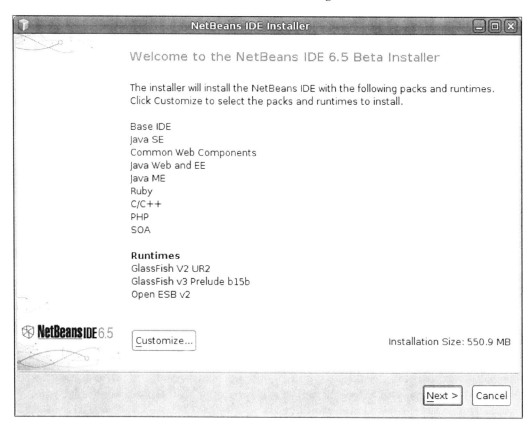

The packs shown may vary depending on the NetBeans pack that was downloaded, the previous screen shot is for the **All** pack.

At this point we should click on the button labeled **Next>** to continue the installation.

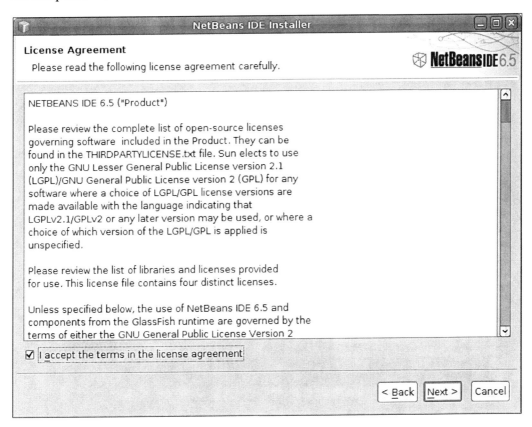

NetBeans is dual licensed. Licenses for NetBeans include the **GNU Public License (GPL)** version 2 with CLASSPATH exception, and the **Common Development and Distribution License (CDDL)**. Both of these licenses are approved by the **Open Source Initiative (OSI)**.

To continue installing NetBeans, click on the checkbox labeled **I accept the terms in the license agreement** and click on the button labeled **Next>**.

At this point the installer will prompt us for a NetBeans installation directory, and for a JDK to use with NetBeans. We can either select new values for these or take the provided defaults.

Once we have selected the appropriate installation directory and JDK, we need to click on the button labeled **Next>** to continue the installation.

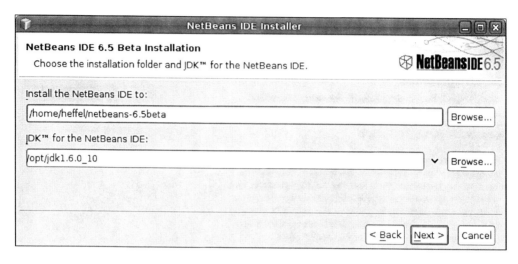

The installer will now prompt us for an installation directory, JDK and other information for the GlassFish 2 application server, usually the defaults are sensible, but we can change them if we have a reason to.

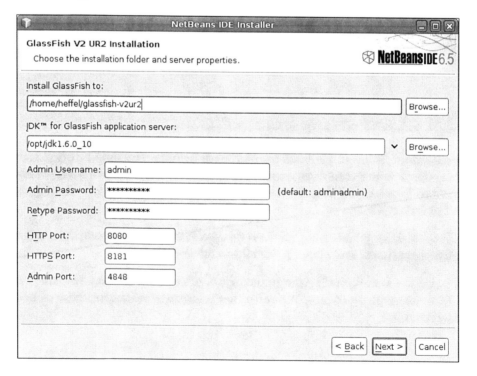

At this point the installer will prompt us for an installation directory for the GlassFish 3 application server, providing a sensible default.

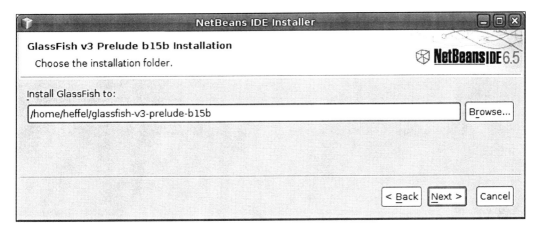

At this point the installer will display a summary of our choices, after reviewing the summary, we need to click on the button labeled **Install** to begin the installation.

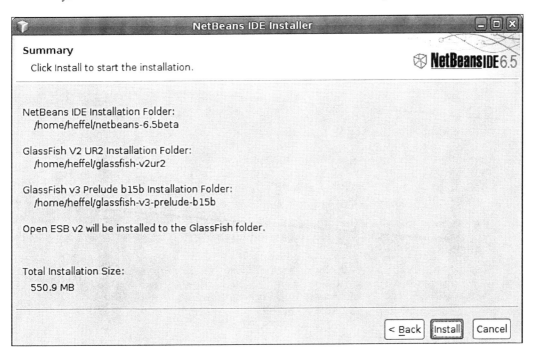

At this point installation will begin, the installer displays a progress bar indicating how far along in the installation it is.

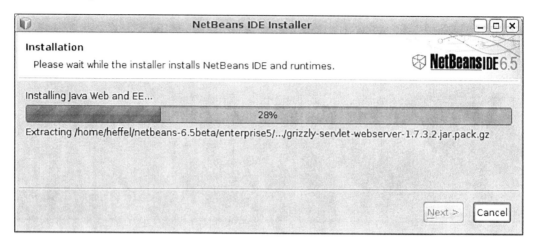

After NetBeans and all related components have been installed, the installer indicates a successful installation.

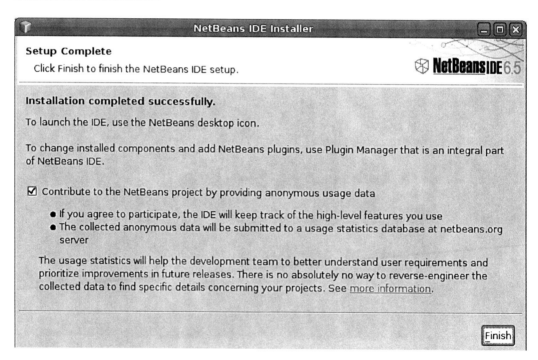

On most platforms, the installer places a NetBeans icon on the desktop, the icon should look like the following image:

Starting NetBeans for the First Time

We can start NetBeans by double-clicking on its icon. We should see the NetBeans splash screen while it is starting up.

 If NetBeans was installed from an OS independent zip file, then the NetBeans icon will not be present in the desktop. For this particular case, NetBeans needs to be started by executing the appropriate binary under the `netbeans/bin directory`.

Once NetBeans starts, we should see a page with links to demos, tutorials, sample projects, and so on.

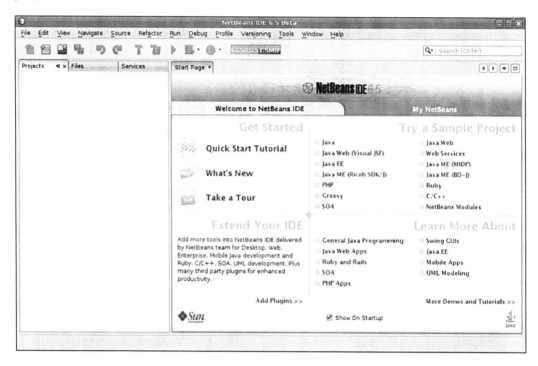

NetBeans defaults to showing this start page every time it is started, if we don't wish for this page to be displayed automatically every time NetBeans is started, we can disable this behavior by unchecking the checkbox labeled **Show on Startup** at the bottom of the page. We can always get the start page back by going to **Help | Start Page**.

Configuring NetBeans for Java EE Development

NetBeans comes pre-configured with the GlassFish 2 application server, and with the JavaDB RDBMS. If we wish to use the embedded GlassFish 2 and JavaDB RDBMS, then there is nothing we need to do to configure NetBeans.

We can, however, integrate NetBeans with other Java EE application servers such as GlassFish 1, Sun Java Application Server, JBoss, Weblogic, or WebSphere. We can also integrate NetBeans with several versions of Tomcat.

Integrating NetBeans with a Third Party Application Server

Integrating NetBeans with an application server is very simple. To do so, we need to take the following steps:

 In this section we will illustrate how to integrate NetBeans with JBoss 4.2.2 (the latest stable release at the time of writing). The procedure is very similar for other application servers or servlet containers.

First, we need to click on the tab labeled **Services**, it can be found at the top-right of the NetBeans main window.

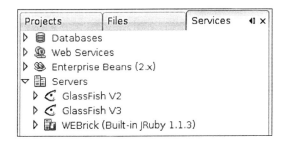

Next, we need to right-click on the node labeled **Servers** in the tree inside the **Services** tab, and select **Add Server...** from the resulting pop-up menu.

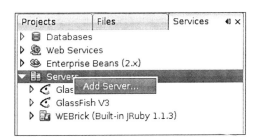

Then we need to select the server to install from the list in the resulting window, and click on the button labeled **Next>**.

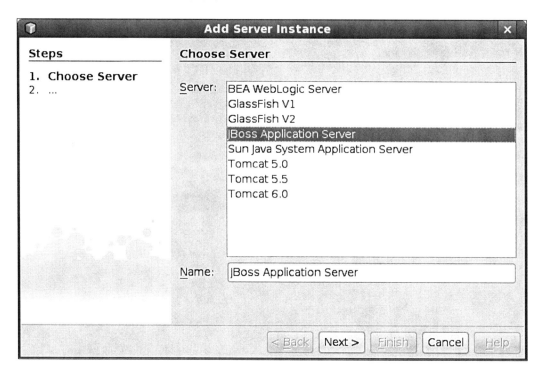

We then need to enter a location in the file system where the application server is installed and click **Next>**.

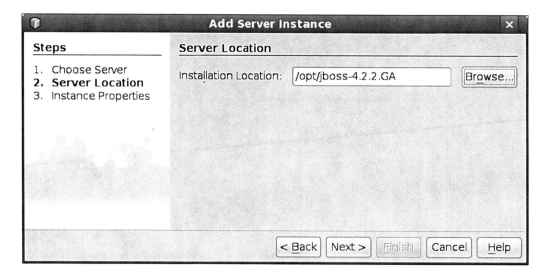

Finally, we need to select a **Domain**, **Host**, and **Port** for our application server, then click on the **Finish** button.

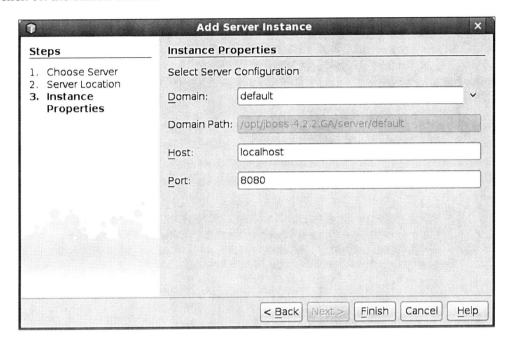

The **Services** tab should now display our newly added application server.

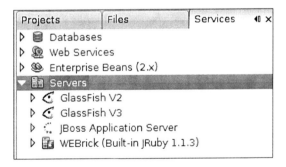

That's it! We have successfully integrated NetBeans with a third party application server.

Integrating NetBeans with a Third Party RDBMS

NetBeans comes with built-in integration with the JavaDB RDBMS system. Additionally, it comes with JDBC drivers for other RDBMS systems such as MySQL and PostgreSQL, as well as the JDBC-ODBC bridge driver to connect to RDBMS systems that don't natively support JDBC or for which a JDBC driver is not readily available.

Although the JDBC-ODBC bridge allows us to connect to most RDBMS systems without having to obtain a JDBC driver, it is usually a better idea to obtain a JDBC driver for our RDBMS. The JDBC-ODBC bridge does not offer the best performance and there are JDBC drivers available for the vast majority of RDBMS systems.

In this section, we will create a connection to HSQLDB, an open source RDBMS written in Java, to illustrate how to integrate NetBeans with a third party RDBMS. The procedure is very similar for other RDBMS systems such as Oracle, Sybase, SQL Server, and so on.

Adding a JDBC Driver to NetBeans

Before we can connect to a third party RDBMS, we need to add its JDBC driver to NetBeans. To add the JDBC driver, we need to right-click on the **Drivers** node under the **Databases** node in the **Services** tab.

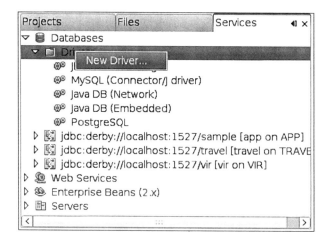

We then need to select a JAR file containing the JDBC driver for our RDBMS. NetBeans guesses the name of the driver class containing the JDBC driver. If more than one driver class is found in the JAR file, the correct one can be selected from the drop-down menu labeled **Driver Class**. We need to click the **OK** button to add the driver to NetBeans.

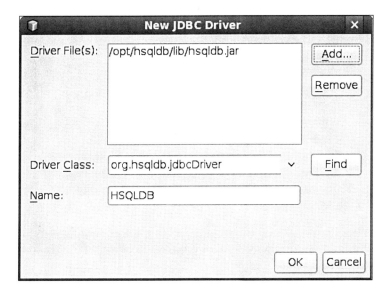

Once we have followed the above procedure, our new JDBC driver is displayed in the list of registered drivers.

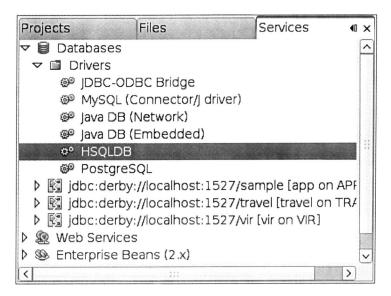

Connecting to a Third Party RDBMS

Once we have added the JDBC driver for our RDBMS to NetBeans, we are ready to connect to the third party RDBMS.

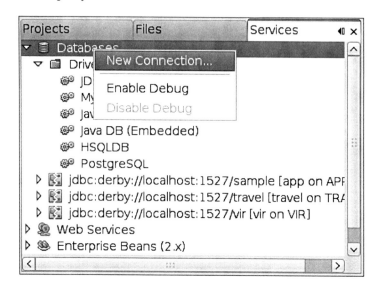

Then we need to enter the JDBC URL, username, and password for our database.

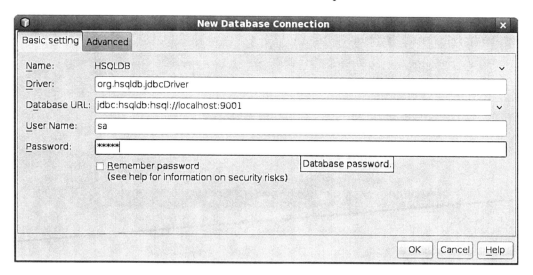

After clicking the **OK** button, NetBeans may ask us to select a database schema.

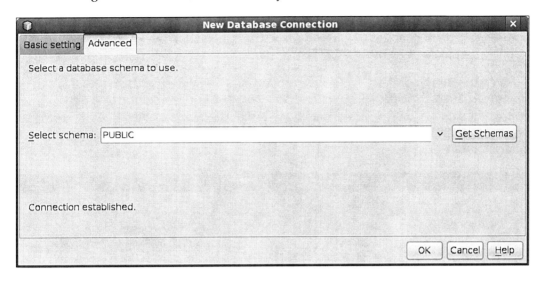

After selecting the schema and clicking the **OK** button, our database is shown in the list of databases in the **Services** tab. We can connect to it by right-clicking on it, selecting **Connect** from the resulting pop-up, then entering our username and password for the database (if we chose not to allow NetBeans to "remember" the password when we added the database).

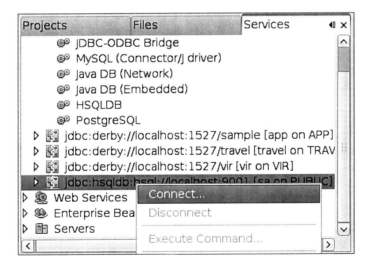

We have now successfully connected NetBeans to a third party RDBMS.

Deploying Our First Application

NetBeans comes pre-configured with a number of sample applications. To make sure everything is configured correctly, we will now deploy one of the sample applications to the integrated GlassFish application server that comes with NetBeans.

To open the sample project, we need to go to **File | New Project**, then select **Samples | Web | Visual JSF** from the categories list in the resulting pop-up window. Once we have selected **Visual JSF** from the categories list, a list of projects is displayed in the **Projects** list. For this example we need to select the **Corporate Travel Center** project.

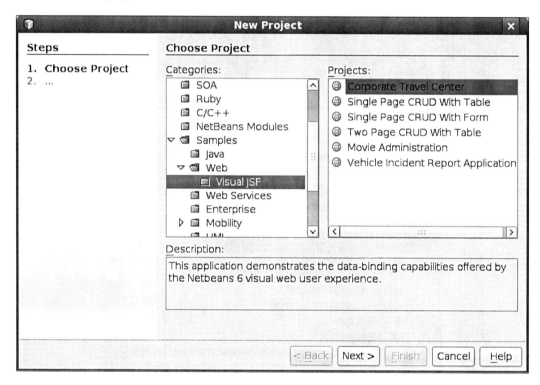

Clicking on the **Next>** button, we are prompted to enter a **Project Name** and **Project Location**. Typically the defaults are sensible.

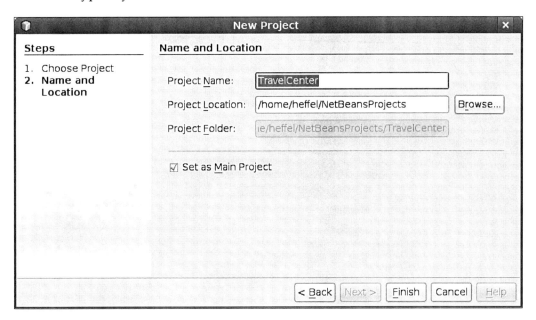

Once we click the **Finish** button, our new project is displayed in the **Projects** tab.

We can compile, package, and deploy our project all in one shot by right-clicking on it and selecting **Run** from the resulting pop-up menu.

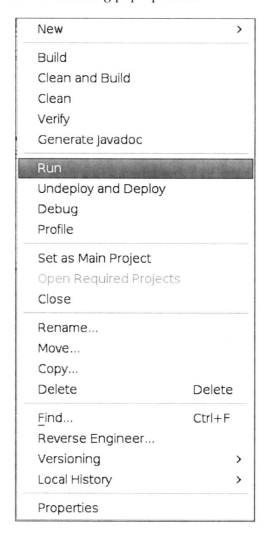

At this point we should see the output of the build script. Also, both the integrated GlassFish application server and the integrated JavaDB RDBMS system should automatically start. The application server and RDBMS will only be started the first time we deploy our project, therefore the delay due to their initialization will not occur in subsequent deployments.

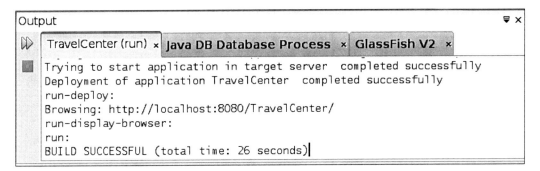

Once the project is deployed we should see NetBean's HTTP monitor. The HTTP monitor is a tool that helps us better develop web applications by providing values of request parameters, request, session and application attributes, request headers, and so on. The HTTP monitor will be discussed in detail in the next chapter.

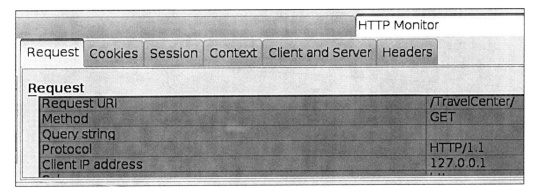

As soon as our application was deployed, a new browser should have automatically started, displaying the default page for our new application. We can select the browser that NetBeans will use by going to **Tools | Options**, then selecting the appropriate browser from the **Web Browser** drop-down in the **General** tab.

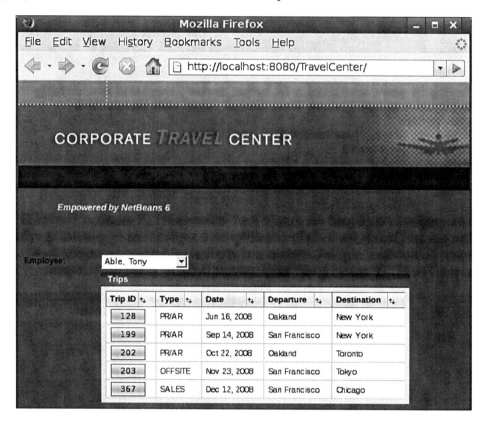

The sample web application we just deployed is a Visual JSF application. The application uses a JDBC connection to the sample travel database included with NetBeans. The application uses the Woodstock JSF components that are bundled with NetBeans, and interacts with data stored in the sample travel database included with NetBeans.

 Visual JSF Development, a NetBeans feature that allow us to build JSF applications graphically, is covered in detail in Chapter 6, *Visual Web JSF Development*.

If our browser is displaying a page similar to the one above, then we can be certain that NetBeans, GlassFish, and JavaDB are all working properly and we are ready to start developing our own Java EE applications.

NetBeans Tips for Effective Development

Although NetBeans offers a wide array of features that make Java EE development easier and faster, it also has a lot of features that make Java development in general easier. In the following few sections we'll cover some of the most useful features.

Code Completion

The NetBeans code editor includes very good code completion. For example, if we wish to create a private variable, we don't need to type the whole "private" word, we can simply write the first three letters ("pri"), then hit *Ctrl+Space*, and NetBeans will complete the word `private` for us.

Code completion also works for variable types and method return values. For example, if we want to declare a variable of type `java.util.List`, we simply need to type the first few characters of the type, then hit *Ctrl+Space*. NetBeans will try to complete with types in any packages we have imported in our class. To make NetBeans attempt to complete with any type in the `CLASSPATH`, we need to hit *Ctrl+Space* again.

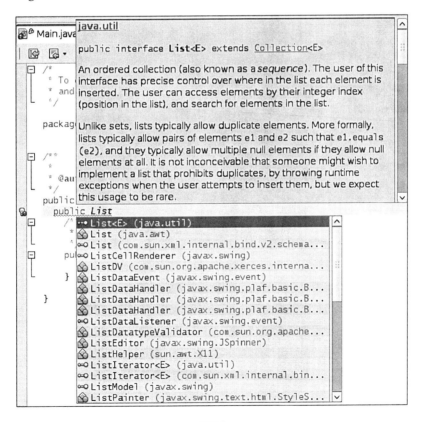

As we can see in the previous screenshot, NetBeans displays JavaDoc for the class we select from the code completion options. Another time saving feature is that the class we select from the options is automatically imported into our code.

Once we have the type of our variable, we can hit *Ctrl+Space* again, right after the variable, and NetBeans will suggest variable names.

```
public class Main {
    public List
        /**
        * @par    □ 1
                  □ list  the command line arguments
        */
        public static void main(String[] args) {
            // TODO code application logic here
        }
```

When we want to initialize our variable to a new value, we can simply hit *Ctrl+Space* again and a list of valid types is shown as options for code completions.

In our example, our type (java.util.List) is an interface, therefore all classes implementing this interface are shown as possible candidates for code completion. Had our type been a class, both our class and all of its subclasses would have been shown as code completion candidates.

When we are ready to use our variable, we can simply type the first few characters of the variable name, then hit *Ctrl+Space*.

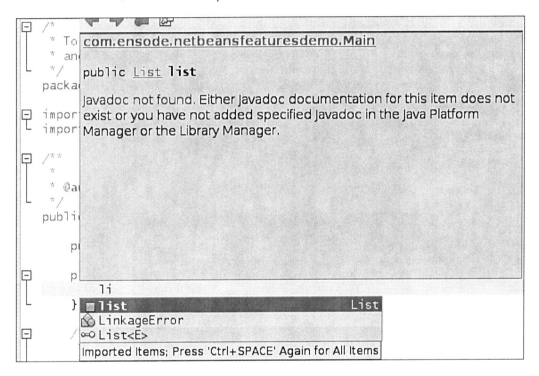

When we wish to invoke a method in our object, we simply type the dot at the end of the variable name, and all available methods are displayed as code completion options.

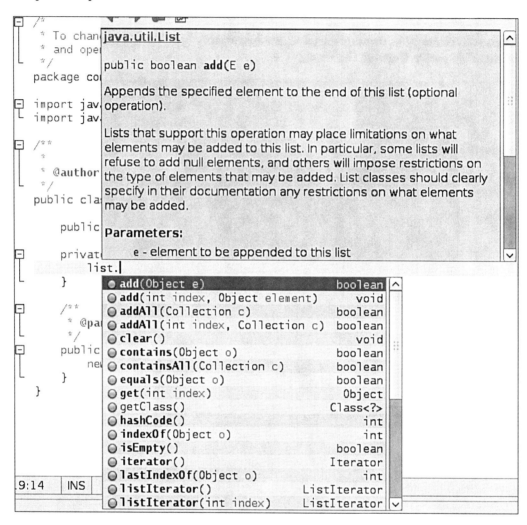

Notice how the JavaDoc for the selected method is automatically displayed.

Code completion also works for methods. We simply need to type the first few characters of our method name and NetBeans will automatically complete the method name, and it will also try to guess the values to pass as parameters.

Code Templates

Code templates are abbreviations for frequently used code snippets. To use a code template, we simply type it into the editor and hit the *Tab* key to expand the abbreviations into the full code snippet it represents.

For example, typing `sout` and pressing the *Tab* key will expand into `System.out.println("");`, with the caret placed between the two double quotes.

Some of the most useful code templates are listed in the table below, please note that code templates are case sensitive.

Abbreviation	Example Expanded Text	Description
Psf	`public static final`	Useful when declaring public static final variables.

forc	`for (Iterator it = list.`
	`iterator();`
	`    it.hasNext();) {`
	`    Object object = it.next();`
	`}`
		Use a standard for loop to iterate through a collection.

fore	`for (Object object : list) {`
	
	`}`
		Use the enhanced for loop to iterate through a collection.

ifelse	`if (boolVar) {`
	
	`} else {`
	
	`}`
		Generate an if-else conditional.

psvm	`public static void main(String[]`
	`args) {`
	
	`}`
		Generate a main method for our class.

soutv	`System.out.println("boolVar = " +` `        boolVar);`	Generate a `System.out.println()` statement displaying the value of a variable.

trycatch	`try {`
	
	`} catch (Exception exception) {`
	`}`
		Generate a try/catch block.

whileit	`while (iterator.hasNext()) {`
	`        Object object = iterator.`
	`next();`
	`    }`
		Generate a while loop to iterate through an Iterator.

To see the complete list of code templates, click on **Tools | Options**. Click on the **Editor** icon, then on the **Code Templates** tab.

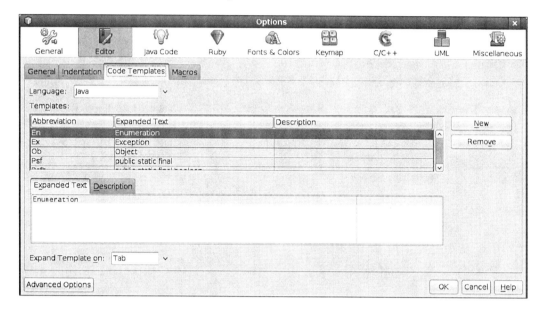

We can add our own templates by clicking on the **New** button. We will be prompted for the template's abbreviation. Once we enter it our new template will be added to the template list and will automatically be selected. We can then enter the expanded text for our template in the **Expanded Text** tab.

Keyboard Shortcuts

NetBeans offers several keyboard shortcuts that allow very fast navigation between source files. Memorizing these keyboard shortcuts allow us to develop code a lot more effectively than relying on the mouse. Some of the most useful NetBeans keyboard shortcuts are listed in this section, but this list is by no means exhaustive. The complete list of NetBeans keyboard shortcuts can be found online at `http://wiki.netbeans.org/wiki/view/KeymapProfileFor60`.

One useful keyboard shortcut that allows us to quickly navigate within a large Java file is *Ctrl+F12*. This keyboard shortcut will present an outline of the current Java file in the editor and show all of its methods and member variables.

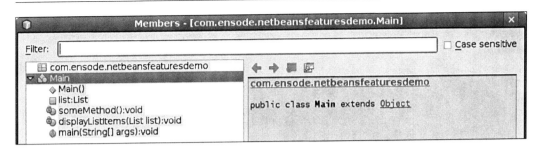

Typing in the text field labeled **Filter** narrows the list of member variables and methods shown. This keyboard shortcut makes it very fast to navigate through large files.

Hitting *Alt+F12* will result in a pop-up window outlining the class hierarchy of the current Java class.

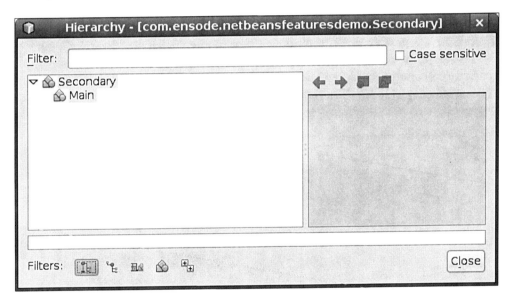

We can use the above shortcut to quickly navigate to a superclass or a subclass of the current class.

Another useful keyboard shortcut is *Alt+Insert*. This keyboard shortcut can be used to generate frequently used code such as constructors, getter and setter methods, and so on.

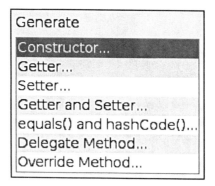

The code will be generated at the current location of the caret.

Additionally, when the caret is right next to an opening or closing brace, clicking *Ctrl+[* results in the caret being placed in the matching brace. This shortcut works for curly braces, parenthesis, and square brackets. Hitting *Ctrl+shift+[* has a similar effect, but this key combination not only places the caret in the matching brace, it also selects the code between the two carets.

```
private void displayListItems(List list) {
    int i = 0;

    for (Object object : list) {
        System.out.println(list.get(i++));
    }

}
```

Sometimes, we would like to know all the places in our project where a specific method is invoked; hitting *Alt+F7* while the method is highlighted allows us to easily find out this information.

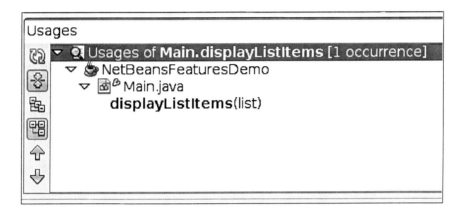

The above keyboard shortcut works with variables as well.

NetBeans will indicate compilation errors in our code by underlining the offending line with a squiggly red line. Placing the caret over the offending code and hitting *Alt+Enter* will allow us to select from a series of suggestions to fix our code.

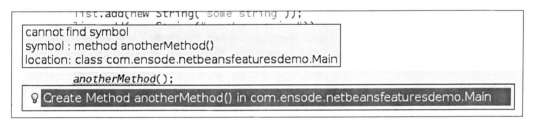

Sometimes navigating through all the files in a project can be a bit cumbersome, especially if we know the name of the file we want to open but we are not sure of its location. Luckily, NetBeans provides the *Shift+Alt+O* keyboard shortcut that allows us to quickly open any file in our project.

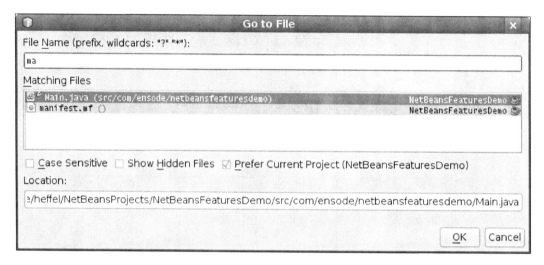

Additional useful keyboard shortcuts include *Shift+Alt+F*; this shortcut quickly formats our code. *Ctrl+E* erases the current line, much faster than highlighting the line and hitting backspace. Sometimes we import a class into our code and later decide not to use it, some of us delete the lines where the class is used but forget to delete the import line at the top of the source file. NetBeans will generate a warning about the unused import, hitting *Ctrl+Shift+I* will delete all unused imports in one fell swoop.

One last thing worth mentioning, even though it is not strictly a keyboard shortcut, a very useful feature of the NetBeans editor is that left-clicking on a method or variable while pressing *Ctrl* will turn the method or variable into a hyperlink, and NetBeans will navigate to the method or variable declaration.

Understanding NetBeans Visual Cues

In addition to offering keyboard shortcuts, code templates, and code completion, NetBeans offers a number of visual cues that allow us to better understand our code at a glance. Some of the most useful are illustrated in the next screenshot.

```
package com.ensode.netbeansfeaturesdemo;

import java.util.Collection;

/**
 *
 * @author heffel
 */
public class Secondary extends Main implements SomeInterface {

    public static int someInt = 3;
    public int anotherInt=4;

    @Override
    public void someMethod() {
        anotherInt = 5;
        super.someMethod();
    }

    public void doSomething() {
        int i = 2;
        foo = 3;
    }
}
```

When there is a warning in our code, NetBeans will alert us in two ways: it will underline the offending line with a squiggly yellow line, and it will place the icon shown below in the left margin of the offending line.

The light bulb in the icon indicates that NetBeans has a suggestion on how to fix the problem, moving the caret to the offending line and hitting *Alt+Enter* will result in NetBeans offering one or more ways of fixing the problem.

Similarly, when there is a compilation error, NetBeans will underline the offending line with a red squiggly line, and place the icon shown below on the left margin of said line.

Again the light bulb indicates that NetBeans has suggestions on how to fix the problem. Hitting *Alt+Enter* in the offending line will allow us to see the suggestions that NetBeans has.

NetBeans not only provides visual cues for errors in our code, it also provides other cues, for example, placing the caret next to an opening or closing brace will highlight both the opening and closing brace, as shown in the doSomething() method in the above screenshot.

Additionally, if one of our methods overrides a method from a parent class, the icon shown below will be placed in the left margin next to the method declaration.

The icon is an upper case **O** inside a circle, the O, of course, stands for "override".

Similarly, when one of our methods is an implementation of one of the interfaces that our class implements, the icon shown below will be placed in the left margin of the method declaration.

The icon is an uppercase **I** inside a green circle, which stands for "implements".

NetBeans also provides visual cues in the form of fonts and font colors, for example, static methods and variables are shown in *italics*, member variables are shown in green, and Java reserved keywords are shown in blue. All of the above cues can be seen in the screenshot at the beginning of this section.

Another nice feature of the NetBeans editor is that highlighting a method or variable highlights it everywhere it is used in the currently open file.

Summary

In this chapter, we provided an introduction to NetBeans as an IDE, explaining the different ways that NetBeans can be obtained, we also covered how to install NetBeans for the different platforms it supports.

Additionally, we looked at how to set up NetBeans with third party Java EE application servers and with third party Relational Database Systems, including how to register a JDBC driver for the RDBMS in question.

We also built and deployed our first Java EE application, and took a first look at the NetBeans HTTP monitor, which helps us better understand how our code behaves "under the hood" by providing request headers, request attributes, session attributes, at a glance.

Finally, we covered some of the NetBeans features such as code completion, code templates, keyboard shortcuts and visual cues that allow us to do our job as software developers more effectively.

2

Developing Web Applications with Servlets and JSPs

In this chapter we will be covering how to develop Java EE web applications taking advantage of the Servlet API. We will also see how to develop Java Server Pages (JSPs) to better separate application business logic from presentation. Some of the topics covered in this chapter include:

- Developing JSPs for display of dynamic web content
- Developing servlets for server side processing of Java web applications
- Securing web applications
- Extracting common markup into JSP fragments
- Using NetBeans HTTP monitor to examine application behavior

Creating Our First Web Application

NetBeans provides a Web category for web applications. To create a new web application, we need to click on **File | New Project** (or press *Ctrl+Shift+N* simultaneously) to create a new project, then select **Web** as the project category, and **Web Application**.

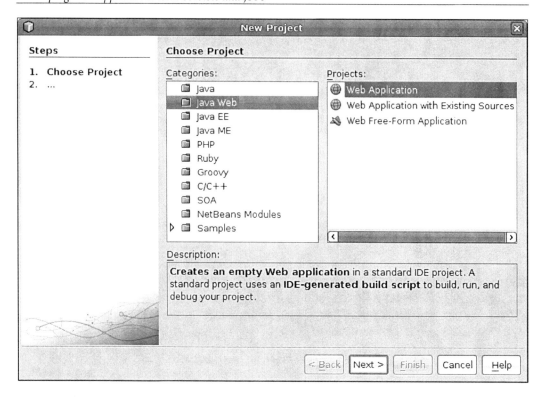

We then need to select a project name for our project. As we type the name for our project, the project location, project folder, and context path are updated automatically. Although we can override default values for these fields if we wish, it is always a good idea to use them since this makes our projects more maintainable (since developers familiar with NetBeans defaults will know the values for these fields without having to look them up).

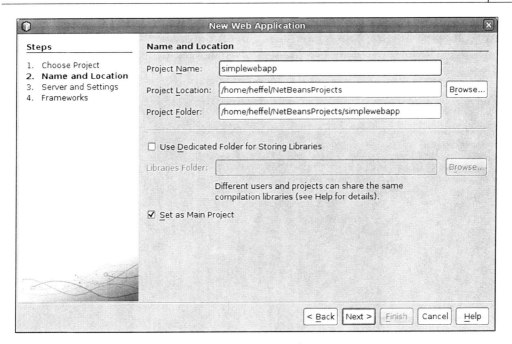

Clicking on the **Next>** button takes us to the next page in the New Web Application wizard.

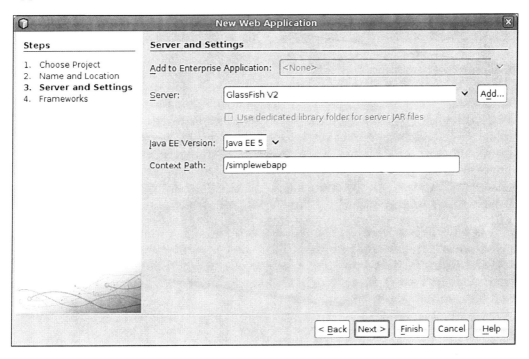

At this stage in the wizard we select what server our application will be deployed to, as well as the Java EE version to use and the context path (the "root" URL) for our application. Default values are usually sensible. Clicking the **Next>** button takes us to the next page in the wizard.

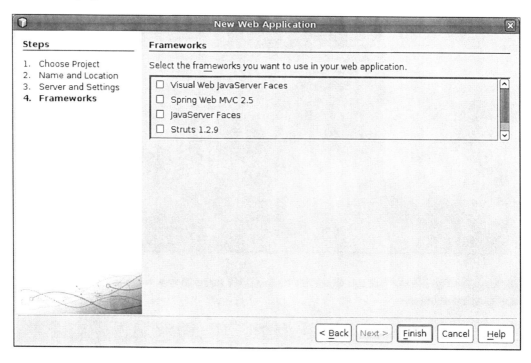

Developing web applications using nothing but servlets and JSPs typically results in having to code a lot of repetitive functionality "by hand". Several web application frameworks have been developed over the years to automate a lot of the repetitive functionality. **Java Server Faces (JSF)** is the standard web application framework for Java EE 5. It is covered in detail in Chapter 5. Additionally, NetBeans includes functionality to create JSF applications visually, by dragging and dropping components from a palette into a design window. This functionality is covered in detail in Chapter 6. For this particular application we will not be using any framework, we should click on the **Finish** button to create our new project.

At this point NetBeans creates a simple, but complete, Java web application. The newly created project contains a single JSP, which is automatically opened in the NetBeans editor. Since the project is a complete Java web application, we can deploy it immediately. We can do so by right-clicking on the project name and selecting **Run** from the resulting pop-up menu.

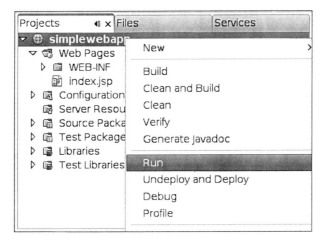

At this point the integrated GlassFish application server and the integrated JavaDB RDBMS are automatically started, tabs for both of them, plus another tab for the build process to execute our project, are created in the NetBeans output window. The **Java DB Database Process** tab will display the contents of the database's log file, similarly, the **GlassFish V2** tab will display the contents of the application server's log file, and the **build process** tab will display the output of the NetBeans generated build script for our application.

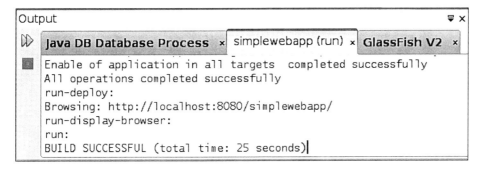

A few seconds later, the application is deployed. At this point the NetBeans HTTP monitor pops up and the default web browser opens and displays the project's JSP file.

We will be covering the HTTP monitor in detail later in this chapter.

The generated JSP is very simple; if we examine its source we can see that it consists almost entirely of standard HTML tags.

```
<%--
    Document   : index
    Created on : Jan 14, 2008, 2:52:32 PM
    Author     : heffel
--%>

<%@page contentType="text/html" pageEncoding="UTF-8"%>
<!DOCTYPE HTML PUBLIC "-//W3C//DTD HTML 4.01 Transitional//EN"
    "http://www.w3.org/TR/html4/loose.dtd">

<html>
    <head>
        <meta http-equiv="Content-Type" content="text/html;
charset=UTF-8">
        <title>JSP Page</title>
    </head>
    <body>
        <h2>Hello World!</h2>
    </body>
</html>
```

The `<%--` and `--%>` tags delineate JSP comments, therefore everything between those two tags is ignored by the JSP compiler. These types of comments will not be rendered on the page. Additionally, we can use standard HTML comments, delineated by `<!--` and `-->`. These type of comments will be placed on the rendered page and, just like with standard HTML pages, they will only be visible by viewing the source of the rendered page.

The next line we see that isn't standard HTML is a JSP page directive. JSP page directives define attributes that apply to the entire page. A JSP page can have more than one page directive, and each directive defines one or more page attributes. The contentType attribute sets the mime type and, optionally, the character set for the page. The pageEncoding attribute sets the character encoding the page uses to render itself.

We can see all valid attributes (and their descriptions) for the page directive by typing <%@page then hitting *Ctrl+Space*. Rather than repeating this information here, readers are encouraged to see it "live" in NetBeans by performing this action.

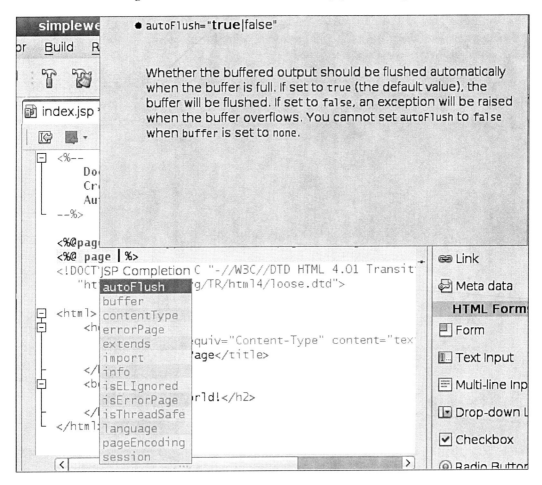

We will now write our own web application using NetBeans' generated code and markup as a base.

Modifying NetBeans' Generated Code

In this section we will develop a simple web application. The application will be a simple survey asking software developers what programming languages they are familiar with. We need to develop two pages: an input page where information from the user will be collected, and an output page where the information entered by the user will be displayed. The output page will serve as a confirmation page where the user can verify that his or her input was collected properly.

Developing the Input Page

NetBeans has a palette where we can drag-and-drop many HTML and JSP elements into the page. For all HTML and JSP elements, whether available in the palette or not, NetBeans offers code completion.

We need to modify our page so that it has an appropriate header and title and some instructions for the user.

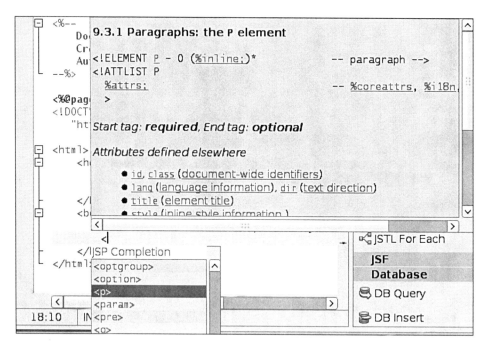

Changing the title and header is trivial, we simply need to modify the body of the tags that were already in the page. We would like to display the instructions inside an HTML <p> tag. We can of course type the tag directly or we can type the opening angled bracket and hit *Ctrl+Space* to invoke code completion. We can then select the tag from the list.

At this point the page should look like this:

```
<%@page contentType="text/html" pageEncoding="UTF-8"%>
<!DOCTYPE HTML PUBLIC "-//W3C//DTD HTML 4.01 Transitional//EN"
"http://www.w3.org/TR/html4/loose.dtd">
<html>
    <head>
        <meta http-equiv="Content-Type" content="text/html;
            charset=UTF-8">
        <title>Developer Survey</title>
    </head>
    <body>
        <h2>Welcome To The Developer Survey</h2>
        <p>
            Please indicate which programming languages you are
            familiar with.
        </p>
    </body>
</html>
```

Modifications to the page are highlighted. As most readers are probably aware, all HTML input fields need to be nested inside an HTML form, therefore the first thing we need to do to our page is to add a form tag to it. We can either type the HTML directly into the page, or we can drag-and-drop the form from the NetBeans palette into the page.

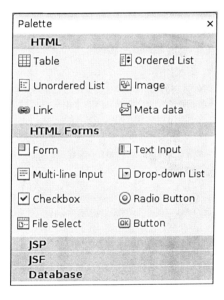

After dragging the form element from the palette and dropping it onto the page, the following window pops up:

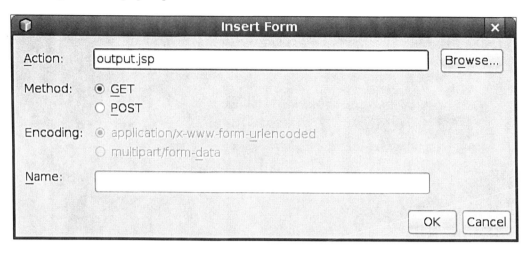

At this point we need to enter an action for the form. The action is the URL that will be executed when the form is submitted. In this case we will execute a JSP called **output.jsp**. We also need to select a method to use for the HTTP request generated when our form is submitted; valid methods are GET and POST. In this case we will use the default **GET** method. Had we selected **POST**, we would also have had to select an encoding for the form. Unless our form has a file upload field, the encoding should always be the default **application/x-www-form-urlencoded**. One more field we can optionally enter is a **Name** for our form.

 GET and POST are generally used for different reasons, GET methods are typically used for retrieving data or for bookmarkable pages and POST methods are typically used for modifying data.

After dropping the form into the page and formatting the code (*Shift+Alt+F*), its markup should now look like this:

```
<%@page contentType="text/html" pageEncoding="UTF-8"%>
<!DOCTYPE HTML PUBLIC "-//W3C//DTD HTML 4.01 Transitional//EN"

"http://www.w3.org/TR/html4/loose.dtd">

<html>
    <head>
        <meta http-equiv="Content-Type" content="text/html;
            charset=UTF-8">
        <title>Developer Survey</title>
```

```
</head>
<body>
    <h2>Welcome To The Developer Survey</h2>
    <p>
        Please enter your name and the technologies and APIs
        you are familiar with.
    </p>
    <form action="output.jsp">
    </form>
</body>
```

The easiest way to lay out input fields in an HTML form is to place them in a table. HTML table is one of the elements that can be dragged and dropped from the NetBeans palette to the page. After doing so, the following window pops up.

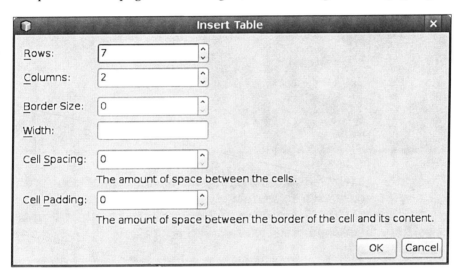

In the above window we can select the properties for our table. In this case we want a table with **7** rows, **2** columns, a **Border Size** of **0**, default **Width** and **Cell Spacing**, and **Cell Padding** of **0**.

After selecting the table properties and clicking **OK**, the markup for our table is placed in the location where we dropped it.

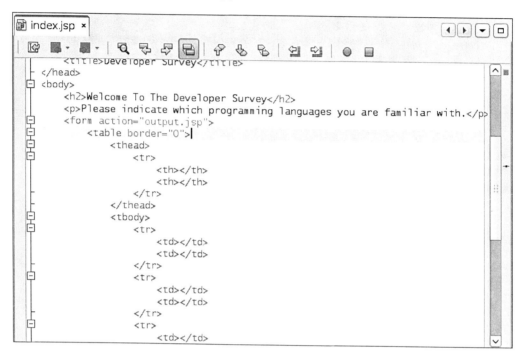

Notice that NetBeans automatically adds a **<thead>** element to our table. In this particular case it is not needed, therefore we will delete it. At this point we need to add input fields to our form. Again we can either type them directly or drop them from the palette into the appropriate location on the page.

After dragging an HTML Text Input element and dropping it into the appropriate location 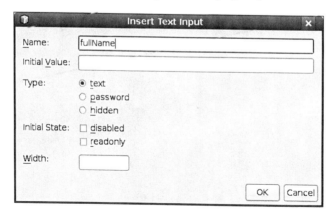 in the page the following window pops up:

In this window we can enter a **Name** for our field (entering a name is good practice since that name will later be used to retrieve the value of the field). We can optionally enter an **Initial Value** for the field. Additionally we can select the type of the input field, our options are: **text** (for standard text fields), **password** (for password fields, fields of this type will not display characters as they are typed into the field, instead either asterisks or dots will be shown, depending on the browser), and **hidden** (fields that are not displayed on the rendered page but are part of the page's markup).

Additionally, we can set the initial state of our field to either **disabled** or **readonly**, plus we can select a **Width** for our input field. **Initial State** and **Width** are only applicable when the type is either **text** or **password**.

After dropping our component into its proper place in the page, selecting its properties and clicking on the **OK** button, then entering some text in the adjacent table cell to be used as a label for our field, the markup for our page now looks like this:

```
index.jsp ×

      <title>Developer Survey</title>
    <head>
  <body>
      <h2>Welcome To The Developer Survey</h2>
      <p>Please indicate which programming languages you are familiar with.</p>
      <form action="output.jsp">
          <table border="0">
              <tbody>
                  <tr>
                      <td>Full Name:</td>
                      <td><input type="text" name="fullName" value="" /></td>
                  </tr>
                  <tr>
                      <td></td>
                      <td></td>
                  </tr>
```

At this point we need to add checkboxes for our developers to select what programming languages they are familiar with, unsurprisingly, dropping a checkbox element into the ☑Checkbox page results in a window prompting us to enter properties for the checkbox to pop-up.

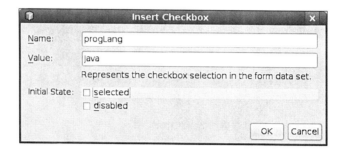

Again we should enter a **Name** for our checkbox, since this name will be used to get the value of the checkbox after the form is submitted. We should also enter a **Value** for the checkbox. This value will only be present in the request object created when the form is submitted only if the checkbox is **selected** when submitting the form.

After adding additional checkboxes for different programming languages and entering their corresponding labels, the markup for the page should now look like this:

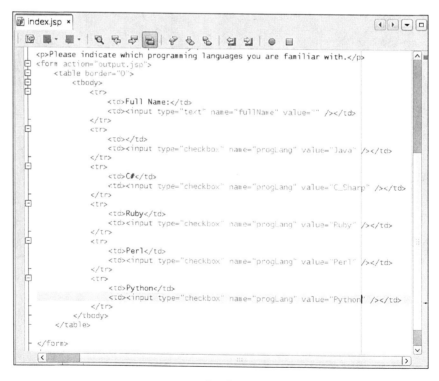

Notice that the name for each checkbox is the same. The reason for this is that when the page is submitted, the values of all selected checkboxes will be retrieved as an array of strings from the HTTP request. We will talk about this in detail when we discuss the output page.

The last thing we need to do is to add a **Submit** button to our page. After dropping the button element from the palette into the page, we are prompted to enter properties for the button.

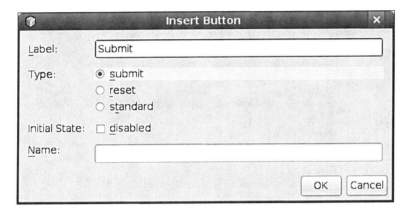

In this window we can enter the button's **Label**.

We can also select a type: **submit** buttons submit a form, **reset** buttons reset a form's values to what they were when the page was loaded, and **standard** buttons are typically used to fire JavaScript events. Since our button will be used to submit a form, the appropriate type for our button is **submit**.

We can also set the button's **Initial State** to be **disabled**, doing this would result in the button being grayed out and the users would be unable to submit the form.

We could optionally enter a name for our button; in most cases this is not necessary for submit buttons. The only case where entering a name for a submit button would be useful would be if a form had more than one submit button, and different actions needed to take place depending on what button was pressed. In a case like this, each button would have the same name, this name would then become a parameter in the HTTP request, the value for this parameter would be the label of the button that was pressed to submit the form.

We now have a fully functional (although admittedly not too elegant) page.

```html
<table border="0">
    <tbody>
        <tr>
            <td>Full Name:</td>
            <td><input type="text" name="fullName" value="" /></td>
        </tr>
        <tr>
            <td>Java</td>
            <td><input type="checkbox" name="progLang" value="Java" /></td>
        </tr>
        <tr>
            <td>C#</td>
            <td><input type="checkbox" name="progLang" value="C_Sharp" /></td>
        </tr>
        <tr>
            <td>Ruby</td>
            <td><input type="checkbox" name="progLang" value="Ruby" /></td>
        </tr>
        <tr>
            <td>Perl</td>
            <td><input type="checkbox" name="progLang" value="Perl" /></td>
        </tr>
        <tr>
            <td>Python</td>
            <td><input type="checkbox" name="progLang" value="Python" /></td>
        </tr>
        <tr>
            <td></td>
            <td><input type="submit" value="Submit" /></td>
        </tr>
    </tbody>
</table>
```

With this, our input page is ready. We can view the way it is displayed in the browser by right-clicking on it and selecting **Run File** (or by pressing *Shift+F6*).

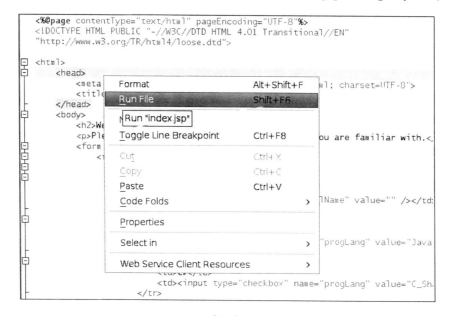

At this point both GlassFish and JavaDB start up, if they weren't already started. Our application is automatically deployed and our page is displayed in the browser.

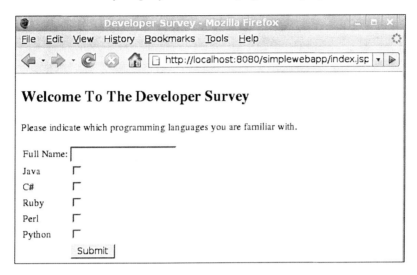

The page now renders properly in the browser. Before the form input can be processed successfully, we need to develop a page that will process it and display an appropriate message.

Developing the Output Page

In order to develop our output page, we need to create a new JSP file, NetBeans can assist us by providing a file we can use as a starting point. To create a new JSP, we can right-click on the project and select **New | JSP**.

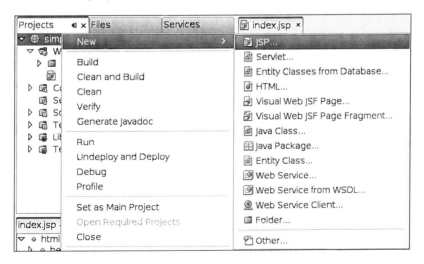

We are then prompted to enter additional information for our page.

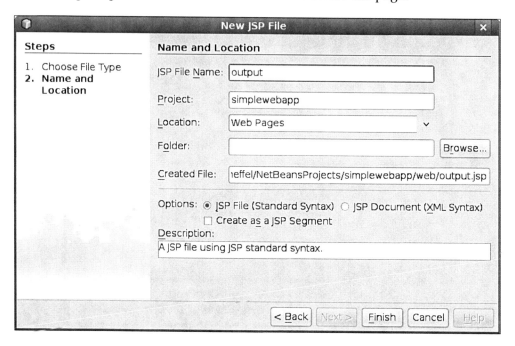

In this particular case we only need to enter the **JSP File Name** and accept all the defaults.

 Notice that we shouldn't enter the file name extension for our JSP since NetBeans will automatically append the appropriate extension to the file name.

We could optionally enter additional information for our page, such as what project to use (provided we had more than one web project open, which isn't the case in our example), a folder to place our page (the selected folder must be under the Web Pages folder; in our example there are no folders in this location, therefore we are unable to select a folder).

The **Created File** field is not editable and is automatically populated based on the choices we made on previous fields.

We are then given the option of creating a JSP file using standard syntax (default), a JSP using XML syntax, or a JSP fragment. In our experience, most JSPs are developed using standard syntax, and NetBeans provides us with a lot more help if we choose this syntax. An alternate syntax for JSP files is the XML syntax. This syntax is less popular than standard syntax and, other than code completion, NetBeans doesn't offer a lot of help when working with it. For this reason we chose to use standard syntax for our pages.

 NetBeans generated JSPs when developing Java Server Pages applications via the visual web development functionality use XML syntax. Visual web page markup is for the most part automatically generated, leaving us to manually code little or no markup in the generated JSPs. Visual web development will be covered in detail in Chapter 6.

We are also given the option of creating a JSP segment. JSP segments (or fragments) are pages containing common markup that is contained in many pages in an application. JSP fragments typically contain navigation menus, header information, and so on. They can then be included dynamically into JSPs in the application. The advantage of JSP fragments is that this common markup can be maintained separately instead of having to update several JSPs in the application. We will cover JSP fragments later in this chapter.

After entering all appropriate data in the New JSP File pop-up window, NetBeans generates a JSP file we can use as a starting point. We need to modify this file to obtain the data that was entered in the previous page.

```
<%--
    Document    : output
    Created on  : Jan 20, 2008, 1:27:46 PM
    Author      : heffel
--%>
<%@page contentType="text/html" pageEncoding="UTF-8"%>
<!DOCTYPE HTML PUBLIC "-//W3C//DTD HTML 4.01 Transitional//EN"
    "http://www.w3.org/TR/html4/loose.dtd">

<html>
    <head>
        <meta http-equiv="Content-Type" content="text/html;
            charset=UTF-8">
        <title>Thank You!</title>
    </head>
    <body>
        <h2>Thanks for taking our survey</h2>
        <p>
```

```
<%= request.getParameter("fullName") %>,
you indicated you are familiar with the following
programming languages:</p>
<ul>
    <%
    String[] selectedLanguages =
        request.getParameterValues("progLang");
    if (selectedLanguages != null) {
        for (int i = 0; i < selectedLanguages.length;
            i++) {
    %>
    <li>
        <%= selectedLanguages[i] %>
    </li>
    <%}
    }
    %>
</ul>
</body>
</html>
```

As we can see, this page is composed of both static HTML elements and JSP expressions and scriptlets.

JSP expressions are enclosed in `<%=` and `%>` delimiters. Inside these delimiters we can place any valid Java expression returning a value. The value is automatically converted to a `String` and displayed on the page. To simplify expressions, JSPs contain a number of implicit objects. One of these implicit objects is `request`. This object contains the HTTP request that was generated when navigating to the page. The first JSP expression on our output page uses the implicit request object. It is used to retrieve the value of the request parameter named `fullName`. Notice that the `String` we passed to this method matches the name of the text input field used to collect the user's full name in the previous page. When that page is submitted, a request parameter is automatically generated with this name and the user entered input as its value. Invoking this method allows us to retrieve the data that the user entered.

Hitting *Ctrl+Space* between `<%=` and `%>` or `<%` and `%>` delimiters results in all implicit objects available to JSP pages being displayed.

```
■ application          ServletContext
□ config               ServletConfig
□ exception            Throwable
□ jspContext           JspContext
□ out                  JspWriter
□ page                 Object
□ pageContext          PageContext
□ request              HttpServletRequest
□ response             HttpServletResponse
□ session              HttpSession
```

The following table briefly describes all implicit JSP objects.

Implicit Object	Implicit Object Type	Implicit Object Description
application	`javax.servlet.ServletContext`	This object can have attributes attached that are visible across user sessions.
config	`javax.servlet.ServletConfig`	Typically used to obtain initialization parameters.
exception	`java.lang.Throwable`	Provides access to the exception that was thrown that led to the page being invoked. This implicit object is only accessible if the page directive's `isErrorPage` attribute is set to `true`.
jspContext	`javax.servlet.jsp.JspContext`	Provides methods for setting, retrieving, and removing attributes from the different scopes (page, request, session, application).
out	`javax.servlet.jsp.JspWriter`	Used to output text on the page.
page	`java.lang.Object`	Returns a reference to the current JSP. This implicit object is not typically used by JSP page authors.
pageContext	`javax.servlet.jsp.PageContext`	Provides all functionality provided by `jspContext` plus additional methods specific to a servlet environment.

Implicit Object	Implicit Object Type	Implicit Object Description
request	javax.servlet. ServletRequest	Commonly used to obtain HTTP request parameters and attributes.
response	javax.servlet. ServletResponse	Contains several methods to manipulate the HTTP response sent to the browser. Can be used to add HTTP headers, cookies, etc.
session	javax.servlet.http. HttpSession	Typically used to set and retrieve attributes that are specific to each user session.

After typing an implicit object followed by a dot, NetBeans will present a list of all available methods for that object, along with a description of each method.

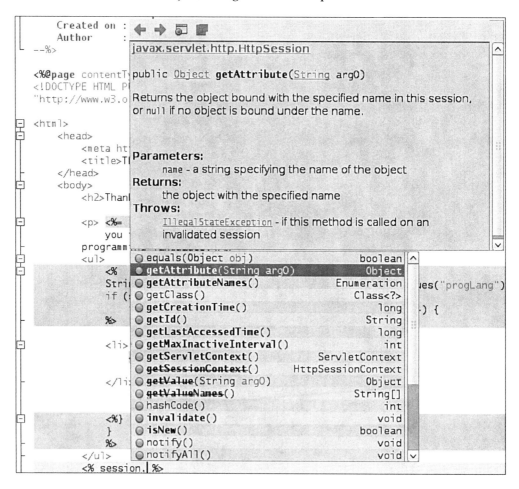

This feature can be used both as a learning tool so that we can see what functionality is available, and as a reference for more experienced developers.

In addition to JSP expressions, our page contains JSP scriptlets. Scriptlets can contain any arbitrary Java code and have access to all implicit objects. In our example, the first scriptlet obtains the values of the request parameter named `progLang`; this is the name we used on the input JSP for all checkboxes. Using the same name for several checkboxes has the effect of creating a request parameter whose value is an array of `String` objects containing the values of the checkboxes that were checked. Our JSP obtains this array and assigns it to a variable named `selectedLanguages`; it then iterates through this array and outputs the value to the page as an unordered list (bullet points).

Notice that scriptlets can be "interrupted", to add static content or expressions inside them. In our example, there is both a condition and a loop started in the first scriptlet, then there is some static markup to generate an item in the list and an expression to display the current element in the list. The next scriptlet closes both the condition and the loop.

At this point, we are ready to test the new page. We should redeploy our application by right-clicking on it in the project window and selecting `Run`. At this point the input page should show up automatically on the browser. Assuming the user entered "David Heffelfinger" as the full name and selected "Java" and "Perl" from the checkboxes, then submitted the form by clicking on the **Submit** button, our new page should be displayed on the screen.

We have now completed a simple but complete application using JSPs.

Servlet Development

Although the application developed in the previous section was fairly easy to develop, the resulting code isn't very maintainable. One of the JSPs has both business logic and presentation logic embedded in it. It is considered a best practice for JSPs to have only presentation logic, and keep the business logic elsewhere.

One common way to approach this problem is to use the **Model-View-Controller (MVC)** design pattern. This pattern provides a clean separation of concerns, providing artifacts that solely act as data (model), while other artifacts are solely responsible for displaying the data (view) and another artifact (or artifacts) is responsible for manipulating the data and transferring control to the view (controller). In Java web applications, JSPs typically act as the view, servlets act as controllers, and custom JavaBeans act as the model.

In this section we will modify the application we developed previously so that it follows this pattern.

Adding a Servlet to Our Application

NetBeans provides functionality that allows us to easily create a servlet. In order to create our servlet, we need to go to **File | New**. Choose **Web** from the **Categories** list, then **Servlet** from the **File Types** list.

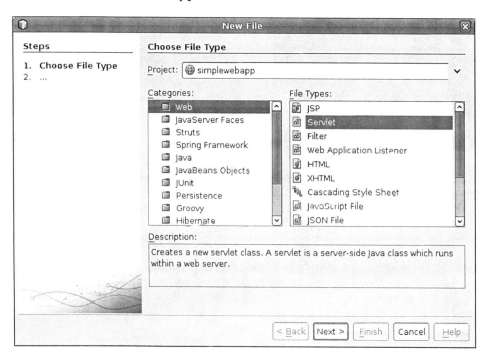

When we click on **Next>**, we should enter a **Class Name** and **Package** for our servlet.

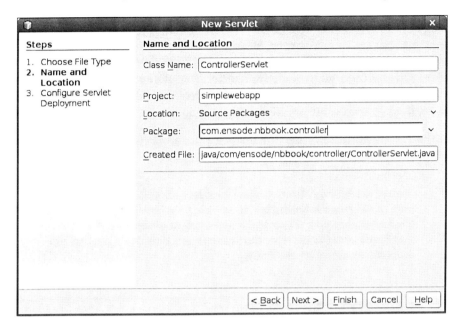

In the next page in the servlet wizard, we are given the opportunity to specify a logical name for our servlet, as well as a **URL Pattern(s)** that will be used to execute our servlet.

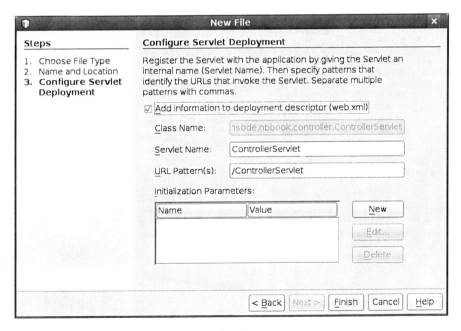

We can also add initialization parameters for our servlets. These parameters can be read by our servlet by invoking the `getInitParameter()` method defined in the `javax.servlet.GenericServlet` class. All servlets in a web application extend `javax.servlet.http.HttpServlet`, which in turn extends `javax.servlet. GenericServlet`, therefore this method is available to all of our servlets via inheritance. This method takes the initialization parameter as a `String` object and returns its value as a `String`. In our particular servlet we don't need initialization parameters, therefore we don't need to enter any in the NetBeans servlet wizard.

Clicking the **Finish** button creates our servlet, plus adds the appropriate entries to our web application's `web.xml` deployment descriptor.

> Every Java web application must contain a configuration file called
> `web.xml`. This file has information needed when the application is
> deployed, therefore it is called a deployment descriptor. If we use
> NetBeans wizards to create our servlets and JSPs this file is created
> behind the scenes by NetBeans.

```java
public class ControllerServlet extends HttpServlet {

    /**
     * Processes requests for both HTTP <code>GET</code> and <code>POST</code> methods.
     * @param request servlet request
     * @param response servlet response
     */
    protected void processRequest(HttpServletRequest request, HttpServletResponse response)
    throws ServletException, IOException {
        response.setContentType("text/html;charset=UTF-8");
        PrintWriter out = response.getWriter();
        try {
            /* TODO output your page here
            out.println("<html>");
            out.println("<head>");
            out.println("<title>Servlet ControllerServlet</title>");
            out.println("</head>");
            out.println("<body>");
            out.println("<h1>Servlet ControllerServlet at " + request.getContextPath () + "<
            out.println("</body>");
            out.println("</html>");
            */
        } finally {
            out.close();
        }
    }

    HttpServlet methods. Click on the + sign on the left to edit the code.
}
```

NetBeans creates a servlet using the class name and package we specified in the wizard. The generated servlet contains a processRequest() method that will be executed every time the servlet receives an HTTP GET or an HTTP POST request from the browser. This method takes an instance of javax.servlet.http. HttpServletRequest and an instance of javax.servlet.HttpServletResponse as parameters. These parameters are equivalent to the request and response implicit objects in JSPs.

The processRequest() method is a NetBeans-specific method that is generated when we use the NetBeans servlet wizard to create a method. The reason this method is created is because in most cases we would like the servlet to execute the same code regardless of if the servlet received an HTTP GET or an HTTP POST request from the browser. These two requests are handled by the doGet() and doPost() methods, respectively. These methods are inherited from the javax.servlet.http. HttpServlet class, which is the parent class of all servlets in a Java web application.

Notice at the bottom of our class we can see that there is some code in our servlet that is collapsed (using NetBeans code folding feature). Clicking on the plus (+) sign next to the collapsed code we can expand it and examine it.

```java
// <editor-fold defaultstate="collapsed" desc="HttpServlet methods. Click on the
/**
 * Handles the HTTP <code>GET</code> method.
 * @param request servlet request
 * @param response servlet response
 */
protected void doGet(HttpServletRequest request, HttpServletResponse response)
throws ServletException, IOException {
    processRequest(request, response);
}

/**
 * Handles the HTTP <code>POST</code> method.
 * @param request servlet request
 * @param response servlet response
 */
protected void doPost(HttpServletRequest request, HttpServletResponse response)
throws ServletException, IOException {
    processRequest(request, response);
}

/**
 * Returns a short description of the servlet.
 */
public String getServletInfo() {
    return "Short description";
}
// </editor-fold>
```

As we can see, the **doPost()** and **doGet()** methods for our servlet simply invoke the generated **processRequest()** method, passing along the **request** and **response** parameters. If we wish our servlet to handle only POST request, we should delete the generated **doGet()** method; similarly, if we wish the servlet to handle only GET request, the **doPost()** method should be deleted.

We need our servlet to process data entered by the user in the application's input page, then invoke the output page, which will be modified to obtain its data from an attribute in the HTTP request.

```
protected void processRequest(HttpServletRequest request, HttpServletResponse response)
        throws ServletException, IOException {

    SurveyData surveyData = new SurveyData();
    surveyData.setFullName(request.getParameter("fullName"));
    surveyData.setProgLangList(request.getParameterValues("progLang"));
    request.setAttribute("surveyData", surveyData);
    request.getRequestDispatcher("output.jsp").forward(request, response);
}
```

In our example we modified the **processRequest()** method of our servlet so that it creates an instance of a JavaBean called **SurveyData** and populates it with values from the request parameters.

SurveyData is a very simple JavaBean with two private properties and corresponding getters and setters. Since it is so simple, it is not shown; it is part of this book's code download. This bean's role is to be the model in our MVC architecture.

The instance of SurveyData is then stored as a request attribute by invoking the setAttribute() method in the request object. Request attributes are visible as long as no new HTTP request is generated from the application. We can navigate to other pages by forwarding the request and its attributes will be preserved. Redirecting the HTTP response, clicking on a link, submitting a page or entering a URL directly in the browser's location field are all actions that generate a new request, causing previous request attributes to be lost.

A different way of transferring control to another URL is by using the sendResponseRedirect() method of HttpServletResponse. This method takes a single String argument containing the URL we wish to redirect to. This method creates a new request, therefore any pre-existing request attributes and parameters are lost. The URL used as a parameter can be a page on any server, where forwarding the request is limited to pages or resources in the same server as the one where the servlet or JSP doing the forwarding is deployed.

Objects can also be stored by a servlet as attributes at the session, or application scope. Had we wished to store the `SurveyData()` instance as a session attribute, we would have added the following line to the `processRequest()` method:

```
request.getSession().setAttribute("surveyData", surveyData);
```

The `getSession()` method of the `javax.servlet.http.HttpServletRequest` interface returns an instance of `javax.servlet.http.HttpSession` representing the user's session. Session attributes are visible to all pages in a user's session, and are preserved across requests.

Storing the instance of `SurveyData` at the application scope would have been accomplished by the following line in the `processRequest()` method:

```
getServletContext().setAttribute("surveyData", surveyData);
```

The `getServletContext()` method is defined in `javax.servlet.GenericServlet`, which is the parent class of `javax.servlet.http.HttpServlet`, which in turn is the parent class of every servlet in a web application. This method returns an instance of `javax.servlet.ServletContext`. Storing an object as an attributes of the servlet context makes it visible across user sessions, therefore all users in the application have access to the attribute.

Request, session, and application attributes can be retrieved by invoking the `getAttribute()` method. This method exists in `HttpServletRequest`, `HttpSession`, and `ServletContext`. In all instances it takes a `String` parameter indicating the parameter to obtain, and returns an instance of `java.lang.Object`, which then needs to be cast to the appropriate type. If there is no attribute of the specified name, the method returns null.

The last thing we need to do in our example is to forward the request to the output JSP, this is accomplished by obtaining an instance of `javax.servlet.RequestDispatcher`, this instance is obtained by invoking the `getRequestDispatcher()` method of `javax.servlet.http.HttpRequestServlet`, this method has a single parameter, which is a String indicating the relative or absolute URL of the page or servlet we wish to navigate to. In our example we are using the relative URL of `output.jsp`. We know the URL is relative because all absolute URLs begin with a forward slash (/). Once we have an instance of `javax.servlet.RequestDispatcher`, we simply invoke its `forward()` method to navigate to the desired page.

We need to make one minor modification to the input JSP page so that it invokes our servlet when its form is submitted.

The line:

```
<form action="output.jsp">
```

Needs to be modified as follows:

```
<form action="ControllerServlet" method="post">
```

What we did was change the value of the action attribute of the HTML `<form>` element to be the URL of our servlet (we defined this URL in the servlet wizard when we were creating our servlet; it is permanently stored in the application's `web.xml` configuration file).

```
<servlet-mapping>
        <servlet-name>ControllerServlet</servlet-name>
        <url-pattern>/ControllerServlet</url-pattern>
</servlet-mapping>
```

Additionally, we added a method attribute to the `<form>` element, and gave it a value of `post`. This step wasn't strictly necessary, however by default a form uses a method of `get`, and HTTP GET requests have a disadvantage: parameter names and values are shown in the browser's location text field, and malicious user's might attempt to break our application by modifying the displayed URL by giving invalid values to the request parameters. HTTP POST requests have no such disadvantage; therefore it is a good idea to use POST requests whenever possible.

We also need to make a few modifications to the output JSP so that it retrieves values from the JavaBean that is stored.

The first thing we need to do is to add a `<jsp:useBean>` tag to our JSP. This tag can be either typed in directly, or can be dragged from the palette and dropped into the page. Dragging and dropping the tag into the page results in the following window popping up.

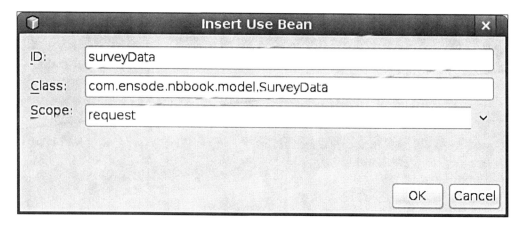

The value of the **ID** field must match the value that was used to store the bean as a request attribute. The value of the **Class** field must be the fully qualified name of the bean's type. The value of the **Scope** field must be the scope we wish to retrieve the bean from; valid values include page, request, session, or application. The scope where the bean is placed affects when and where the bean can be accessed. The following table summarizes all valid scopes.

Scope	Description
page	Bean is only accessible in the current page, including any JSP page fragments included in the page.
request	Bean is only accessible withing a single HTTP request, usually from the page to be displayed after the request is processed.
session	Bean is accessible across requests in a single HTTP session, typically this means there is a single instance of the bean per user of the application.
application	Bean is accessible across HTTP sessions, typically this means there is a single instance of the bean accessible to all users of the application.

After filling out all fields, NetBeans inserts the following markup code in the location where we dropped the component:

```
<jsp:useBean id="surveyData" scope="request"
            class="com.ensode.nbbook.model.SurveyData" />
```

The next thing we need to do is replace the JSP expression retrieving the **fullName** request parameter with the `<jsp:getProperty>` tag. This tag retrieves the value of a JSP property. Again we can either type the tag in the appropriate location, or drag it from the palette and drop it into the page. As usual, NetBeans pops up a window when the tag is dropped into the page.

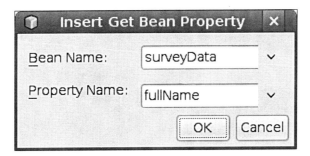

The **Bean Name** drop-down options show all valid beans in the page, the value for this field must match the bean's ID from the `<jsp:useBean>` tag. After we select one, the **Property Name** drop-down is populated with all properties in the bean. Once we select the appropriate bean and property, NetBeans generates the following markup code:

```
<jsp:getProperty name="surveyData" property="fullName" />
```

The value of the `name` attribute matches the value we selected in the **Bean Name** drop-down, and the value of the `property` attribute matches the values selected in the **Property Name** drop-down.

The last change we need to make to the page is to modify the scriptlet so that the array containing the programming languages selected by the user is obtained from the bean instead of directly from the HTTP request.

To accomplish this, the line:

```
String[] selectedLanguages = request.getParameterValues("progLang");
```

Needs to be changed to:

```
String[] selectedLanguages = surveyData.getProgLangList();
```

Notice that the bean's id (surveyData, in our case) can be used in scriptlets as a variable name.

After implementing all of the above changes, our output page now looks like this:

```
<%@page contentType="text/html" pageEncoding="UTF-8"%>
<!DOCTYPE HTML PUBLIC "-//W3C//DTD HTML 4.01 Transitional//EN"

    "http://www.w3.org/TR/html4/loose.dtd">
<jsp:useBean id="surveyData"
    type="com.ensode.nbbook.model.SurveyData"
    scope="request"/>
<html>
    <head>
        <meta http-equiv="Content-Type" content="text/html;
            charset=UTF-8">
        <title>Thank You!</title>
    </head>
    <body>
        <h2>Thanks for taking our survey</h2>

        <p>
          <jsp:getProperty name="surveyData"
```

```
                property="fullName"/>
            ,you indicated you are familiar with the
    following programming languages:</p>
        <ul>
            <%
            String[] selectedLanguages =
                    surveyData.getProgLangList();
            if (selectedLanguages != null) {
                for (int i = 0; i < selectedLanguages.length; i++) {
            %>

            <li>
                <%= selectedLanguages[i] %>
            </li>
            <%}
            }
            %>
        </ul>
    </body>
</html>
```

We can execute our application by right-clicking on the project and selecting **Run**. At this point the application will be deployed and opened automatically in the default browser. With one minor exception, it should behave exactly like it did before we introduced the servlet. The one exception is that the URL displayed on the browser's location text field when the form is submitted is the servlet's URL. The reason for this is that the URL displayed in the browser does not change when the HTTP request is forwarded, like we did in our servlet.

We have now successfully re-architected our application to use the industry standard Model-View-Controller design pattern. We followed standard practices in Java web applications of having JavaBeans serve as the model, JSPs serving as the view, and a servlet serving as the controller.

Securing Web Applications

It is a common requirement to only allow certain users to access certain pages in a web application. Before a web application can be secured, a **security realm** needs to be set up in the application server where the application will be deployed. Security realms are essentially collections of users and security groups.

Each security realm allows the application server to obtain security information from some sort of permanent storage. This security information could be stored in a simple flat file, a relational database, an LDAP repository, or any other kind of persistent storage. Configuring the application server to obtain the security information from any kind of persistent storage allows us as application developers not to have to worry about the specific implementation. We simply configure our application to use a defined security realm for authentication.

Each user can belong to one or more security groups. Secured pages in a web application are only accessible by certain security groups.

 The procedure of setting up a security realm varies from application server to application server, consult your application server documentation for details. In this section we will use a pre-configured GlassFish security realm called "file". Consult your application server documentation for information on how to configure security realms.

There are four different ways we can authenticate a user. When accessing a page using **Basic Authentication**, a browser pop-up window is displayed asking the user to enter his credentials.

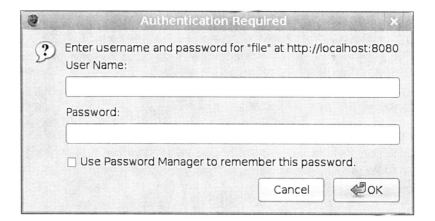

The advantage of this approach is that it is the easiest to implement. Disadvantages of this approach include the fact that by default passwords are not encrypted, and that the login page is not very elegant. Another disadvantage of this approach is that there is no way for the user to log out, other than closing the browser window.

The second approach we can use for authentication is to use **Digest Authentication**. This approach works much like basic authentication, with the exception that passwords are encrypted when sent to the server.

 Digest Authentication is not in widespread use, and many application servers do not support it, therefore its use is discouraged.

The third approach we can use to authenticate users is to use a **client-side certificate**. These certificates are issued by certificate authorities such as Verisign or Thawte. Client-side certificates are essentially a file in the user's hard drive. The user's browser needs to be configured to use the client-side certificate for authentication. Although applications using client-side certificates tend to be very secure, they are not very common due to the expense and lack of convenience of issuing client-side certificates.

The fourth and most common approach to user authentication is to use **form-based authentication**. When using this type of authentication, we need to develop a JSP or HTML page used to collect user credentials. The advantages of this approach include the ability to make login pages as elaborate or as simple as we wish; additionally, the user name and password can be easily encrypted by setting up the page to use the HTTPS (HTTP over SSL).

Implementing Form Based Authentication

To implement form-based authentication, a few steps need to be followed:

1. A login page needs to be created.
2. A login error page needs to be created, this page will be displayed when a user enters incorrect credentials.
3. The web application needs to be configured to use a security realm for authentication.

Implementing the Login Page

The first step to follow to implement form-based authentication is to create a login page. A fairly simple and "bare bones" login page is shown in the following listing.

```
<%@ page language="java" contentType="text/html; charset=UTF-8"
  pageEncoding="UTF-8"%>
<!DOCTYPE html PUBLIC "-//W3C//DTD HTML 4.01 Transitional//EN"
    "http://www.w3.org/TR/html4/loose.dtd">
<html>
<head>
```

```
<meta http-equiv="Content-Type" content="text/html; charset=UTF-8">
<title>Login</title>
</head>
<body>
<p>Please enter your username and password to access the
    application</p>
<form method="POST" action="j_security_check">
<table cellpadding="0" cellspacing="0" border="0">
  <tr>
    <td align="right">Username: </td>
    <td>
      <input type="text" name="j_username">
    </td>
  </tr>
  <tr>
    <td align="right">Password: </td>
    <td>
     <input type="password" name="j_password">
    </td>
  </tr>
  <tr>
    <td></td>
    <td><input type="submit" value="Login"></td>
  </tr>
</table>
</form>
</body>
</html>
```

Every login page created for form based authentication must contain an HTML `form` with a method of `POST` and an action of `j_security_check`. Every Java EE compliant application server will have a security servlet already deployed on installation. This servlet is mapped to the `j_security_check` URL, as such, its `doPost()` method is executed when the form is submitted.

Each form-based authentication login page must also have two additional fields: a text field named `j_username`, and a password field named `j_password`. The security servlet will then check that these values match those in the security realm when the form is submitted. Needless to say, the form needs a submit button so that user entered credentials can be sent to the servlet.

We need a way to display an authentication error if the user enters incorrect credentials.

Implementing a Login Error Page

The next step we need to do to implement form based authentication is to develop a page to be displayed when login fails. A common practice is to allow the user to attempt to log in again from the error page, this practice is followed in our login error page.

```
<%@ page language="java" contentType="text/html; charset=UTF-8"
        pageEncoding="UTF-8"%>
<!DOCTYPE html PUBLIC "-//W3C//DTD HTML 4.01 Transitional//EN"
    "http://www.w3.org/TR/html4/loose.dtd">
<html>
  <head>
    <meta http-equiv="Content-Type" content="text/html;
     charset=UTF-8">
    <title>Login Error</title>
  </head>
  <body>
    There was an error logging in. Please try again.
    <br />
    <form method="POST" action="j_security_check">
      <table cellpadding="0" cellspacing="0" border="0">
        <tr>
          <td align="right">Username: </td>
          <td>
           <input type="text" name="j_username">
         </td>
        </tr>
        <tr>
          <td align="right">Password: </td>
          <td><input type="password" name="j_password"></td>
        </tr>
        <tr>
          <td></td>
          <td><input type="submit" value="Login"></td>
        </tr>
      </table>
    </form>
  </body>
</html>
```

If a user enters incorrect credentials when attempting to log in to our application, he/she will automatically be directed to this page. In our particular implementation of the login error page, we chose to display an error message and allow the user to try to log in again (a fairly common practice).

Configuring Our Application for Form-Based Authentication

When an unauthenticated user attempts to access a secured page, our application must redirect the user to the login page. Once the user has successfully authenticated via the application's security realm, the user is presented with the page he/she was trying to access. If the user does not successfully authenticate, the application must direct the user to our login error page. All of this needs to be configured in the application's web.xml deployment descriptor.

By default, NetBeans opens the web.xml deployment descriptor in a visual editor. After opening our application's web.xml (located under **Configuration Files**), and clicking the **Security** button in the toolbar, we can enter security information for our application.

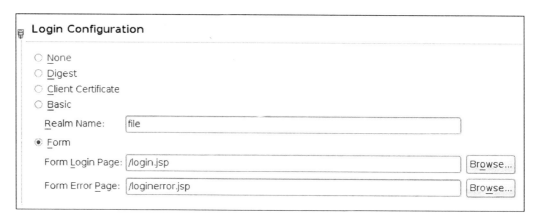

In the **Login Configuration** section, we need to choose the type of authentication the application will use. For form based authentication, we also need to indicate the login and login error pages.

In the **Security Roles** section, we add security roles for our web application.

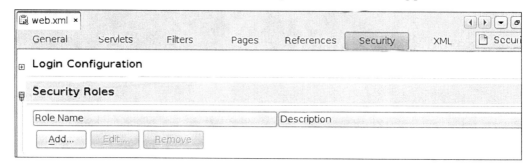

Security roles can be added by clicking on the **Add...** button.

We can then add a **Role Name** and an optional **Description**. After clicking the **OK** button, we can see our newly added **Security Roles** in the NetBeans **web.xml** visual editor.

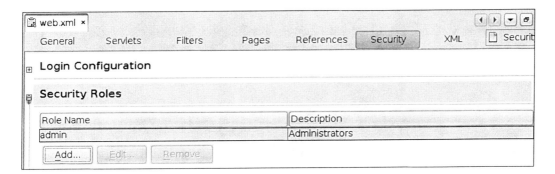

 Our application requires two security roles: admin and user. The procedure to add each security role is identical, therefore adding the user role is not shown.

Next, we need to specify what roles have access to what pages. We can do this by clicking on the **Add Security Constraint** button.

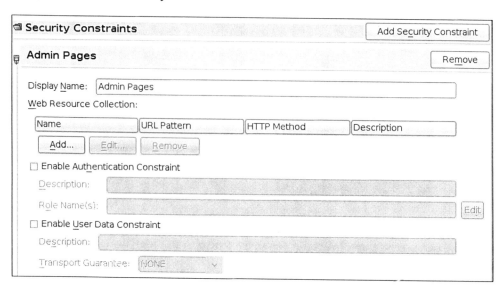

It is recommended to modify the default for the **Display Name** field, giving it a descriptive value. We then need to specify the pages that belong to our security constraint. We do this by clicking on the **Add...** button under the **Web Resource Collection** section.

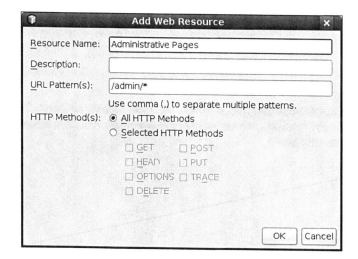

Next, we then need to provide a **Resource Name**, an optional **Description**, and **URL Pattern(s)** for the pages belonging to our security constraint. A common practice is to group all pages belonging to a security constraint under a sub folder of the Web Pages folder, a practice we followed in our example. All administrative pages are under the **admin** folder, therefore the URL pattern to access them is /admin/*, meaning any URL beginning with /admin, after the context root of our application. In our application we will have a single JSP named admin.jsp in the admin folder. This JSP will only be accessible after the user enters a valid username/password combination.

```
<%@page contentType="text/html" pageEncoding="UTF-8"%>
<!DOCTYPE HTML PUBLIC "-//W3C//DTD HTML 4.01 Transitional//EN"

    "http://www.w3.org/TR/html4/loose.dtd">

<html>
    <head>
        <meta http-equiv="Content-Type" content="text/html;
            charset=UTF-8">
        <title>JSP Page</title>
    </head>
    <body>
        <h2>Admin Page</h2>
        <p>
            Had this been a real admin page, you would have been
            able to administer the system from here!
        </p>
    </body>
</html>
```

GlassFish-Specific Security Configuration

The configuration presented in this section is part of the Java EE specification, and, as such, must take place regardless of what application server we are using to deploy our application. Application server vendors may optionally require additional steps. In this section we will cover the steps needed to deploy on GlassFish, the Java EE application server bundled with NetBeans. Consult your application server documentation for additional information on other application servers.

When deploying our application to GlassFish, we need to modify `sun-web.xml`, a GlassFish-specific deployment descriptor. This deployment descriptor is automatically generated when we create a web application. It can be found under the **Configuration Files** folder in our project. The file opens in the NetBeans visual `sun-web.xml` editor.

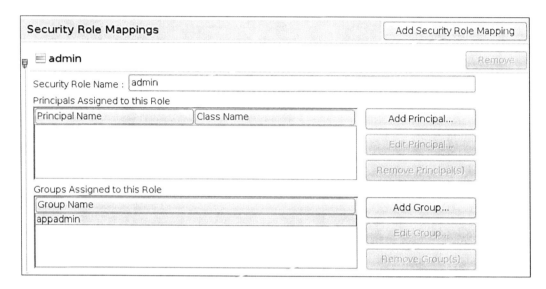

We now need to enter a **Security Role Name**. This name must match the name of a security role defined in the application's **web.xml** deployment descriptor. Then we need to enter one or more groups to be assigned to this role. Groups can be added by clicking the **Add Group...** button and entering the **Group Name**, which must match the name of a security group defined in the security realm our application is using for authentication.

The last thing we need to do to finish configuring application security is to create our users and groups in the security realm used by our application. To do this with the pre-configured file realm in GlassFish, we need to open the GlassFish admin console by going to the **Services** window, right-clicking on the GlassFish node on the server, and selecting **View Admin Console**.

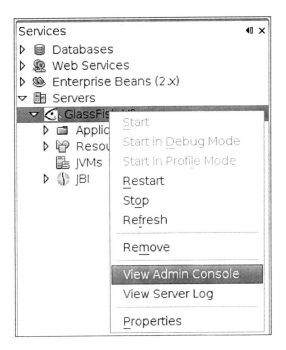

 We need to use the username/password combination we chose when installing NetBeans. The default username/password combination for the GlassFish admin console is admin/adminadmin.

In the GlassFish console, we need to expand the **Configuration** node, followed by **Security**, followed by **Realms**, then click on the **file** realm.

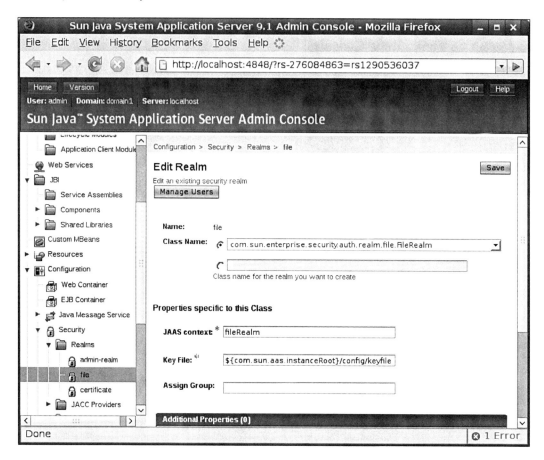

We can add users by clicking on the **Manage Users** button.

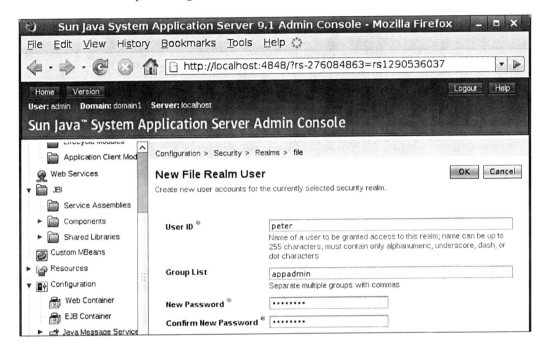

We need to enter the following information for our user, a **User ID**, one or more groups, and a password. The groups our user belongs to must match one of the group names we used in the application's sun-web.xml deployment descriptor. After entering this data and clicking the **OK** button, we are now ready to test our application's security.

After deploying our application and pointing the browser to a protected page (`http://localhost:8080/simplewebapp/admin/admin.jsp` in our example), the user is automatically directed to the application's login page.

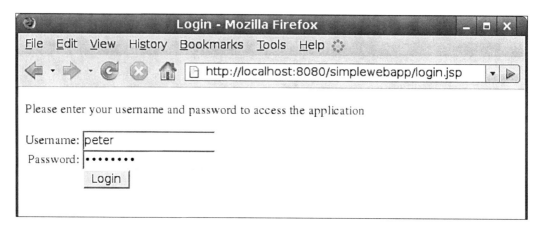

After entering correct credentials we are allowed to access the protected page.

JSP Fragments

In a typical web application, most pages share certain common areas such as a navigation menu, a header, footer, and so forth. Since these areas must be identical across pages, maintaining them can be a tedious process since every change in one of these areas must be done in each and every page in the application. To avoid this situation in Java web applications, we can create JSP fragments that can be included in every page. This way if we need to make a change, we only need to do it in the JSP fragment.

In the previous section, we created a login form on both the `login.jsp` and `loginerror.jsp` pages. If we wish to change the look of this login form, we would have to do it twice, once in each page. This form is a perfect candidate to be extracted to a JSP fragment.

Creating a JSP Fragment in NetBeans

To create a JSP fragment in NetBeans, we simply need to go to **File | New**, select **Web** as the category, then **JSP** as the file type. We then fill out all the information in the **New JSP File** window as usual, making sure to check the **Create as JSP Segment** checkbox.

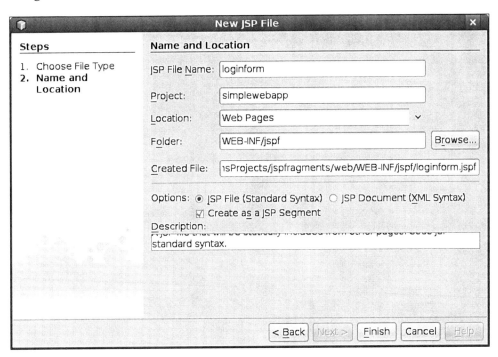

NetBeans suggests placing the JSP fragment under `WEB-INF/jspf`. The reason for this is that any files under the `WEB-INF` folder are not directly accessible via the web browser. Since JSP fragments are not full JSPs, most of the time they won't render properly in a web browser by themselves, therefore it is a good idea to follow NetBeans' suggestion.

 NetBeans will automatically create the `WEB-INF/jspf` folder for us if it doesn't already exist.

At this point, NetBeans generates our page with some trivial content meant to be replaced with something else.

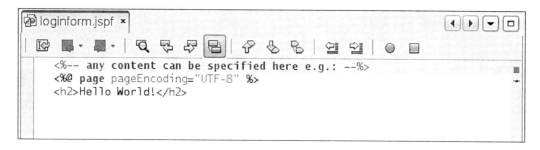

In our case what we want to do is extract the form used in both `login.jsp` and `loginerror.jsp` into the page fragment.

```
loginform.jspf ×

<form method="POST" action="j_security_check">
    <table cellpadding="0" cellspacing="0" border="0">
        <tr>
            <td align="right">Username: </td>
            <td><input type="text" name="j_username"></td>
        </tr>
        <tr>
            <td align="right">Password: </td>
            <td><input type="password" name="j_password"></td>
        </tr>
        <tr>
            <td></td>
            <td><input type="submit" value="Login"></td>
        </tr>
    </table>
</form>
```

We simply copied the form from `login.jsp` and pasted it into the JSP fragment.

The next thing we need to do is modify `login.jsp` and `loginerror.jsp` to use the JSP fragment by replacing the HTML form with a JSP include directive. The modified version of `login.jsp` is shown next.

```
<%@ page language="java" contentType="text/html; charset=UTF-8"
        pageEncoding="UTF-8"%>
<!DOCTYPE html PUBLIC "-//W3C//DTD HTML 4.01 Transitional//EN"
    "http://www.w3.org/TR/html4/loose.dtd">
<html>
```

```
<head>
<meta http-equiv="Content-Type" content="text/html; charset=UTF-8">
<title>Login</title>
</head>
<body>
<p>Please enter your username and password to access the application</p>
<%@ include file="WEB-INF/jspf/loginform.jspf" %>
</body>
</html>
```

The include directive inserts the contents of the JSP fragment into our page. The value of its file attribute is a relative path to the file we want to include. When the page is rendered in the browser, the contents of the included `file` are placed where we placed our include directive.

> *Ctrl+Space* code completion works between the double quotes for the file attribute.

After making this change in `loginerror.jsp`, we have successfully extracted the common markup between both pages into a single JSP fragment. Our application will behave exactly as it did before, but it is now more maintainable since changes to the HTML form have to be done only once.

Monitoring Web Applications with NetBeans HTTP Monitor

When deploying any application by right-clicking on the project and selecting **Run**, the HTTP monitor pops up at the bottom of the NetBeans main window.

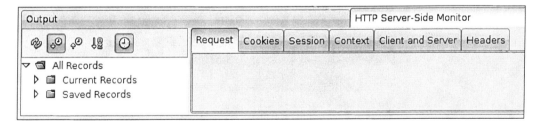

The HTTP monitor allows us to easily see request parameters and attributes, as well as cookies, session attributes, context (application) attributes, information about the client (browser) and server, as well as request headers.

Expanding the node labeled **Current Records** on the left pane of the HTTP monitor, then clicking on one of its child nodes, results in the right pane displaying information about the selected record.

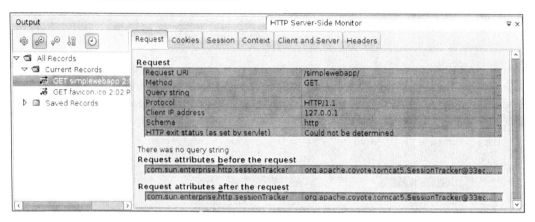

At a glance we can see a lot of information such as the request URI, HTTP method, query string, etc. Notice that we can see an object stored as a request attribute. This request attribute is set behind the scenes by GlassFish, which is the application server we are using to deploy our application.

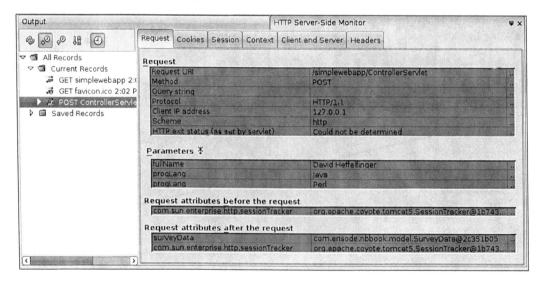

Notice that now we can see some additional information, the name and values of the request parameters corresponding to the fields in the input JSP file, we can also see the instance of `SurveyData` we stored as a request attribute when the `processRequest()` method of our servlet was executed.

The different tabs in the HTTP monitor allows us to examine different pieces of information. The **Cookies** tab allows us to see any incoming or outgoing cookies.

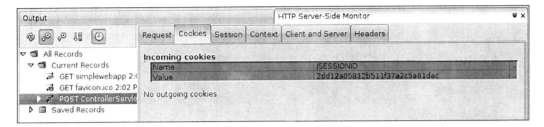

Incoming cookies are cookies that were set *before* our code (JSP or servlet) executed. Outgoing cookies are cookies that were set *while* our code executed. In the previous screen shot, we can see that a cookie was automatically added by the application server. This cookie is used to track the user session.

> We can add our own cookies by invoking the `addCookie()` method on the `response` object. This method takes an instance of `javax.servlet.http.Cookie` as its sole parameter. Right after the code invoking this method has executed, the cookie will be displayed as an outgoing cookie; it will be displayed as an incoming cookie afterwards.

The **Session** tab indicates if the session was created as a result of the request, or if it existed previously.

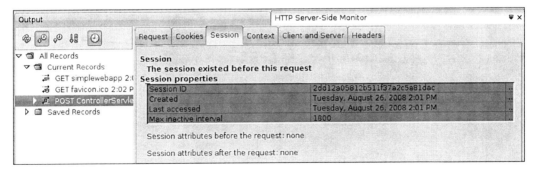

It also displays session properties such as the session ID, the session creation date, the date the session was last accessed, and the allowed time of inactivity (in seconds) allowed before the session expires.

The session tab also shows session attributes that existed before the request (if any) and session attributes that were created during the request (if any).

The **Context** tab displays context information, including context attributes and initialization parameters.

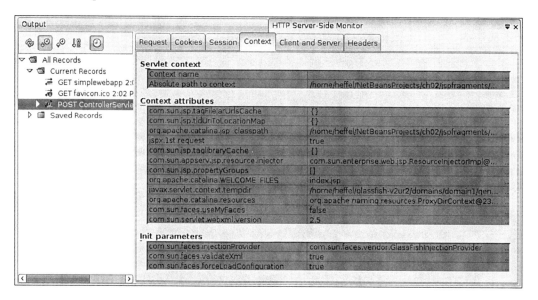

We can once again see attributes that were set by the application server. Had our code stored objects as context attributes, they would be shown on this tab as well.

We can also see some initialization parameters that were added by the application server. We can add initialization parameters by modifying the application's web.xml deployment descriptor. Adding the following lines to our application's web.xml would result in an initialzation parameter named admin_email with a value of admin@nowhere.com to be added to the servlet context.

```
<context-param>
    <param-name>admin_email</param-name>
    <param-value>admin@nowhere.com</param-value>
</context-param>
```

Had we done this for our application, we would have seen our initialization parameter listed under the **Init parameters** section of the **Context** tab.

 An alternate way of adding context parameters to our web application is to use NetBeans' web.xml visual editor, in the **General** tab.

Recall that the servlet context is available from any servlet or JSP in our application. In a servlet, it can be obtained by invoking the getServletContext() method, which returns an instance of javax.servlet.ServletContext, and is defined in the javax.servlet.GenericServlet class, which is a "grandparent" class of all servlets in a web application. We can obtain the value of an initialization parameter by invoking the getInitParameter() method on this instance of ServletContext. This method takes the parameter name as a String, and returns the parameter value as a String.

The **Client and Server** tab of the HTTP monitor displays information about the server where the application is deployed and about the browser used to access the application.

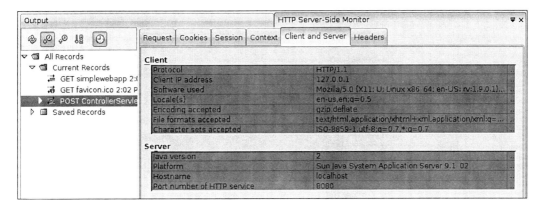

Lastly, the **Headers** tab displays any HTTP headers present when the page was rendered.

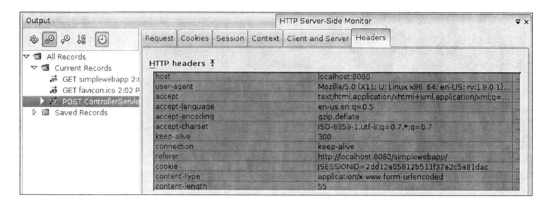

No doubt the ability to inspect request parameters, cookies, attributes in all scopes, and so on, is very useful when working with web applications, but the benefits of NetBean's HTTP monitor don't end there. One very nice feature of the HTTP monitor is the ability to "replay" records.

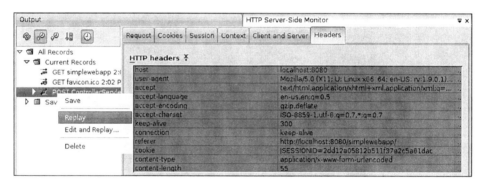

Doing this allows us to navigate directly to the page we are working with, without having to go through any previous pages in our web application. In our little example application there is only one page we need to get to before displaying the page we are using, but in many applications we need to go through several pages before we can get to the page in question. Navigating directly to the page frequently does not work since the page typically needs certain request parameters, or attributes in a scope or another, so that it can be rendered properly. The NetBeans HTTP monitor allows us to save a lot of time by placing any required attributes or request parameters where they belong before navigating to our page.

Additionally, as can be seen in the above screenshot, we can edit the record we are working with. This way we can test our page or servlet with different request parameters, cookies or headers.

After right-clicking on the HTTP Monitor record we wish to work with, then selecting **Edit and Replay...**, the following window pops up.

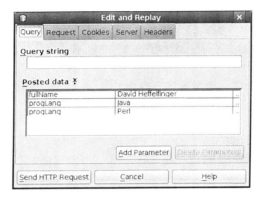

We can add request parameters by clicking on the **Add Parameter** button.

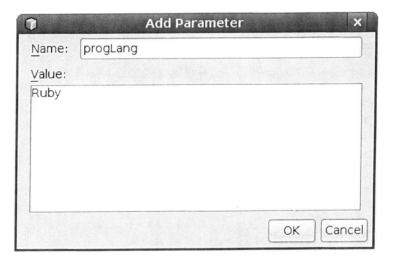

After clicking **OK**, then clicking on the **Send HTTP Request** button, the browser is opened and the application behaves as if the user had entered additional data.

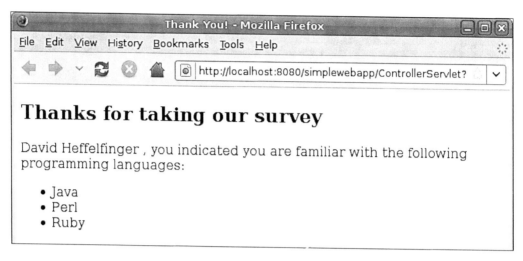

Cookies can be added in the **Cookies** tab and headers can be added in the **Headers** tab. The procedure is very similar to adding a request parameter.

Summary

In this chapter we covered how to develop JSPs to display both static and dynamic content in a web browser. We also saw how to implement the Model-View-Controller design pattern by using JavaBeans as the model component, JSPs as the view, and servlets as controllers. Additionally, we learned how to secure web applications via form based authentication. We also covered how to extract common markup across pages into a single JSP fragment, easing maintenance of web applications. Finally, we saw how the NetBeans HTTP monitor allows us to easily keep track of what is happening to our web application, by allowing us to easily see request, session, and application attributes, request parameters, HTTP headers, and so forth.

3
Enhancing JSP Functionality with JSTL and Custom Tags

In the previous chapter, we covered how to write applications using Servlets and JSPs using NetBeans. In this chapter we will see how NetBeans allows us to easily use the **JSP Standard Tag Library** (**JSTL**) to build JSPs that are readable and maintainable, by relying less on JSP scriptlets.

Topics covered in this chapter include:

- NetBeans support for Core JSTL tags that, among other things, allow us to implement conditional logic and loops in JSPs without resorting to scriptlets
- NetBeans support for SQL JSTL tags that allow us to insert, retrieve, or update data in a relational database
- Using NetBeans to create JSP tags that can help us create more maintainable JSPs by abstracting common markup into a single file

JSTL allows us to add functionality to our pages without having to rely on scriptlets, which tend to create pages that are hard to maintain.

Core JSTL tags allow us to control how pages are displayed, for example, conditionally rendering segments of the page or iterating through a collection of objects to dynamically generate markup from said collection.

SQL JSTL tags allow us to access a database and run SQL queries by simply adding some tags to our JSPs.

Since using JSTL allows us to avoid scriptlets, our pages become more maintainable and easier to read. NetBeans allows us to use both Core JSTL tags and SQL JSTL tags by simply dragging items from the NetBeans palette into our JSPs.

Core JSTL Tags

NetBeans allows us to easily use three core JSTL tags, the `<c:if>` tag used to conditionally render segments of a page; the `<c:choose>` tag, which allows us to render part of a page differently based on a boolean condition; and the `<c:forEach>` tag, which allows us to iterate through an instance of a class implementing `java.util.Collection` or through an array. These tags can be dragged from the NetBeans palette into our page.

Before we can use core JSTL tags, we need to add a **taglib directive** to our page. The taglib directive tells our JSP that we will be using custom tags in the page. For core JSTL tags, the taglib directive looks like this:

```
<%@ taglib prefix="c" uri="http://java.sun.com/jsp/jstl/core" %>
```

The value of the `prefix` attribute is the prefix to be used before any tags in the tag library. By convention, the prefix of `c` is used for JSTL core tags. The value of the `uri` attribute is a **Unique Resource Identifier** that will let our page know where to find the custom tags. Each tag library defines its URI in a tag library descriptor file. For JSTL core tags, the value of the `uri` attribute must always be `http://java.sun.com/jsp/jstl/core`.

Conditionally Displaying Part of a Page with the <c:if> Tag

The JSTL `<c:if>` tag allows us to conditionally display or hide part of a page, based on a boolean condition. With NetBeans, all we need to do to add a JSTL `<c:if>` tag to one of our JSP pages is to drag the **JSTL If** item from the palette to the location in our page where we wish to place the tag.

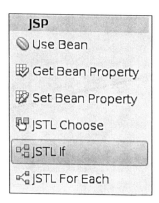

After dragging the **JSTL If** item to our page, NetBeans prompts us for additional information.

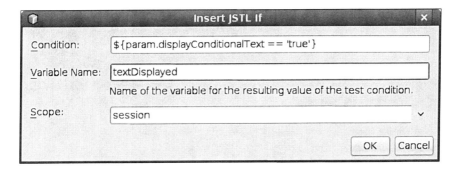

The value of the **Condition** field must be enclosed in **${}**; this denotes this value as a **JSTL expression**. In our particular example, we are looking for a request parameter named **displayConditionalText**, whose value is **true**. If (and only if) the request parameter is present and has the expected value, then the text inside the `<c:if>` tag will be rendered in the generated HTML page from our JSP.

In the above screenshot, `param` is a **JSTL implicit object** to obtain the value of a request parameter. **param.displayConditionalText** is equivalent to `request.getParameter("displayConditionalText")`. As we can see, using the implicit object allows us to save quite a bit of typing, and it makes our expression a lot more readable. There are a lot of JSTL implicit objects, the most common ones are `param`, `applicationScope`, `sessionScope`, `requestScope`, and `pageScope`. Like we already saw, `param` allows us to easily retrieve request parameters. The others in the list allow us to retrieve attributes in the application, session, request, and page scopes, respectively. They all use the dot notation we saw in the `param` implicit object, with the key used to store the attribute following the dot, and return the object attached to the appropriate scope with said key.

To see all implicit JSTL objects, simply invoke code completion (*Ctrl+Space*) between the two curly braces in a JSTL expression (${ }).

Back to our example, the **Variable Name** field is optional, if entered. It will be used to store the value of the conditional expression in a Boolean variable. The **Scope** field is also optional. If a value is selected, this will be the scope of the variable entered in the **Variable Name** field; if no value is selected for the **Scope** field, and a value is entered for the **Variable Name** field, then the variable will have a default scope of page.

After filling out the fields in the **Insert JSTL If** window, as shown in the screenshot, and clicking **OK**, the following markup is generated in our page.

```
<c:if test="${param.displayConditionalText == 'true'}"
    var="textDisplayed" scope="session">
</c:if>
```

We, of course, need to add some markup between the `<c:if>` and `</c:if>` tags, Whatever we add between these two tags will only be rendered if the condition inside the `test` attribute is true.

After adding some markup both before, inside, and after the `<c:if>` tag, the body of our page now looks like this:

```
<body>
        <h2>Hello World!</h2>
        <p>
            This paragraph will always be displayed.
        </p>
        <c:if test="${param.displayConditionalText == 'true'}"
            var="textDisplayed" scope="session">
            <p>
                This paragraph will only be displayed if the request
                parameter named "displayConditionalText" has a value
                of "true".
            </p>
        </c:if>
        <p>
            This paragraph will also always be displayed.
        </p>
</body>
```

We can see how the page is displayed in the browser by right-clicking on it and selecting **Run File** from the resulting pop-up menu.

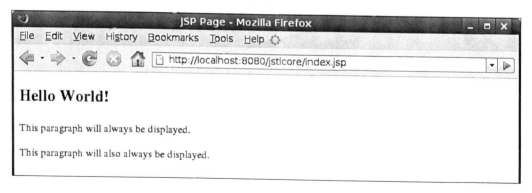

Since the request parameter used in the `<c:if>` tag condition was not present, the markup in its body was not rendered. Modifying the URL, so that the parameter is there and has the expected value, results in the conditional markup being rendered.

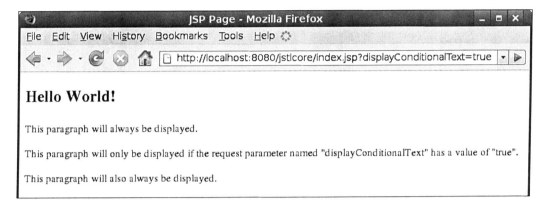

Displaying Mutually Exclusive Markup with the <c:choose> Tag

One disadvantage of the `<c:if>` JSTL tag, discussed in the previous section, is that there is no way to display markup if (and only if) the expression in its `test` attribute evaluates to `false`. If we need this kind of functionality, we need the JSTL `<c:choose>` tag.

Just like with the `<c:if>` tag, we can drag-and-drop the **JSTL Choose** item from the NetBeans palette into our page.

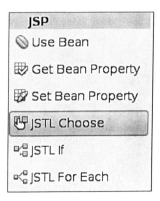

After dropping the **JSTL Choose** item into the appropriate location in our page, we are prompted for additional information.

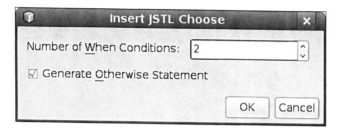

The JSTL `<c:when>` tag needs to have one or more nested `<c:when>` tags, and optionally, a `<c:otherwise>` tag. In the **Insert JSTL Choose** window we indicate how many `<c:when>` tags we need, and if we need a `<c:otherwise>` statement.

After filling out the fields in the **Insert JSTL Choose** window, as shown in the screenshot, the following markup is generated in our page.

```
<c:choose>
    <c:when test="">
    </c:when>
    <c:when test="">
    </c:when>
    <c:otherwise>
    </c:otherwise>
</c:choose>
```

We of course need to fill the body and the value of the test attribute for each `<c:when>` tag, and the body of the `<c:otherwise>` tag. After doing just that and adding some additional markup both before and after the `<c:choose>` tag, the body of our page now looks like this:

```
<body>
  <h2>Hello World!</h2>
  <p>
    This paragraph will always be displayed.
  </p>
  <p>
    <c:choose>
      <c:when
          test="${param.displayConditionalText == '1'}">
        This paragraph will only be displayed if the request
        parameter named "displayConditionalText" has a value
```

```
            of "1".
        </c:when>
        <c:when
            test="${param.displayConditionalText == '2'}">
            This paragraph will only be displayed if the request
            parameter named "displayConditionalText" has a value
            of "2".
        </c:when>
        <c:otherwise>
            This paragraph will only be displayed if the request
            parameter named "displayConditionalText" is either not
            present or has a value different from "1" or
            "2".
        </c:otherwise>
    </c:choose>
    </p>
    <p>
        This paragraph will also always be displayed.
    </p>
    </body>
```

When executing the JSP by right-clicking on it and selecting **Run File**, no request parameter is added to the URL, therefore we see the text inside the `<c:otherwise>` tag displayed in the rendered page.

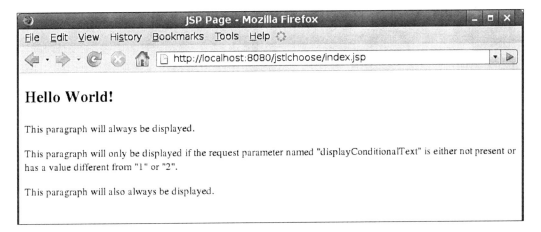

Modifying the URL so that it has the `displayConditionalText` request parameter and one of the expected values results in the corresponding markup to be rendered in the page.

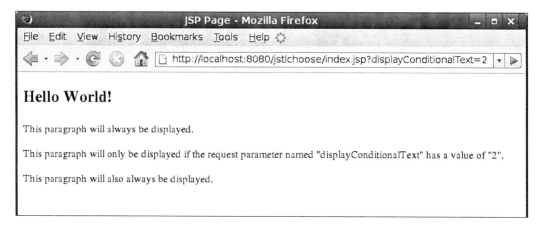

Just like the JSTL `<c:if>` tag, the JSTL `<c:when>` tag has access to all JSTL implicit objects.

In our examples we have been using the equality logical operator (`==`) to compare two objects. This operator is equivalent to the `equals()` method in `java.lang.Object`. There are several other operators that can be used in JSTL expressions. The following table summarizes the most commonly used ones:

Operator Type	Operators
Arithmetic	`+`, `-`, `*`, `/` (or `div`), `%` (or `mod`)
Logical	`&&` (or `and`), `||` (or `or`), `!` (or `not`), `empty`
Relational	`==` (or `eq`), `>` (or `gt`), `<` (or `lt`), `>=` (or `ge`), `<=` (or `le`)

All of these operators should be intuitive to any moderately experienced Java programmer. Notice that many of the operators have both symbolic and textual versions. The reason for the textual versions is that they do not invalidate XML pages, allowing us to use JSTL in XHTML or any other XML markup.

Iterating through Arrays or Collections with the <c:forEach> Tag

Many times it is necessary to repeatedly generate markup which is almost identical. A typical example is the need to generate table rows. The only difference between the markup for each row is the contents of each cell, other than that the markup is identical. In cases like this, it is useful to iterate through an array or collection of objects, generating the required markup in each iteration.

For cases like this, JSTL provides the <c:forEach> tag, just like tags previously discussed in this chapter. The <c:forEach> tag can be dragged from the NetBeans palette and dropped into our page.

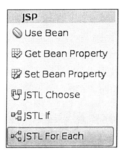

After dropping the **JSTL For Each** item into the appropriate location in our page, we are prompted for additional information.

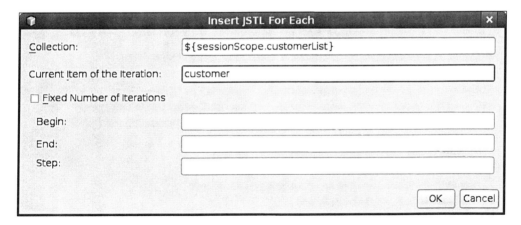

The value of the **Collection** text field must be a JSTL expression resolving to either a class implementing the java.util.Collection interface, or to an array. In our example, we are retrieving an ArrayList attached to the session scope with the name **customerList**.

The value of the **Current item of the Iteration** text field is the name we wish to use to refer to the current iteration item inside the body of the tag. In our example, we chose to name the current item **customer**.

Although we typically wish to iterate through the whole collection or array, the JSTL `<c:forEach>` tag allows us to specify the index of the element in the array or `Collection` to begin iterating from, where the first element has an index of `0`. To do this, we need to check the **Fixed Number of Iterations** check box, and specify the index of the element we wish to start iterating from as the value of the **Begin** text field.

Similarly, if we wish to stop iterating at a specific element in the array or collection, we can specify the index of the element we wish to end iterating by entering its index as the value of the **End** text field.

If we don't wish to process every item in the array or collection we are iterating through, and instead we wish to process every other item, or every three items, we can specify this by entering a value for the **Step** text field. For example, if we wished to process every other item, we would enter a value of **2** for this field.

After filling out the fields of the **Insert JSTL for Each** field window, as shown in the above screenshot, and clicking **OK**, the following markup is added to our page:

```
<c:forEach var="customer" items="{sessionScope.customerList}">
</c:forEach>
```

We then modify the page, adding a scriptlet to create the `ArrayList` we are iterating through and adding it as a session attribute, plus adding some markup inside the body of the `<c:forEach>` tag, as well as before and after the tag.

```
<%@page contentType="text/html" pageEncoding="UTF-8"%>
<%@page import="java.util.ArrayList" %>
<%@page import="com.ensode.nbbook.CustomerBean" %>
<%@ taglib prefix="c" uri="http://java.sun.com/jsp/jstl/core" %>
<!DOCTYPE HTML PUBLIC "-//W3C//DTD HTML 4.01 Transitional//EN"

  "http://www.w3.org/TR/html4/loose.dtd">
<%
  ArrayList<CustomerBean> customerList = new
      ArrayList<CustomerBean>();

  customerList.add(new CustomerBean("David", "Heffelfinger"));
  customerList.add(new CustomerBean("Jeff", "Wu"));
  customerList.add(new CustomerBean("Jacqueline", "Smith"));

  session.setAttribute("customerList", customerList);
```

```
%>
<html>
    <head>
        <meta http-equiv="Content-Type" content="text/html;
                                    charset=UTF-8">
        <title>JSP Page</title>
    </head>
    <body>
        <h2>Hello World!</h2>
        <table border="1" cellpadding="1" cellspacing="0">
            <thead>
                <tr>
                    <th>First Name</th>
                    <th>Last Name</th>
                </tr>
            </thead>
            <tbody>
                <c:forEach var="customer"
                    items="${sessionScope.customerList}">
                    <tr>
                        <td>${customer.firstName}</td>
                        <td>${customer.lastName}</td>
                    </tr>
                </c:forEach>
            </tbody>
        </table>

    </body>
</html>
```

Notice at the top of the JSP, that the ArrayList we attach to the session contains instances of a class called CustomerBean. This class is a simple JavaBean with two properties, firstName and lastName. In the body of the <c:forEach> tag, we access the getter methods for these properties by simply entering the name of the property after the name we gave for the current item in the list (customer). For example, to invoke the getFirstName() getter method in CustomerBean, we simply need to type ${customer.firstName} inside the body of the <c:forEach> tag. This notation allows us to easily invoke getter methods in JavaBeans from JSTL scriptlets. The notation can be used with any expression that resolves to a JavaBean; it is not limited to the body of a <c:forEach> tag.

As we have seen before, the easiest way to deploy our web application and execute our file in the browser is to right-click anywhere in the file and select **Run File** from the resulting pop-up menu.

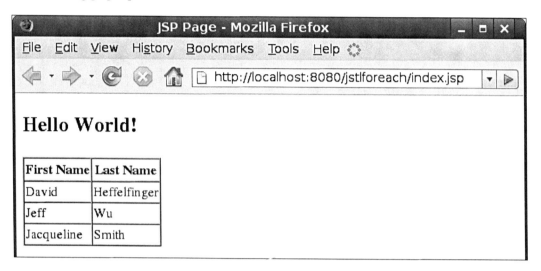

All table rows are generated by iterating through the collection. The values we see in each cell are the values of the `firstName` and `lastName` of each instance of `CustomerBean` in the `ArrayList` we iterated through.

SQL JSTL Tags

JSTL includes an SQL tag library that allows us to quickly and easily write web applications that interact with a relational database. NetBeans supports the most commonly used tags in the SQL tag library, allowing us to use these tags by simply dragging them from its palette into our JSP pages.

All JSTL tags are supported in NetBeans, however only a subset of them is available in the NetBeans palette to be dropped in our JSPs. For tags not included in the palette, we simply need to type the appropriate tag in the page markup.

Although SQL JSTL tags allow us to quickly create web applications that interact with a database, they tend to create applications that are hard to maintain, since they mix database access with display logic. For this reason, these tags are suitable for prototyping and for "**throwaway**" applications.

In order to successfully use the SQL JSTL tags, we need to create a connection pool and data source in the application server we are using to deploy our application. NetBeans comes pre-configured with a sample database, and the integrated GlassFish application server included with NetBeans comes with a datasource to access this sample database out of the box. In this section we will be using the sample database and its corresponding datasource. In Chapter 5 we will explain how to configure NetBeans and GlassFish to interact with a relational database that hasn't been pre-configured.

Before we can interact with a relational database through the JSTL SQL tags, we need to configure our application to have access to the data source providing access to the appropriate relational database. We can accomplish this by adding a resource reference in our application's web.xml deployment descriptor.

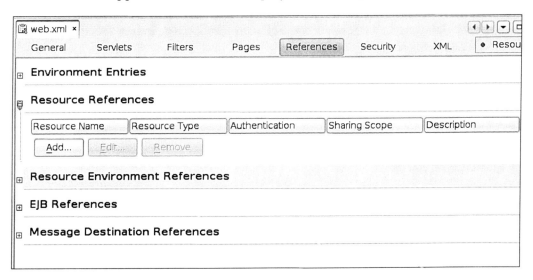

We can add this resource reference by opening our application's `web.xml` deployment descriptor (located under the **Configuration Files** folder), clicking on the **References** button in the tool bar, then expanding the **Resource References** node, and clicking on the **Add...** button.

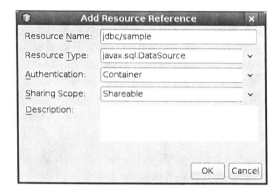

For our purposes, all we need to do is add a value for the **Resource Name** text field. The value of this field must be the **Java Naming and Directory Interface (JNDI)** name of the data source we wish to use with our application. In our specific example, this JNDI name is `jdbc/sample`.

After entering the resource name for our datasource and clicking **OK**, we can see it listed in the **Resource References** section of our application's `web.xml`.

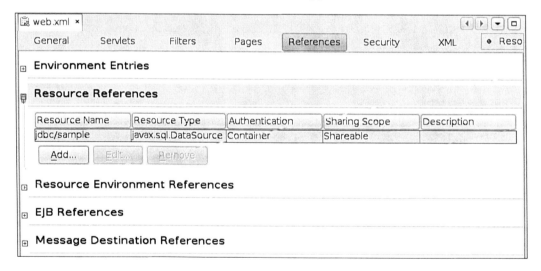

At this point we are ready to use the JSTL SQL library. Just like with any other tag library, we need to add a `taglib` directive at the top of any JSP that will use the JSTL SQL tags.

```
<%@ taglib prefix="sql" uri="http://java.sun.com/jsp/jstl/sql" %>
```

By convention, the prefix of `sql` is used for the JSTL SQL tag library, its `uri` (Uniform Resource Identifier) is always `http://java.sun.com/jsp/jstl/sql`.

Retrieving Database Data with the <sql:query> Tag

The first JSTL SQL tag that we will cover is the `<sql:query>` tag. This tag allows us to execute an SQL `SELECT` statement, and store it in an object implementing the `javax.servlet.jsp.jstl.sql.Result` interface. We can then iterate through this object with the standard JSTL `<c:forEach>` tag.

The `javax.servlet.jsp.jstl.sql.Result` interface defines a number of methods that we can call from a `<c:forEach>` tag in order to display database data on the page. These methods are outlined in the following table.

Method Name	Description
`getColumnNames()`	Returns an array of `String` objects containing the column names in the result set.
`getRowCount()`	Returns an `int` indicating the number of rows in the result set.
`getRows()`	Returns an array of `java.util.SortedMap` objects. Each element in the array represents a row in the result set. Keys in each `SortedMap` are `String` objects containing the column names; values are objects representing the value for the column in the current row.
`getRowsByIndex()`	Returns a bi-dimensional array of Objects representing the rows and columns of the result set.
`isLimitedByMaxRows()`	Returns a boolean indicating if the maximum number of rows in the result set was limited by the `maxRows` attribute of the `<sql:query>` tag.

As we can see, all methods defined in the `javax.servlet.jsp.jstl.sql.Result` interface are getter methods that conform to the JavaBean specification, therefore these methods can be accessed as JavaBean properties from JSTL tags.

The easiest way to add an `<sql:query>` tag to one of our JSPs is to simply drag the **DB Query** item from the NetBeans palette into our page.

After dropping this item into our page, we are prompted for additional information.

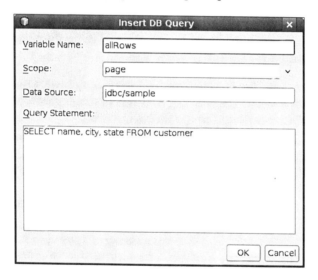

The **Variable Name** field is the name that will be given to the variable that will hold the result set generated by our query. The **Scope** field is the scope where this variable will be stored; the variable can be stored on any valid scope (**page**, **request**, **session**, or **application**). The **Data Source** field is for the JNDI name of the data source we will be using to obtain a connection to the database, this data source must be added as a resource reference to our web application's `web.xml` deployment descriptor, as explained in the previous section.

After entering appropriate values for all fields and clicking **OK**, the following markup is generated in our page:

```
<sql:query var="allRows" dataSource="jdbc/sample">
    SELECT name, city, state FROM customer
</sql:query>
```

The values of the `var` and `dataSource` attributes of the tag correspond to the values we entered in the **Variable Name** and **Data Source** fields in the **Insert DB Query** window. Since page scope is the default scope, we don't see an attribute defining the variable scope. Had we picked a scope different from page, NetBeans would have added a scope attribute to the tag, containing the scope for the variable as its value (that is `scope="session"`).

We then need to add some logic to our page to traverse the result set. This is typically done through the `<c:forEach>` tag. After adding the required markup, the body of our page now looks like this:

```
<body>
    <h2>Hello World!</h2>
    <sql:query var="allRows" dataSource="jdbc/sample">
        SELECT name, city, state FROM customer
    </sql:query>
    <table border="1">
        <thead>
            <tr>
                <th>Name</th>
                <th>Location</th>
            </tr>
        </thead>
        <tbody>
            <c:forEach var="currentRow"
                items="${allRows.rows}">
                <tr>
                    <td>${currentRow.name}</td>
                    <td>${currentRow.city},
                        ${currentRow.state}
                    </td>
                </tr>
            </c:forEach>
        </tbody>
    </table>
</body>
```

Notice how we dynamically generate table rows with the `<c:forEach>` tag.

After deploying our application we can see the resulting page.

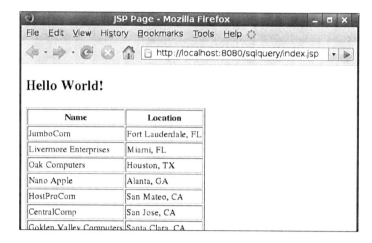

The technique illustrated in this example is very common. Very frequently an `<sql:query>` tag is used, followed by a `<c:forEach>` tag used to generate a database table from the result set. Since the technique is so common, NetBeans provides an item in its palette to generate both the `<sql:query>` tag and the `<c:forEach>` tag, including the static markup for the table just before and after the `<c:forEach>` tag. To take advantage of this functionality, we simply drag the **DB Report** item from the NetBeans palette into our page.

After dropping the **DB Report** item into our page, we get a window that is very similar to the one we get when dropping the **DB Query** item. After entering values for the **Variable Name**, **Scope**, **Data Source**, and **Query Statement** fields, the following markup is generated in the location where we dropped the **DB Report** item.

```
<sql:query var="result" dataSource="jdbc/sample">
    SELECT name, city, state FROM customer
</sql:query>

<table border="1">
    <!-- column headers -->
```

```
<tr>
    <c:forEach var="columnName"
        items="${result.columnNames}">
        <th><c:out value="${columnName}"/></th>
    </c:forEach>
</tr>
<!-- column data -->
<c:forEach var="row" items="${result.rowsByIndex}">
    <tr>
        <c:forEach var="column" items="${row}">
            <td><c:out value="${column}"/></td>
        </c:forEach>
    </tr>
</c:forEach>
</table>
```

Notice that the generated `<c:forEach>` tags dynamically generate the table header by invoking the `getColumNames()` method of the `javax.servlet.jsp.jstl.sql.Result` interface as a JavaBean property. Similarly, the bi-dimensional array returned by the `getRowsByIndex()` method is used to traverse the result set and display its contents on the page.

Modifying Database Data with the <sql:update> Tag

The JSTL `<sql:update>` tag allows us to modify database data either through SQL `INSERT`, `UPDATE`, or `DELETE` statements. Just like other JSTL tags we have discussed so far, the easiest way to use this tag with NetBeans is to drag the appropriate item from the NetBeans palette into our page.

Inserting Database Data

To execute an `INSERT` statement, we can drag the **DB Insert** item from the NetBeans palette into our page.

After dropping the **DB Insert** item into our page, we are prompted for additional information.

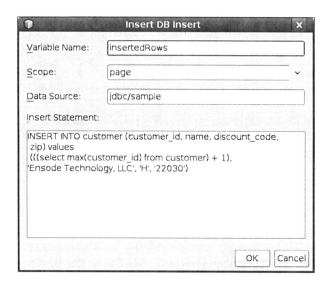

The value of the **Variable Name** field is a variable of type `java.lang.Integer` which will hold the number of rows that were inserted into the database after the `INSERT` statement was executed.

The **Scope** field must contain the scope where the value of the **Variable Name** field will be stored.

The **Data Source** field must contain the JNDI name of the data source used to obtain a database connection. This data source must be added as a **Resource References** to our application's `web.xml` deployment descriptor as explained earlier in this chapter.

Finally, the value of the **Insert Statement** field allows us to specify the SQL `INSERT` statement to be executed.

After entering the appropriate data for all fields in the **Insert DB Insert** window, the following markup is generated in our page:

```
<sql:update var="insertedRows" dataSource="jdbc/sample">
    INSERT INTO customer (customer_id, name,
    discount_code,zip) values
    (((select max(customer_id) from customer) + 1),
    'Ensode Technology, LLC', 'H', '22030')
</sql:update>
```

The attributes and the body of the generated `<sql:update>` tag get populated from the data we entered in the **Insert DB Insert** window.

We can add a **DB Report** item from the NetBeans palette, so that we can see the value we inserted into the database. After doing so, the body of our page looks like this:

```
<body>
    <h2>Hello World!</h2>
    <sql:update var="insertedRows" dataSource="jdbc/sample">
        INSERT INTO customer (customer_id, name,
        discount_code, zip) values
        (((select max(customer_id) from customer) + 1),
        'Ensode Technology, LLC', 'H', '22030')
    </sql:update>

    <sql:query var="result" dataSource="jdbc/sample">
        SELECT customer_id, name, discount_code, zip FROM
      customer where name like ?
        <sql:param value="Ensode%" />
    </sql:query>

    <table border="1">
        <!-- column headers -->
        <tr>
            <c:forEach var="columnName"
                    items="${result.columnNames}">
                <th><c:out value="${columnName}"/></th>
            </c:forEach>
        </tr>
        <!-- column data -->
        <c:forEach var="row" items="${result.rowsByIndex}">
            <tr>
                <c:forEach var="column" items="${row}">
                    <td><c:out value="${column}"/></td>
                </c:forEach>
            </tr>
        </c:forEach>
    </table>
</body>
```

Notice that inside the body of the `<sql:query>` tag we added a `<sql:param>` tag, this tag is used to dynamically substitute items in the WHERE clause of the SQL SELECT statement in the tag, in a matter similar to the way the `java.sql.PreparedStatement` interface works. In the query, question marks are used to indicate parameters that need to be substituted with `<sql:param>` tags. Should our query have multiple parameters (for example, when the values of two or more columns are used in its WHERE clause), we can use a question mark for each parameter in the query. The body of the `<sql:query>` tag must have a `<sql:param>` tag for each question mark in the query; the first `<sql:param>` will contain the value for the first question mark, the second one will contain the value for the second question mark, and so forth. The `value` attribute of the `<sql:param>` tag can contain a String literal or a JSTL expression.

By deploying our application and pointing the browser to our page (or simply right-clicking on the page and selecting **Run File**), we can see the `<sql:update>` tag in action.

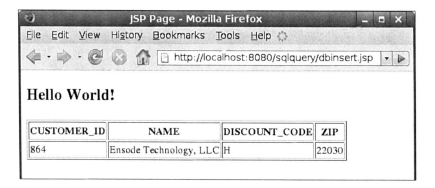

Every time we reload our page, a new row is added to the database, and the table on the page is updated accordingly.

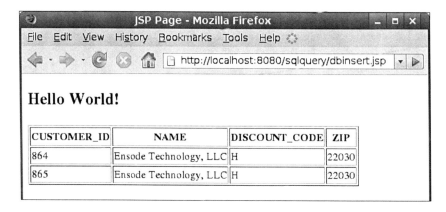

Updating Database Data

Like we mentioned earlier, the `<sql:update>` tag can be used for executing both SQL INSERT and UPDATE statements in the database. The easiest way to use this tag to execute an SQL UPDATE statement is to drag the **DB Update** item from the NetBeans palette into our page.

Like most JSTL SQL tags discussed so far, the easiest way to create an `<sql:update>` statement that updates existing rows in a database table is to drag the **DB Update** item from the NetBeans palette into our page.

After doing so, we are prompted for the usual additional information.

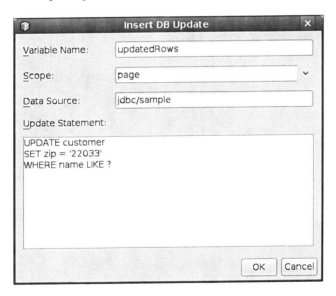

Here we see the same fields we saw when we were using this tag to insert a row into a database table. In this case the **Variable Name** field indicates the number of rows that were updated by the UPDATE statement. When clicking the **OK** button, the following markup is generated in the location where we dropped the **DB Update** palette item.

```
<sql:update var="updatedRows" dataSource="jdbc/sample">
    UPDATE customer
    SET zip = '22033'
    WHERE name LIKE ?
</sql:update>
```

Since we have a parameter in our query, we need to add a `<sql:param>` tag inside our `<sql:update>` tag.

```
<sql:update var="updatedRows" dataSource="jdbc/sample">
    UPDATE customer
    SET zip = '22033'
    WHERE name LIKE ?
    <sql:param value="Ensode%"/>
</sql:update>
```

Just like we did in our last page, we can add a **DB Report** item from the NetBeans palette so that we can visually inspect the effect of the `<sql:update>` tag. After doing so, the body of our page looks like this:

```
<body>
    <h2>Hello World!</h2>
    <sql:update var="updatedRows" dataSource="jdbc/sample">
        UPDATE customer
        SET zip = '22033'
        WHERE name LIKE ?
        <sql:param value="Ensode%"/>
    </sql:update>

    <sql:query var="result" dataSource="jdbc/sample">
        SELECT customer_id, name, discount_code, zip
        FROM customer where name like ?
        <sql:param value="Ensode%" />
    </sql:query>

    <table border="1">
        <!-- column headers -->
        <tr>
            <c:forEach var="columnName"
```

```
            items="${result.columnNames}">
            <th><c:out value="${columnName}"/></th>
        </c:forEach>
    </tr>
    <!-- column data -->
    <c:forEach var="row" items="${result.rowsByIndex}">
        <tr>
            <c:forEach var="column" items="${row}">
                <td><c:out value="${column}"/></td>
            </c:forEach>
        </tr>
    </c:forEach>
</table>
</body>
```

After deploying our application and opening our page in the browser, we can see the results or our SQL UPDATE statement.

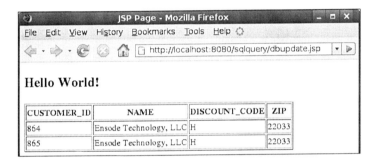

As we can see, the zip codes for all rows we inserted earlier were modified by our SQL UPDATE statement.

Deleting Database Data

The <sql:update> tag can be used to delete data from the database. This can be done by placing an SQL DELETE statement inside its body. With NetBeans, we can simply drag the **DB Delete** item from the NetBeans palette into our page.

After doing so, we are asked for the usual additional information.

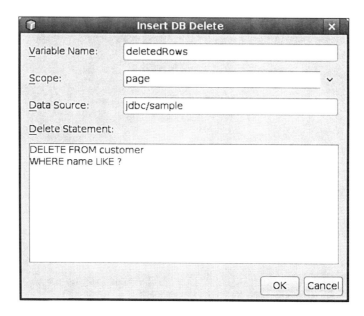

In this case the **Variable Name** field will hold the number of rows that were deleted, the **Scope** and **Data Source** fields hold the scope for the **Variable Name** field and the JNDI name for the data source to be used to connect to the database, respectively. The **Delete Statement** field contains the SQL DELETE statement we will use to delete data from the database. Notice in our example, we used a question mark as a placeholder for an <sql:param> tag.

After clicking the **OK** button, the following markup is generated in our page:

```
<sql:update var="deletedRows" dataSource="jdbc/sample">
    DELETE FROM customer
    WHERE name LIKE ?
</sql:update>
```

In order to substitute the question mark with the appropriate value, we need to add a <sql:param> tag inside the <sql:update> tag.

```
<sql:update var="deletedRows" dataSource="jdbc/sample">
    DELETE FROM customer
    WHERE name like ?
    <sql:param value="Ensode%"/>
</sql:update>
```

Just like we have done in previous examples, we will drag the **DB Report** item from the NetBeans palette into our page, so that we can see the effect that the DELETE statement had in the database. After doing so, the body of our page now looks like this:

```
<body>
    <h2>Hello World!</h2>
    <sql:update var="deletedRows" dataSource="jdbc/sample">
        DELETE FROM customer
        WHERE name like ?
        <sql:param value="Ensode%"/>
    </sql:update>

    <sql:query var="result" dataSource="jdbc/sample">
        SELECT customer_id, name, discount_code, zip FROM customer
                where name like ?
        <sql:param value="Ensode%" />
    </sql:query>

    <table border="1">
        <!-- column headers -->
        <tr>
            <c:forEach var="columnName"
                        items="${result.columnNames}">
                <th><c:out value="${columnName}"/></th>
            </c:forEach>
        </tr>
        <!-- column data -->
        <c:forEach var="row" items="${result.rowsByIndex}">
            <tr>
                <c:forEach var="column" items="${row}">
                    <td><c:out value="${column}"/></td>
                </c:forEach>
            </tr>
        </c:forEach>
    </table>
</body>
```

After executing our page by right-clicking on it and selecting **Run File** from the pop-up menu, we can see the results of our DELETE statement.

Since we deleted all rows matching the criteria in the WHERE clause of the <sql: query> tag generated by the **DB Report** item we dragged into our page, all we see in the rendered page is a table containing only column headers.

Closing Remarks about JSTL

We covered all the JSTL tags supported by NetBeans via drag-and-drop functionality. Additional JSTL tags exist, however they aren't used very frequently, and therefore not included in the NetBeans palette. NetBeans certainly supports code completion for these tags. For more information about JSTL, see the JSTL site at http://java.sun.com/products/jsp/jstl/.

Custom JSP Tags

Sometimes we need to add very similar snippets of HTML to our pages. For example, we might have a calendar component used to input all dates in our system, or we might have a specific format for all address input fields in our application.

Although we can certainly copy and paste the code throughout all JSP pages that need it in our application, this approach is not very desirable, since, if we need to make a change to the common code, we need to go through all the pages and make individual modifications. When using JSPs, we can create custom JSP tags. These JSP tags allow us to create the HTML code we need in one place, then we simply use the tag in any page that requires it. NetBeans has great support for helping us develop custom JSP tags.

Creating a JSP tag is not much different than creating a JSP. To create a JSP tag, a **tag file** is created, it needs to be placed under the WEB-INF/tags folder in our application, or in any subdirectory of this directory.

To create a custom JSP tag file in NetBeans, we need to go to **File** | **New**, select the
Web category, and the **Tag File** file type.

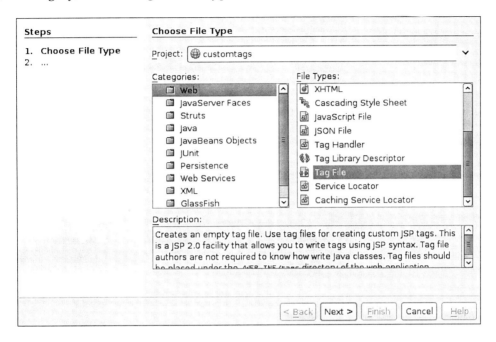

After clicking **Next>**, we are presented with additional choices.

Entering the **Tag File Name** into the first field will result in the value of the **Created** File field to be filled automatically. Default values for all other fields are sensible and in most cases there is no need to modify them.

At this point, NetBeans creates an initial tag file that we can use as a starting point.

```
<%@tag description="put the tag description here" pageEncoding="UTF-8"%>

<%-- The list of normal or fragment attributes can be specified here: --%>
<%@attribute name="message"%>

<%-- any content can be specified here e.g.: --%>
<h2>${message}</h2>
```

Tag files can contain one or more `tag` directives. The `tag` directive is similar to the `page` directive in a JSP. The generated `tag` directive contains two attributes: a `description` attribute used to describe the purpose of the tag, and a `pageEncoding` attribute used to set the page encoding of the tag.

The `attribute` directive allows us to specify what attributes may be sent from the JSP using our tag.

Using the above markup as a starting point, we will now create a tag file that will generate an HTML table containing a series of input fields for entering an address.

```
<%@tag description="Address Input Field" pageEncoding="UTF-8"%>
<jsp:useBean id="addressBean" scope="session"
             class="com.ensode.netbeansbook.AddressBean"/>
<%@ taglib prefix="c" uri="http://java.sun.com/jsp/jstl/core" %>
<%-- The list of normal or fragment attributes can be specified here: --%>
<%@attribute name="addressType" required="true" %>

<table cellpadding="0" cellspacing="0" border="0">
  <tr>
      <td>Line 1: </td>
    <td>
      <input type="text" size="20"
        name="${addressType}_line1"
        id="${addressType}_line1"
        value="${addressBean.line1}"/>
    </td>
  </tr>
```

```
<tr>
  <td>Line 2: </td>
  <td>
    <input type="text" size="20"
      name="${addressType}_line2"
      id="${addressType}_line2"
      value="${addressBean.line2}"/>
  </td>
</tr>
<tr>
  <td>City: </td>
  <td>
    <input type="text" size="20"
      name="${addressType}_city"
      id="${addressType}_city"
      value="${addressBean.city}"/>
  </td>
</tr>
<tr>
  <td>State: </td>
  <td>
    <select name="${addressType}_state"
      id="${addressType}.state">
      <option value=""></option>
      <option value="AL"
        <c:if test="${addressBean.state == 'AL'}">
          selected</c:if>>Alabama
      </option>
      <option value="AK"
        <c:if test="${addressBean.state == 'AK'}">
          selected</c:if>>Alaska
      </option>
      <option value="AZ"
        <c:if test="${addressBean.state == 'AZ'}">
          selected</c:if>>Arizona
      </option>
      <option value="AR"
        <c:if test="${addressBean.state == 'AR'}">
          selected</c:if>>Arkansas</option>
      <option value="CA"
        <c:if test="${addressBean.state == 'CA'}">
          selected</c:if>>California
      </option>
    </select>
```

```
      </td>
    </tr>
    <tr>
      <td>Zip: </td>
      <td><input type="text"
              name="${addressType}_zip"
              id="${addressType}.zip"
              value="${addressBean.zip}" />
      </td>
    </tr>
  </table>
```

Notice that a tag file is not much different from a JSP, it can use JSTL and other tag libraries, it has access to the same implicit objects that a JSP has access to. In our example we use the `<jsp:useBean>` tag to access a JavaBean of type `net.ensode.netBeansbook.AddressBean`, this is a simple JavaBean containing a default no argument constructor and a few arguments.

 Since the `AddressBean` is so simple, its code is not shown, however it is available as part of this book's code download.

Our tag file also uses the JSTL core tag library to implement some conditional logic.

Like we mentioned earlier, a tag file can contain one or more attributes. Our tag file contains a single simple attribute, named `addressType`. This attribute is a `String` we use to append to the names of all input fields in the tag file. The reason we do this is to allow a single JSP to use multiple instances of our tag, allowing fields generated by each tag in the page to have a unique name. Tags can be optional or required. To make a tag required, the `required` attribute of the attribute directive its used, setting its value to `true`. Since not passing the `addressType` attribute to our tag would potentially generate duplicate input field names and id's in a single page, we made this attribute required in our custom address tag.

Notice the comment generated by NetBeans states that normal or fragment attributes can be defined. Fragment attributes allow the page using our tag to send snippets of HTML code to our tag; fragment attributes are defined.

```
<%@attribute name="myattribute" fragment="true"%>
```

Setting the `fragment` attribute to `true` indicates that this attribute is a fragment attribute.

To render the fragment attribute in our tag, the `<jsp:invoke>` standard action:

```
<jsp:invoke fragment="myattribute"/>
```

The JSP using our tag file would need to send it the fragment via the `<jsp:fragment>` action.

```
<prefix:tagname>
  <jsp:attribute name="myattribute">
    <!-- Any HTML or JSP markup can be put here -->
  </jsp:attribute>
</prefix:tagname>
```

The rest of our example generates an HTML table with input fields and tables (for simplicity and brevity, only US addresses are supported, and only a small subset of US states are used as drop-down options).

A JSP invoking our tag would need to include our tag library via the `taglib` directive:

```
<%@ taglib prefix="ct" tagdir="/WEB-INF/tags/" %>
```

Our custom tag library would consist of all custom tags placed in the `WEB-INF/tags` directory in our web application. For our custom tags, we used the `tagdir` attribute of the `taglib` directive to indicate the location of our tags.

 All of our tags must be either directly under `WEB-INF/tags` or in a subdirectory of `WEB-INF/tags`. A custom tag library consists of all custom tags under a single directory.

Our tag can then be invoked by placing the following markup in the JSP file:

```
<ct:address addressType="home"/>
```

Custom JSP tags can contain a body. The JSP invoking our tag would look like the following example:

```
<prefix:sometag>
    <b>Hello there!</b>
</prefix:sometag>
```

 If our tag contains `<jsp:attribute>` actions, we need to place its body between `<jsp:body>` and `</jsp:body>` tags.

Any HTML or JSP markup can be placed in the body of our tag. Our tag renders its body by placing a `<jsp:doBody>` action in the location where we wish to render its body.

Summary

In this chapter we covered how to use NetBeans graphical tools to add JSTL tags to our JSP pages. We saw how JSTL can enhance JSP functionality while at the same time making our JSP's more readable by minimizing the use of scriptlets.

We also saw how to develop our own custom JSP tags to encapsulate JSP markup and functionality, and how NetBeans can generate an initial tag file we can use as a starting point to develop our own custom tags.

Developing Web Applications using JavaServer Faces

In the previous two chapters we covered how to develop web applications in Java using Servlets and JSPs. Although a lot of applications have been written using these APIs, most modern Java applications are written using some kind of web application framework. As of Java EE 5, the standard framework for building web applications is Java Server Faces (JSF). In this chapter we will see how using JSF can simplify web application development.

The following topics will be covered in this chapter:

- Creating a JSF project with NetBeans
- Generating a form to capture user data by draging a JSF form from the NetBeans palette into our page
- Laying out JSF tags by taking advantage of the JSF `<h:panelGrid>` tag
- Using static and dynamic navigation to define navigation between pages
- Using the NetBeans **New JSF Managed Bean** wizard to create a JSF managed bean and automatically add it to the application's `<faces-config.xml>` configuration file
- Using the NetBeans Page Flow editor to establish page navigation by graphically connecting pages
- Implementing custom JSF validators
- Displaying tabular data in our pages by dragging-and-dropping the **JSF Data Table** item from the NetBeans palette into our page

Introduction to JavaServer Faces

Before JSF was developed, Java web applications were typically developed using non-standard web application frameworks such as Apache Struts, Tapestry, Spring Web MVC, or many others. These frameworks are built on top of the Servlet and JSP standards, and automate a lot of functionality that needs to be manually coded when using these APIs directly.

Having a wide variety of web application frameworks available (at the time of writing, Wikipedia lists 35 Java web application frameworks, and this list is far from extensive!), often resulted in "analysis paralysis", that is, developers often spend an inordinate amount of time evaluating frameworks for their applications.

The introduction of JSF to the Java EE 5 specification resulted in having a standard web application framework available in any Java EE 5 compliant application server.

 We don't mean to imply that other web application frameworks are obsolete or that they shouldn't be used at all, however, a lot of organizations consider JSF the "safe" choice since it is part of the standard and should be well supported for the foreseeable future. Additionally, NetBeans offers excellent JSF support, making JSF a very attractive choice.

Strictly speaking, JSF is not a web application framework as such, but a component framework. In theory, JSF can be used to write applications that are not web-based, however, in practice JSF is almost always used for this purpose.

In addition to being the standard Java EE 5 component framework, one benefit of JSF is that it was designed with graphical tools in mind, making it easy for tools and IDEs such as NetBeans to take advantage of the JSF component model with drag-and-drop support for components. NetBeans provides a Visual Web JSF Designer that allow us to visually create JSF applications. This tool is discussed in detail in Chapter 6.

Developing Our first JSF Application

From an application developer's point of view, a JSF application consists of a series of JSP pages containing custom JSF tags, one or more **JSF managed beans**, and a configuration file named `faces-config.xml`. The `faces-config.xml` file declares the managed beans in the application, as well as the navigation rules to follow when navigating from one JSF page to another.

Creating a New JSF Project

To create a new JSF project, we need to go to **File | New Project**, select the **Java Web** project category, and **Web Application** as the project type.

After clicking **Next>**, we need to enter a **Project Name**, and optionally change other information for our project, although NetBeans provides sensible defaults.

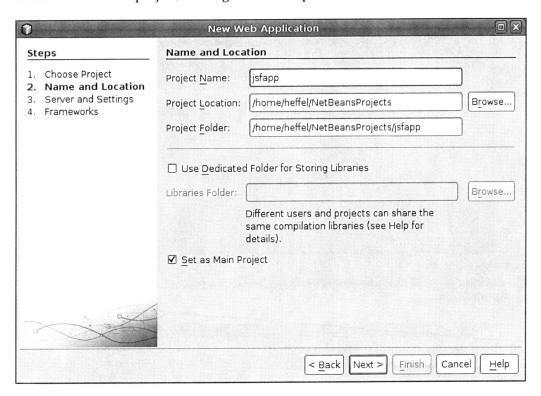

On the next page in the wizard, we can select the **Server**, **Java EE Version**, and **Context Path** of our application. In our example we will simply pick the default values.

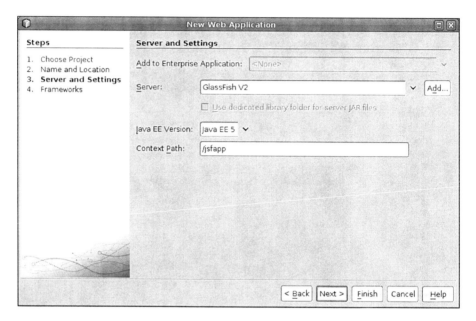

On the next page of the new project wizard, we can select what frameworks our web application will use.

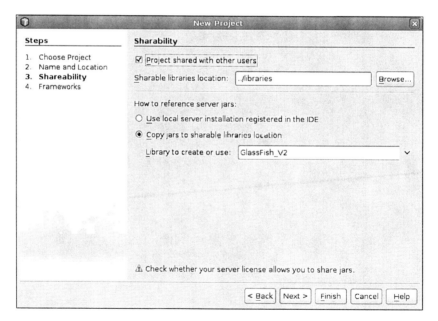

Unsurprisingly, for JSF applications we need to select the JavaServer
Faces framework.

> The Visual Web JavaServer Faces framework allows us to quickly build
> web pages by dragging-and-dropping components from the NetBeans
> palette into our pages. Although it certainly allows us to develop
> applications a lot quicker than manually coding, it hides a lot of the "ins"
> and "outs" of JSF. Having a background in standard JSF development will
> help us understand what the NetBeans Visual Web functionality does
> behind the scenes. Visual Web JSF is covered in Chapter 6.

When clicking **Finish**, the wizard generates a skeleton JSF project for us, consisting
of a single JSP file called `welcomeJSF.jsp`, and a few configuration files: `web.xml`,
`faces-config.xml` and, if we are using the default bundled GlassFish server, the
GlassFish specific `sun-web.xml` file is generated as well.

web.xml is the standard configuration file needed for all Java web applications.
faces-config.xml is a JSF-specific configuration file used to declare JSF-managed
beans and navigation rules. **sun-web.xml** is a GlassFish-specific configuration file
that allows us to override the application's default context root, add security role
mappings, and perform several other configuration tasks.

The generated JSP looks like this:

```
<%@page contentType="text/html"%>
<%@page pageEncoding="UTF-8"%>

<%@taglib prefix="f" uri="http://java.sun.com/jsf/core"%>
<%@taglib prefix="h" uri="http://java.sun.com/jsf/html"%>

<!DOCTYPE HTML PUBLIC "-//W3C//DTD HTML 4.01 Transitional//EN"
    "http://www.w3.org/TR/html4/loose.dtd">

<%--
    This file is an entry point for JavaServer Faces application.
--%>

<html>
    <head>
        <meta http-equiv="Content-Type" content="text/html;
            charset=UTF-8">
        <title>JSP Page</title>
    </head>
    <body>
        <f:view>
            <h1>
                <h:outputText value="JavaServer Faces"/>
            </h1>
        </f:view>
    </body>
</html>
```

As we can see, a JSF enabled JSP file is a standard JSP file using a couple of JSF-specific tag libraries. The first tag library, declared in our JSP by the following line:

```
<%@taglib prefix="f" uri="http://java.sun.com/jsf/core"%>
```

is the core JSF tag library, this library includes a number of tags that are independent of the rendering mechanism of the JSF application (recall that JSF can be used for applications other than web applications). By convention, the prefix f (for faces) is used for this tag library.

The second tag library in the generated JSP, declared by the following line:

```
<%@taglib prefix="h" uri="http://java.sun.com/jsf/html"%>
```

is the JSF HTML tag library. This tag library includes a number of tags that are used to implement HTML specific functionality, such as creating HTML forms and input fields. By convention, the prefix h (for HTML) is used for this tag library.

The first JSF tag we see in the generated JSP file is the `<f:view>` tag. When writing a Java web application using JSF, all JSF custom tags must be enclosed inside an `<f:view>` tag. In addition to JSF-specific tags, this tag can contain standard HTML tags, as well as tags from other tag libraries, such as the JSTL tags discussed in the previous chapter.

The next JSF-specific tag we see in the above JSP is `<h:outputText>`. This tag simply displays the value of its `value` attribute in the rendered page.

The application generated by the new project wizard is a simple, but complete, JSF web application. We can see it in action by right-clicking on our project in the project window and selecting **Run**. At this point the application server is started (if it wasn't already running), the application is deployed and the default system browser opens, displaying our application's welcome page.

Modifying Our JSP to Capture User Data

The generated application, of course, is nothing but a starting point for us to create a new application. We will now modify the generated `welcomeJSF.jsp` file to collect some data from the user.

The first thing we need to do is to add an `<h:form>` tag inside the `<f:view>` tag. The `<h:form>` tag is equivalent to the `<form>` tag in standard HTML pages. We can either type the `<h:form>` tag directly in the page or drag the **JSF Form** item from the palette into the appropriate place in the page markup.

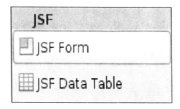

If we choose the second approach, the following window will pop-up:

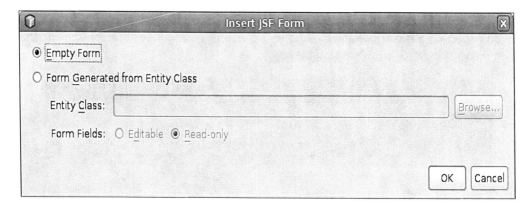

Selecting **Empty Form** will generate an empty `<h:form>` tag which we can use to add our own input fields.

>
> The **Form Generated from Entity Class** selection is a very nice NetBeans feature that allows us to generate a form that will include input fields mapping to all properties in a **Java Persistence API (JPA)** entity. JPA is covered in detail in Chapter 5.

After adding the `<h:form>` tag and a number of additional JSF tags, our page now looks like this:

```
<%@page contentType="text/html"%>
<%@page pageEncoding="UTF-8"%>

<%@taglib prefix="f" uri="http://java.sun.com/jsf/core"%>
<%@taglib prefix="h" uri="http://java.sun.com/jsf/html"%>
```

```
<!DOCTYPE HTML PUBLIC "-//W3C//DTD HTML 4.01 Transitional//EN"
"http://www.w3.org/TR/html4/loose.dtd">

<html>
    <head>
        <meta http-equiv="Content-Type"
        content="text/html; charset=UTF-8">
        <link rel="stylesheet" type="text/css"
        href="../css/style.css">
        <title>JSP Page</title>
    </head>
    <body>
      <f:view>
        <h1><h:outputText value="JavaServer Faces" /></h1>
        <h:form>
          <h:panelGrid columns="3"
            columnClasses="rightalign,leftalign,leftalign">
          <!-- First row begins here -->
          <h:outputLabel value="Salutation: "
            for="salutation"/>
           <h:selectOneMenu id="salutation" label="Salutation"
              value="#{RegistrationBean.salutation}" >
            <f:selectItem itemLabel="" itemValue=""/>
            <f:selectItem itemLabel="Mr." itemValue="MR"/>
            <f:selectItem itemLabel="Mrs." itemValue="MRS"/>
            <f:selectItem itemLabel="Miss" itemValue="MISS"/>
            <f:selectItem itemLabel="Ms" itemValue="MS"/>
            <f:selectItem itemLabel="Dr." itemValue="DR"/>
          </h:selectOneMenu>
          <h:message for="salutation"/>
          <!-- Second row begins here -->
          <h:outputLabel value="First Name:"
            for="firstName"/>
          <h:inputText id="firstName" label="First Name"
             required="true"
            value="#{RegistrationBean.firstName}" />
          <h:message for="firstName" />
          <!-- Third row begins here -->
          <h:outputLabel value="Last Name:" for="lastName"/>
          <h:inputText id="lastName" label="Last Name"
             required="true"
            value="#{RegistrationBean.lastName}" />
          <h:message for="lastName" />
          <!-- Fourth row begins here -->
```

```
                <h:outputLabel for="age" value="Age:"/>
                <h:inputText id="age" label="Age" size="2"
                    value="#{RegistrationBean.age}"/>
                <h:message for="age"/>
                <!-- Fifth row begins here -->
                <h:outputLabel value="Email Address:" for="email"/>
                <h:inputText id="email" label="Email Address"
                    required="true"
                    value="#{RegistrationBean.email}" />
                <h:message for="email" />
                <!-- Sixth row begins here -->
            <h:panelGroup/>
            <h:commandButton id="register" value="Register"
                                            action="submit" />
            </h:panelGrid>
        </h:form>
      </f:view>
     </body>
   </html>
```

The following screenshot illustrates how our page will be rendered at runtime:

All JSF input fields must be inside a `<h:form>` tag. The `<h:panelGrid>` helps us to easily align JSF tags in our page. It can be thought of as a grid where other JSF tags will be placed. The `columns` attribute of the `<h:panelGrid>` tag indicates how many columns the grid will have, each JSF component inside the `<h:panelGrid>` component will be placed in an individual cell of the grid, when the number of components matching the value of the `columns` attribute (three in our example) has been placed inside `<h:panelGrid>`, a new row is automatically started.

The following table illustrates how tags will be laid out inside a `<h:panelGrid>` tag.

First Tag	Second Tag	Third Tag
Fourth Tag	Fifth Tag	Sixth Tag
Seventh Tag	Eighth Tag	Ninth Tag

Each row in our `<h:panelGrid>` consists of an `<h:outputLabel>` tag, an input field, and an `<h:message>` tag.

The `columnClasses` attribute of `<h:panelGrid>` allow us to assign CSS styles to each column inside the panel grid. Its `value` attribute must consist of a comma separated list of CSS styles (defined in a CSS stylesheet). The first style will be applied to the first column, the second style will be applied to the second column, the third style will be applied to the third column, so on and so forth. If our panel grid had more than three columns, then the fourth column would have been styled using the first style in the `columnClasses` attribute, the fifth column would have been styled using the second style in the `columnClasses` attribute, so on and so forth.

 The CSS stylesheet for our example is very simple, therefore it is not shown. However, it is part of the code download for this chapter.

If we wish to style rows in an `<h:panelGrid>`, we can do so with its `rowClasses` attribute, which works the same way that the `columnClasses` works for columns.

`<h:outputLabel>`, generates a label for an input field in the form. The value of its `for` attribute must match the value of the `id` attribute of the corresponding input field.

`<h:message>` generates an error message for an input field. The value of its `for` field must match the value of the `id` attribute for the corresponding input field.

The first row in our grid contains an `<h:selectOneMenu>`. This tag generates an HTML `<select>` tag on the rendered page.

Every JSF tag has an `id` attribute. The value for this attribute must be a string containing a unique identifier for the tag. If we don't specify a value for this attribute, one will be generated automatically. It is a good idea to explicitly state the ID of every component, since this ID is used in runtime error messages (affected components are a lot easier to identify if we explicitly set their IDs).

When using `<h:label>` tags to generate labels for input fields, or when using `<h:message>` tags to generate validation errors, we need to explicitly set the value of the id tag, since we need to specify it as the value of the `for` attribute of the corresponding `<h:label>` and `<h:message>` tags.

Every JSF input tag has a `label` attribute. This attribute is used to generate validation error messages on the rendered page. If we don't specify a value for the `label` attribute, then the field will be identified in the error message by it's ID.

Each JSF input field has a `value` attribute. In the case of `<h:selectOneMenu>`, this attribute indicates which of the options in the rendered `<select>` tag will be selected. The value of this attribute must match the value of the `itemValue` attribute of one of the nested `<f:selectItem>` tags. The value of this attribute is usually a **value binding expression**, which means that the value is read at runtime from a JSF-managed bean. In our example, the value binding expression `#{RegistrationBean.salutation}` is used. What will happen is, at runtime JSF will look for a managed bean named `RegistrationBean`, and look for an attribute named `salutation` on this bean, the `getter` method for this attribute will be invoked, and its return value will be used to determine the selected value of the rendered HTML `<select>` tag.

Nested inside the `<h:selectOneMenu>` there are a number of `<f:selectItem>` tags. These tags generate HTML `<option>` tags inside the HTML `<select>` tag generated by `<h:selectOneMenu>`. The value of the `itemLabel` attribute is the value that the user will see, while the value of the `itemValue` attribute will be the value that will be sent to the server when the form is submitted.

All other rows in our grid contain `<h:inputText>` tags. This tag generates an HTML input field of type `text`, which accepts a single line of typed text as input. We explicitly set the id attribute of all of our `<h:inputText>` fields; this allows us to refer to them from the corresponding `<h:outputLabel>` and `<h:message>` fields. We also set the `label` attribute for all of our `<h:inputText>` tags; this results in user friendlier error messages.

Some of our `<h:inputText>` fields require a value. These fields have their `required` attribute set to `true`, and each JSF input field has a `required` attribute. If we require the user to enter a value for this attribute, then we need to set this attribute to `true`. This attribute is optional, and if we don't explicitly set a value for it, then it defaults to false.

In the last row of our grid, we added an empty `<h:panelGroup>` tag. The purpose of this tag is to allow adding several tags into a single cell of an `<h:panelGrid>`. Any tags placed inside this tag are placed inside the same cell of the grid where `<h:panelGrid>` is placed. In this particular case, all we want to do is to have an "empty" cell in the grid so that the next tag, `<h:commandButton>`, is aligned with the input fields in the rendered page.

`<h:commandButton>` is used to submit a form to the server. The value of it's `value` attribute is used to generate the text of the rendered button. The value of it's `action` attribute is used to determine what page to display after the button is pressed. This is specified in the navigation rules of the application's `faces-config.xml` file, which will be covered later in the chapter.

In our example, we are using **static navigation**. When using JSF static navigation, the value of the `action` attribute of a command button is hard coded in the JSP markup. An alternate to static navigation is **dynamic navigation**. When using dynamic navigation, the value of the `action` attribute of the command button is a value binding expression resolving to a method returning a `String` in a managed bean. The method may then return different values based on certain conditions. Navigation would proceed to a different page, depending on the value of the method.

 As long as it returns a `String`, the managed bean method executed when using dynamic navigation can contain any logic inside it, and is frequently used to save data in a managed bean into a database.

Both when using static or dynamic navigation, the page to navigate to is defined in the application's `faces-config.xml` configuration file. Later in this chapter, we will explain how we can graphically configure navigation rules using the NetBeans Page Flow editor.

Creating Our Managed Bean

JSF-managed beans are standard JavaBeans that are used to hold user-entered data in JSF applications. JSF-managed beans need to be declared in the application's `faces-config.xml` file. NetBeans can help expedite things by automatically adding our managed beans to `faces-config.xml`.

In order to create a new managed bean, we need to go to **File | New**, select **JavaServer Faces** from the category list, and **JSF Managed Bean** from the file type list.

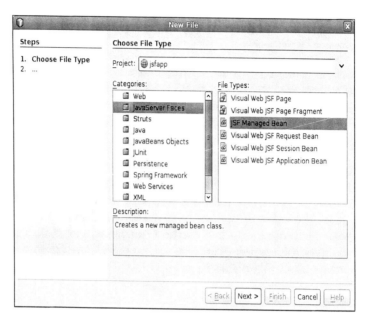

In the next screen in the wizard, we need to enter a name for our managed bean, as well as a package.

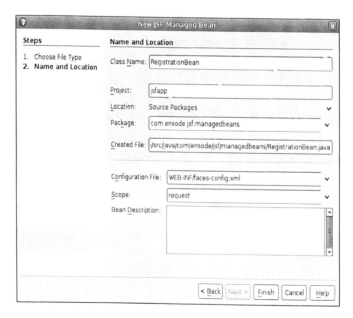

Most default values are sensible and in most cases can be accepted. The only one we should change if necessary is the **Scope** field.

Managed beans can have different scopes. A scope of **request means that** the bean is only available in a single HTTP request. Managed beans **can also have** session scope, in which case they are available in a single user's HTTP **session**. A scope of application means that the bean is accessible to all users in **the application**, across user sessions. Managed beans can also have a scope of none, **which means that the** managed bean is not stored at any scope, but is created on demand as needed. We should select the appropriate scope for our managed bean. In **our** particular example, the default request scope will meet our needs.

After finishing the wizard, two things happen: a boilerplate version of our managed bean is created in the specified package, and our managed bean is added to the application's `faces-config.xml`.

The generated managed bean source simply consists of the class and a public no argument constructor.

```
package com.ensode.jsf.managedbeans;
public class RegistrationBean {
    /** Creates a new instance of RegistrationBean */
    public RegistrationBean() {
    }
}
```

The application's `faces-config.xml` contains our managed bean declaration.

```
<?xml version='1.0' encoding='UTF-8'?>
<faces-config version="1.2"
    xmlns="http://java.sun.com/xml/ns/javaee"
    xmlns:xsi="http://www.w3.org/2001/XMLSchema-instance"
    xsi:schemaLocation="http://java.sun.com/xml/ns/javaee
        http://java.sun.com/xml/ns/javaee/web-facesconfig_1_2.xsd">
    <managed-bean>
        <managed-bean-name>
         RegistrationBean
        </managed-bean-name>
        <managed-bean-class>
         com.ensode.jsf.managedbeans.RegistrationBean
        </managed-bean-class>
        <managed-bean-scope>request</managed-bean-scope>
    </managed-bean>
</faces-config>
```

The value of the `<managed-bean-name>` element matches the value we entered in the **Class Name** field in the wizard. Notice that this value is what we used in the value binding expressions in our page to access the managed bean properties. Although the value we gave the managed bean matches it's class name, this is not mandatory.

The value we entered in the wizard's **Class Name** field is also used as the name of the class that was generated by the wizard, as can be seen by the value of the `<managed-bean-class>` element, which is the fully qualified name of our managed bean class. Unsurprisingly, the package structure matches the value we entered in the **Package** field in the wizard. Finally, we see the scope we selected in the wizard as the value of the **<managed-bean-scope>** element.

At this point, we need to modify our managed bean by adding properties that will hold the user-entered values.

Automatic Generation of Getter and Setter Methods

Netbeans can automatically generate getter and setter methods for our properties. We simply need to click the keyboard shortcut for "insert code", which defaults to *Alt+Insert* in Windows and Linux, then select **Getters and Setters**.

```java
package com.ensode.jsf.managedbeans;

public class RegistrationBean {

    /** Creates a new instance of RegistrationBean */
    public RegistrationBean() {
    }

    private String salutation;
    private String firstName;
    private String lastName;
    private Integer age;
    private String email;

    public String getEmail() {
        return email;
    }

    public void setEmail(String email) {
        this.email = email;
    }
```

```
    public String getFirstName() {
        return firstName;
    }

    public void setFirstName(String firstName) {
        this.firstName = firstName;
    }

    public String getLastName() {
        return lastName;
    }

    public void setLastName(String lastName) {
        this.lastName = lastName;
    }

    public String getSalutation() {
        return salutation;
    }

    public void setSalutation(String salutation) {
        this.salutation = salutation;
    }

    public Integer getAge() {
        return age;
    }

    public void setAge(Integer age) {
        this.age = age;
    }
}
```

Notice that the names of all of the bean's properties (instance variables) match the names we used in the JSP's value binding expressions. These names must match so that JSF knows how to map the bean's properties to the value binding expressions.

Implementing Navigation

The last thing we need to do before we can test our application is to implement application navigation. For our application we need to create a confirmation page, then add navigation rules to our JSP page so that the application navigates from the input page to the confirmation page when the user submits the form.

NetBeans allows us to save some time by allowing us to graphically add navigation rules via the NetBeans **Page Flow Editor**. To do so, we need to open **faces-config. xml** and click on the **PageFlow** button in the toolbar above the file. In our particular case we haven't yet created the confirmation page we wish to navigate to. This is not a problem, since it can be created "on demand" by NetBeans by right-clicking on the **PageFlow** editor and selecting **New File** from the resulting pop-up menu.

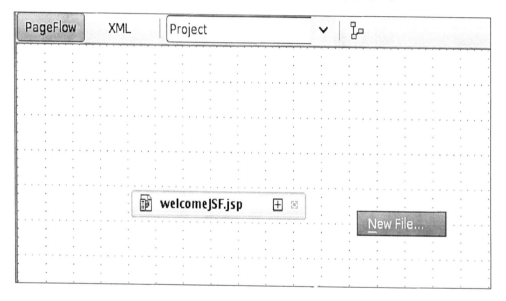

At this point the standard **New JSP File** wizard appears. We enter `confirmation. jsp` as the name of the new JSP. The new page is automatically created and added to the page flow editor.

Refer to Chapter 2 *Developing Web Applications with Servlets and JSPs* for instructions on the **New JSP File** wizard.

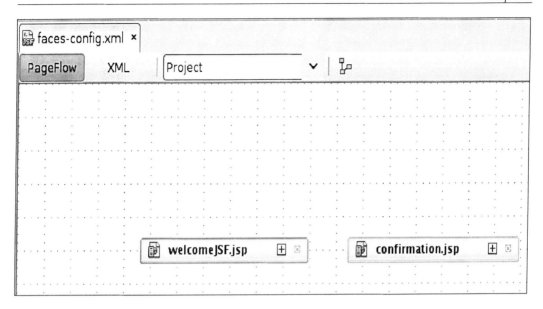

We can graphically connect the two pages by clicking on the connector to the right of **welcomeJSF.jsp** and dragging it to **confirmation.jsp**.

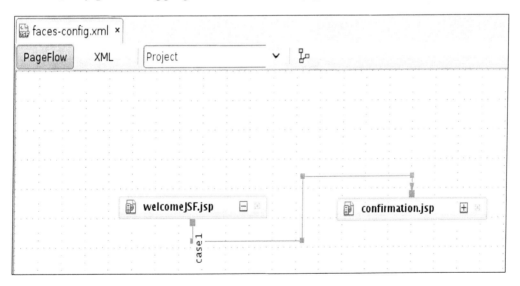

Doing so generates a navigation case from **welcomeJSF.jsp** to **confirmation.jsp**. As we can see, the navigation case is given a default outcome name of **case1**. We need to modify this to be the value of the `action` attribute of the `<h:commandButton>` in `welcomeJSF.jsp`.

To do this, we simply double-click on the text representing the navigation case outcome name, then replace it with the appropriate value.

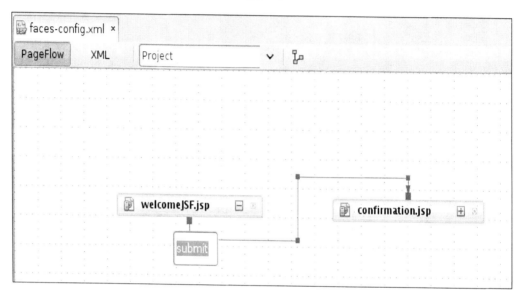

At this point, the navigation case name is updated with the value we entered.

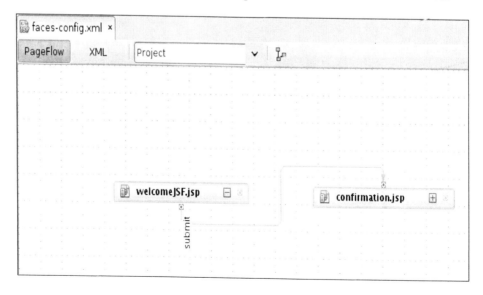

If we had been using dynamic navigation (and, of course, if there were more than two JSP pages in the application), we would simply drag the connector from **welcomeJSF. jsp** to another page to create a different navigation case based on the value of the managed bean method executed when clicking the page's command button.

The NetBeans **PageFlow** editor updates our application's `faces-config.xml` behind the scenes. It adds a `<navigation-rule>` element to it.

```
<navigation-rule>
    <from-view-id>/welcomeJSF.jsp</from-view-id>
    <navigation-case>
        <from-outcome>submit</from-outcome>
        <to-view-id>/confirmation.jsp</to-view-id>
    </navigation-case>
</navigation-rule>
```

The `<from-view-id>` element is the name of the JSP originating the navigation. It is the JSP we drag from in the **PageFlow** editor to create the navigation case. The value of the `<to-view-id>` element is the destination page. It is generated from the JSP we drag the navigation case to in the **PageFlow** editor. The value of the `<from-outcome>` element is the name of the navigation case outcome in the **PageFlow** editor.

If we had been using dynamic navigation, we would have separate `<navigation-case>` elements for each possible return value of the managed bean method bound to the page's command button, the body of the `<from-outcome>` element of each navigation case would be one possible return value, and the body of the `<to-view-id>` would be the page we would navigate to for that particular navigation case.

Notice that the value of the `<from-view-id>` element starts with a forward slash (/). A common mistake when setting up JSF navigation is to forget this initial tag. When this happens, JSF will fail to find the destination JSP and will simply redisplay the page that initiated the navigation. Using NetBean's **PageFlow** editor prevents us from making that mistake.

After setting up our navigation case, we now need to modify the generated `confirmation.jsp` so that it displays the values in our managed bean.

```
<%@page contentType="text/html" pageEncoding="UTF-8"%>
<!DOCTYPE HTML PUBLIC "-//W3C//DTD HTML 4.01 Transitional//EN"
    "http://www.w3.org/TR/html4/loose.dtd">
<%@ taglib prefix="f" uri="http://java.sun.com/jsf/core" %>
<%@ taglib prefix="h" uri="http://java.sun.com/jsf/html" %>
<html>
```

```
<head>
  <meta http-equiv="Content-Type" content="text/html;
      charset=UTF-8">
  <link rel="stylesheet" type="text/css"
      href="../css/style.css">
  <title>Confirmation Page</title>
</head>
<body>
  <h2>Confirmation Page</h2>
  <f:view>
    <h:panelGrid columns="2"
        columnClasses="rightalign-bold,normal">
      <!-- First row begins here -->
      <h:outputText value="Salutation: "/>
      <h:outputText
          value="#{RegistrationBean.salutation}" />
      <!-- Second row begins here -->
      <h:outputText value="First Name:"/>
      <h:outputText value="#{RegistrationBean.firstName}" />
      <!-- Third row begins here -->
      <h:outputText value="Last Name:"/>
      <h:outputText value="#{RegistrationBean.lastName}" />
      <!-- Fourth row begins here -->
      <h:outputText value="Age:"/>
      <h:outputText value="#{RegistrationBean.age}"/>
      <!-- Fifth row begins here -->
      <h:outputText value="Email Address:"/>
      <h:outputText value="#{RegistrationBean.email}" />
    </h:panelGrid>
  </f:view>
</body>
</html>
```

As we can see, our confirmation page is very simple. It consists of a series of
`<h:outputText>` tags containing labels and value binding expressions bound to our
managed bean's properties.

Executing Our Application

We are now ready to execute our JSF application. The easiest way to do so is to
right-click on **welcomeJSF.jsp** and click on **Run File** in the resulting pop-up menu,
or, if our application is set as the main project, we can click directly to the "Run" icon
in the tool bar at the top of the IDE.

At this point GlassFish (or whatever application server we are using for our project) will start automatically, if it hadn't been started already, the default browser will open and it will automatically be directed to our page's URL.

After entering some data on the page, it should look something like the following screenshot.

When we click on the **Register** button, our `RegistrationBean` managed bean is populated with the values we entered into the page. Each property in the field will be populated according to the value binding expression in each input field.

At this point JSF navigation "kicks-in", and we are taken to the **Confirmation Page**.

The values displayed in the confirmation page are taken from our managed bean, confirming that the bean's properties were populated correctly.

JSF Validation

Earlier in this chapter we discussed how the `required` attribute for JSF input fields allows us to easily make input fields mandatory.

If a user attempts to submit a form with one or more required fields missing, an error message is automatically generated.

The error message is generated by the `<h:message>` tag corresponding to the invalid field. The string `First Name` in the error message corresponds to the value of the `label` attribute for the field. Had we omitted the label attribute, the value of the fields `id` attribute would have been shown instead. As we can see, the `required` attribute makes it very easy to implement mandatory field functionality in our application.

Recall that the `age` field is bound to a property of type `Integer` in our managed bean. If a user enters a value that is not a valid integer into this field, a validation error is automatically generated.

Of course, a negative age wouldn't make much sense, however, our application validates that user input is a valid integer with essentially no effort on our part.

The email address input field of our page is bound to a property of type `String` in our managed bean. As such, there is no built-in validation to make sure that the user enters a valid email address. In cases like this, we need to write our own custom JSF validators.

Custom JSF validators must implement the `javax.faces.validator.Validator` interface. This interface contains a single method named `validate()`. This method takes three parameters: an instance of `javax.faces.context.FacesContext`, an instance of `javax.faces.component.UIComponent` containing the JSF component we are validating, and an instance of `java.lang.Object` containing the user entered value for the component. The following example illustrates a typical custom validator.

```
package com.ensode.jsf.validators;

import java.util.regex.Matcher;
import java.util.regex.Pattern;
import javax.faces.application.FacesMessage;
import javax.faces.component.UIComponent;
import javax.faces.component.html.HtmlInputText;
import javax.faces.context.FacesContext;
import javax.faces.validator.Validator;
import javax.faces.validator.ValidatorException;
```

```
public class EmailValidator implements Validator {

    public void validate(FacesContext facesContext,
            UIComponent uIComponent, Object value) throws
            ValidatorException {
        Pattern pattern = Pattern.compile("\\w+@\\w+\\.\\w+");
        Matcher matcher = pattern.matcher(
                (CharSequence) value);
        HtmlInputText htmlInputText = (HtmlInputText) uIComponent;
        String label;

        if (htmlInputText.getLabel() == null ||
                htmlInputText.getLabel().trim().equals("")) {
            label = htmlInputText.getId();
        } else {
            label = htmlInputText.getLabel();
        }

        if (!matcher.matches()) {
            FacesMessage facesMessage =
                    new FacesMessage(label +
                    ": not a valid email address");

            throw new ValidatorException(facesMessage);
        }
    }
}
```

In our example, the `validate()` method does a regular expression match against the value of the JSF component we are validating. If the value matches the expression, validation succeeds, otherwise, validation fails and an instance of `javax.faces.validator.ValidatorException` is thrown.

The primary purpose of our custom validator is to illustrate how to write custom JSF validations, and not to create a foolproof email address validator. There may be valid email addresses that don't validate using our validator.

The constructor of `ValidatorException` takes an instance of `javax.faces.application.FacesMessage` as a parameter. This object is used to display the error message on the page when validation fails. The message to display is passed as a `String` to the constructor of `FacesMessage`. In our example, if the `label` attribute of the component is not `null` nor empty, we use it as part of the error message, otherwise we use the value of the component's `id` attribute. This behavior follows the pattern established by standard JSF validators.

Before we can use our custom validator in our pages, we need to declare it in the application's `faces-config.xml` configuration file. To do so, we need to add a `<validator>` element just before the closing `</faces-config>` element.

```
<validator>
    <validator-id>emailValidator</validator-id>
    <validator-class>
        com.ensode.jsf.validators.EmailValidator
    </validator-class>
</validator>
```

The body of the `<validator-id>` sub element must contain a unique identifier for our validator. The value of the `<validator-class>` element must contain the fully qualified name of our validator class.

Once we add our validator to the application's `faces-config.xml`, we are ready to use it in our pages.

In our particular case, we need to modify the email field to use our custom validator.

```
<h:inputText id="email" label="Email Address"
        required="true" value="#{RegistrationBean.email}">
    <f:validator validatorId="emailValidator"/>
</h:inputText>
```

All we need to do is nest an `<f:validator>` tag inside the input field we wish to have validated using our custom validator. The value of the `validatorId` attribute of `<f:validator>` must match the value of the body of the `<validator-id>` element in `faces-config.xml`.

At this point we are ready to test our custom validator.

When entering an invalid email address into the email address input field and submitting the form, our custom validator logic was executed and the String we passed as a parameter to FacesMessage in our validator() method is shown as the error text by the <h:message> tag for the field.

Displaying Tabular Data

JavaServer Faces includes the <h:dataTable> tag that makes it easy to iterate through an array or collection of objects. With NetBeans, a data table tag can be added to a page by simply dragging the **JSF Data Table** item from the NetBeans palette into our page. In order to demonstrate the usage of this tag, let's create a new **Web Application** project, and add a new JSP named registrationlist.jsp to it.

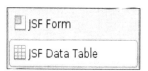

After dragging the **JSF Data Table** item into the appropriate location in our
`registrationlist.jsp` page, the following window pops up.

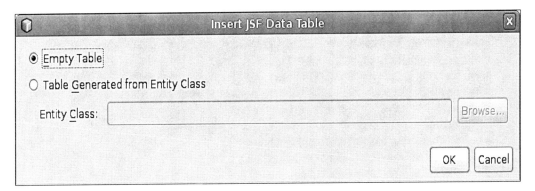

We can either select to create an **Empty Table** or a **Table Generated from an Entity Class**.

 An Entity Class refers to a Java Persistence API (JPA) entity. We will
discuss JPA in detail in Chapter 5 *Interacting With Databases through the
Java Persistence API*.

Selecting to create an empty table generates the following markup in our page:

```
<h:form>
  <h:dataTable value="#{arrayOrCollectionOf}"
      var="item">
  </h:dataTable>
</h:form>
```

Notice that NetBeans automatically wraps the generated `<h:dataTable>` tag in an
`<h:form>` tag. The `<h:form>` tag is necessary if we plan to have any input fields in
our table. Since this is not the case in our example, we can safely delete it.

The value of the `value` attribute of `<h:dataTable>` typically resolves to an array
or collection of objects. NetBeans places the placeholder value binding expression
`#{arrayOrCollectionOf}` as its value; we must replace this with a value binding
expression resolving to one of the appropriate types.

The value of the `var` attribute of `<h:dataTable>` is used to refer to the current
element in the table. As we iterate through the elements of the array or collection
from the `value` attribute, we can use the value of the `item` attribute to refer to the
current element in the array or collection.

We need to add a `<h:column>` tag inside the `<h:dataTable>` tag for each column we wish to add to the table. The following example illustrates typical usage of `<h:dataTable>` and `<h:column>`.

```jsp
<%@page contentType="text/html" pageEncoding="UTF-8"%>
<!DOCTYPE HTML PUBLIC "-//W3C//DTD HTML 4.01 Transitional//EN"
"http://www.w3.org/TR/html4/loose.dtd">
<%@ taglib prefix="f" uri="http://java.sun.com/jsf/core" %>
<%@ taglib prefix="h" uri="http://java.sun.com/jsf/html" %>
 <html>
    <head>
     <meta http-equiv="Content-Type"
           content="text/html; charset=UTF-8">
      <title>JSP Page</title>
    </head>
    <body>
   <f:view>
     <h:form>
       <h:dataTable
         value=
          "#{RegistrationListController.registrationBeanList}"
          var="item"  border="1" cellspacing="0"
          cellpadding="5">
         <h:column>
           <f:facet name="header">
             <h:outputText value="Salutation"/>
           </f:facet>
           <h:outputText value="#{item.salutation}"/>
         </h:column>
         <h:column>
           <f:facet name="header">
             <h:outputText value="First Name"/>
           </f:facet>
           <h:outputText value="#{item.firstName}"/>
         </h:column>
         <h:column>
           <f:facet name="header">
             <h:outputText value="Last Name"/>
           </f:facet>
           <h:outputText value="#{item.lastName}"/>
         </h:column>
         <h:column>
           <f:facet name="header">
             <h:outputText value="Age"/>
```

```
            </f:facet>
            <h:outputText value="#{item.age}"/>
          </h:column>
        </h:dataTable>
      </h:form>
    </f:view>
  </body>
  </html>
```

In this example, we will be iterating through a collection of `RegistrationBean` objects. The objects will be stored as a property named `registrationBeanList` of type `java.util.List` in a managed bean called `RegistrationListController`, therefore we set the value of the `value` attribute of `<h:dataTable>` to `#{RegistrationListController.registrationBeanList}`.

NetBeans creates a sensible value for the `var` attribute, therefore we leave it as is.

`<h:dataTable>` contains a few attributes that allow us to control the look of the generated table. These attributes are identical to attributes in a standard HTML table. In our example, we set a border of 1 pixel in the table by setting the value of the `border` attribute to `1`. We set the spacing between table cells to zero by setting the `cellspacing` attribute to `0`. We also set the spacing (padding) inside table cells to 5 pixels by setting the `cellpadding` attribute to `5`.

> The complete list of attributes for `<h:dataTable>` can be seen by using code completion (*Ctrl+Space*).

Since our table will have four columns, we need to add four nested `<h:column>` tags into our data table (one for each column).

Notice each `<h:column>` tag has a nested `<f:facet>` tag. JSF tags might define one or more facets. Facets are components that are rendered differently from other components in the parent component. Each facet must have a unique name for each parent component. `<h:column>` defines a facet with a name of `header`, this facet will be rendered as the header of the generated table. To render a facet inside a JSF component, the `<f:facet>` tag is used. In our example we give our facet the name of `header` by assigning this value to its `name` property. At runtime, JSF renders the tag inside `<f:facet>` as the header of the column rendered by the facet's parent `<h:column>` tag. Each `<f:facet>` tag must have a single child tag, which can be any HTML JSF tag.

Adding Multiple Child Components to a Facet

Although the `<f:facet>` tag only accepts a single child component, we can add multiple components to it by nesting them inside an `<f:panelGroup>` tag.

Although not shown in the example, `<h:column>` also defines a facet with a name of `footer` that can be used to render a footer for the column. We simply would add a second facet named `footer` inside our `<h:column>` tag.

Next we add the tags that will be displayed as a single cell for the particular column. We can access the current item in the collection or array. We will be iterating, by using the value of the `var` attribute of `<h:dataTable>` (`item`, in our particular example).

In our example we simply display the values for a single property or each item, however any JSF component can be placed inside `<h:column>`.

Before we can deploy our application and see the above page in action, we need to create the `RegistrationListController` managed bean.

Recall that the easiest way to create JSF managed beans is by going to **File | New**, selecting the **JavaServer Faces** category, and **JSF Managed Bean** as the file type. This procedure is covered in detail earlier in this chapter.

Our managed bean is shown next:

```
package com.ensode.jsf;

import java.util.ArrayList;
import java.util.List;

public class RegistrationListController {

    private List<RegistrationBean> registrationBeanList;

    public RegistrationListController() {
    }

    public String populateList() {
        registrationBeanList = new
        ArrayList<RegistrationBean>();
```

```
            registrationBeanList.add(populateBean(
                "MS", "Carol", "Jones", 35));
            registrationBeanList.add(populateBean(
                "MRS", "Glenda", "Murphy", 39));
            registrationBeanList.add(populateBean(
                "MISS", "Stacy", "Clark", 36));
            registrationBeanList.add(populateBean(
                "MR", "James", "Fox", 40));
            registrationBeanList.add(populateBean(
                "DR", "Henry", "Bennett", 53));

            return "success";
        }

        public List<RegistrationBean> getRegistrationBeanList() {
            return registrationBeanList;
        }

        public void setRegistrationBeanList(
            List<RegistrationBean> registrationBeanList) {
            this.registrationBeanList = registrationBeanList;
        }

        private RegistrationBean populateBean(String salutation,
                String firstName, String lastName, Integer age) {
            RegistrationBean registrationBean;

            registrationBean = new RegistrationBean();
            registrationBean.setSalutation(salutation);
            registrationBean.setFirstName(firstName);
            registrationBean.setLastName(lastName);
            registrationBean.setAge(age);

            return registrationBean;
        }
    }
}
```

Notice that the bean has a property named `registrationBeanList` of type `java.util.List`. This is the property we used as the value of the `value` property in the `<h:dataTable>` tag in the page above.

The bean's `populateList()` method will be called from another JSP via dynamic navigation. This method populates the `registrationBeanList` property in the bean.

A real application would more than likely retrieve this information from a relational database. To keep our example simple we are simply populating the bean from new instances of `RegistrationBean` we create on the fly.

Now we need to modify the JSP that will be invoked initially. When creating the project, NetBeans automatically sets it up so that a JSP called `welcomeJSF.jsp` will be invoked when we point the browser to our application's URL. We need to modify this JSP so that it will invoke the `populateList()` method of our `RegistrationBeanList` managed bean when navigating to the page we wrote earlier.

```
<f:view>
  <h:form>
    <h:commandLink value="Populate List"
        action="#{RegistrationListController.populateList}" />
  </h:form>
</f:view>
```

For brevity, we are only showing the relevant parts of the JSP. Our JSP will have an `<h:commandLink>` tag used for navigation. `<h:commandLink>` is functionally equivalent to `<h:commandButton>`, the main difference is that it is rendered as a link as opposed to a button. The value of the `value` attribute of `<h:commandLink>` is used to render the link text; its `action` attribute is used for navigation. In this case we are using dynamic navigation. When using dynamic navigation, a value binding expression is used as the value of the `action` attribute. This value binding expression must resolve to a method that returns a `String`. The method must take no arguments. When using dynamic navigation, the method that the value binding expression resolves to may return different strings depending on its logic. We can have a page navigate to different pages depending on the value returned by this method. To do this we would have to add a `<navigation-case>` element for each possible value that the method may return.

In our example, the `populateList()` method of the `RegistrationListController` managed bean is invoked when a user clicks on the link. This method populates the list that we will iterate through and returns the value of `success`.

Before we deploy our application, we need to define the navigation between our two pages. Normally this is done by manually editing **faces-config.xml**. However, when using NetBeans, it can be done graphically in the NetBeans **PageFlow** editor as explained earlier in this chapter.

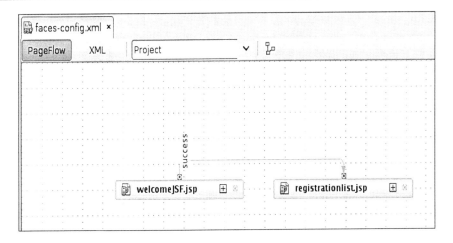

The above screenshot shows the **PageFlow** editor after connecting the initial page containing the `<h:commandLink>` that initiates navigation to the page that iterates through the list of `RegistrationBean` instances, and after changing the default navigation case to `success`. Notice that the text in the navigation case matches the return value of the `populateList()` method in the `RegistrationListController` method. This is how the navigation case is linked to the method's return value.

At this point we are ready to test our application. We can execute the initial `welcomeJSF.jsp` page by right-clicking on it and selecting **Run File**.

At this point, the application server is started (if it hadn't been started previously), the application is deployed, and a browser window opens displaying the page.

Here we can see the link that was generated by the `<h:commandLink>` tag in our JSP. Clicking on that link results in executing the `populateList()` method in the `RegistrationListController` managed bean and navigating to the JSP containing the `<h:dataTable>` tag.

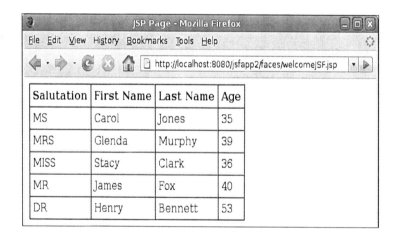

Here we can see the table generated by `<h:dataTable>`, the headers (**Salutation, First Name, Last Name**, and **Age**) are generated by the `<f:facet>` tags inside each `<h:column>`. While iterating through the collection of `RegistrationBean` objects in the `registrationBeanList` property of the `RegistrationListController` managed bean, each cell in each row displays the property corresponding to the `<c:outputText>` tag inside each `<c:column>` tag in the table.

Summary

In this chapter we saw how NetBeans can help us easily create new JSF projects by automatically adding all required libraries and configuration files.

We also saw how we can create JSF forms for data input and data tables for displaying tabular data by simply dragging and dropping icons from the NetBeans palette into our page.

Additionally, we saw how NetBeans can simplify and significantly speed up development of JSF applications by automatically adding managed bean definitions to the application's `<faces-config.xml>` configuration file, and by allowing us to graphically define navigation rules by taking advantage of the NetBeans **PageFlow** editor.

5

Interacting with Databases through the Java Persistence API

The Java Persistence API (JPA) is an object relational mapping API. Object relational mapping tools help us automate mapping Java objects to relational database tables. Earlier versions of J2EE used Entity Beans as the standard approach for object relational mapping. Entity Beans attempted to keep the data in memory always synchronized with database data, a good idea in theory, however, in practice this feature resulted in poorly performing applications.

Several object relational mapping APIs were developed to overcome the limitations of Entity Beans, such as Hibernate, iBatis, Cayenne, and Toplink among others.

With Java EE 5, Entity Beans were deprecated in favor of JPA. JPA took ideas from several object relational mapping tools and incorporated them into the standard. As we will see in this chapter NetBeans has several features that make development with JPA a breeze.

The following topics will be covered:

- Creating our first JPA entity
- Interacting with JPA entities with entity manager
- Generating forms in JSF pages from JPA entities
- Generating JPA entities from an existing database schema
- JPA named queries and JPQL
- Entity relationships
- Generating complete JSF applications from JPA entities

Creating Our First JPA Entity

JPA entities are Java classes whose fields are persisted to a database by the JPA API. JPA entities are **Plain Old Java Objects** (**POJOs**), as such, they don't need to extend any specific parent class or implement any specific interface. A Java class is designated as a JPA entity by decorating it with the `@Entity` annotation.

In order to create and test our first JPA entity, we will be creating a new web application using the JavaServer Faces framework. In this example we will name our application **jpaweb**. As with all of our examples, we will be using the bundled GlassFish application server.

 Consult Chapter 4 *Developing Web Applications using JavaServer Faces* for instructions on creating a new JSF project.

To create a new JPA Entity, we need to right-click on the project and select **New | Entity Class**.

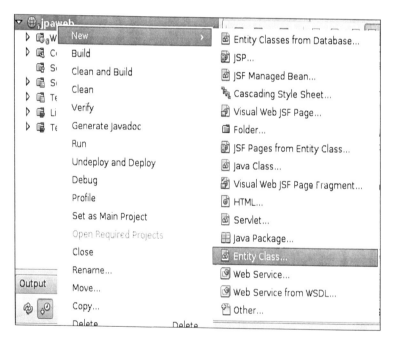

After doing so, NetBeans presents the **New Entity Class** wizard.

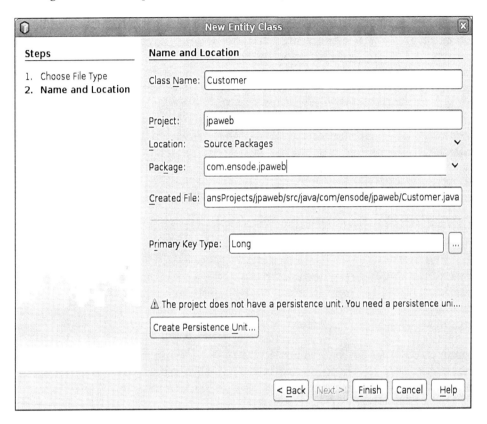

At this point, we should specify the values for the **Class Name** and **Package** fields (**Customer** and **com.ensode.jpaweb** in our example), then click on the **Create Persistence Unit...** button.

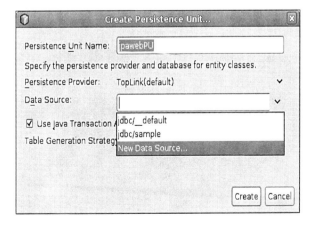

The **Persistence Unit Name** field is used to identify the persistence unit that will be generated by the wizard, it will be defined in a JPA configuration file named `persistence.xml` that NetBeans will automatically generate from the **Create Persistence Unit** wizard. The **Create Persistence Unit...** wizard will suggest a name for our persistence unit, in most cases the default can be safely accepted.

JPA is a specification for which several implementations exist. NetBeans supports several JPA implementations including Toplink, Hibernate, KODO, and OpenJPA. Since the bundled GlassFish application server includes Toplink as its default JPA implementation, it makes sense to take this default value for the **Persistence Provider** field when deploying our application to GlassFish.

Before we can interact with a database from any Java EE 5 application, a database connection pool and data source need to be created in the application server.

A database connection pool contains connection information that allow us to connect to our database, such as the server name, port, and credentials. The advantage of using a connection pool instead of directly opening a JDBC connection to a database is that database connections in a connection pool are never closed, they are simply allocated to applications as they need them. This results in performance improvements, since the operations of opening and closing database connections are expensive in terms of performance.

Data sources allow us to obtain a connection from a connection pool by obtaining an instance of `javax.sql.DataSource` via JNDI, then invoking its `getConnection()` method to obtain a database connection from a connection pool. When dealing with JPA, we don't need to directly obtain a reference to a data source, it is all done automatically by the JPA API, but we still need to indicate the data source to use in the application's Persistence Unit.

NetBeans comes with a few data sources and connection pools pre-configured. We could use one of these pre-configured resources for our application, however, NetBeans also allows creating these resources "on the fly", which is what we will be doing in our example.

To create a new data source we need to select the **New Data Source...** item from the **Data Source** combo box.

A data source needs to interact with a database connection pool. NetBeans comes pre-configured with a few connection pools out of the box, but just like with data sources, it allows us to create a new connection pool "on demand". In order to do this, we need to select the **New Database Connection...** item from the **Database Connection** combo box.

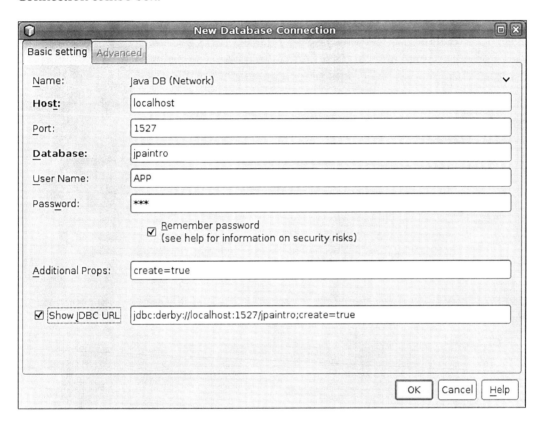

NetBeans includes JDBC drivers for a few **Relational Database Management Systems (RDBMS)** such as JavaDB, MySQL, and PostgreSQL "out of the box". JavaDB is bundled with both GlassFish and NetBeans, therefore we picked JavaDB for our example. This way we avoid having to install an external RDBMS.

For RDBMS systems that are not supported out of the box, we need to obtain a JDBC driver and let NetBeans know of it's location by selecting **New Driver** from the **Name** combo box. We then need to navigate to the location of a JAR file containing the JDBC driver. Consult your RDBMS documentation for details.

JavaDB is installed in our workstation, therefore the server name to use is localhost. By default, JavaDB listens to port 1527, therefore that is the port we specify in the URL. We wish to connect to a database called jpaintro, therefore we specify it as the database name. Since the jpaintro database does not exist yet, we pass the attribute create=true to JavaDB, this attribute is used to create the database if it doesn't exist yet.

Every JavaDB database contains a schema named APP, since each user by default uses a schema named after his/her own login name. The easiest way to get going is to create a user named "APP" and select a password for this user.

Clicking on the **Show JDBC URL** checkbox reveals the JDBC URL for the connection we are setting up.

The **New Database Connection** wizard warns us of potential security risks when choosing to let NetBeans remember the password for the database connection. Database passwords are scrambled (but not encrypted) and stored in an XML file under the .netbeans/[netbeans version]/config/Databases/Connections directory. If we follow common security practices such as locking our workstation when we walk away from it, the risks of having NetBeans remember database passwords will be minimal.

Once we have created our new data source and connection pool, we can continue configuring our persistence unit.

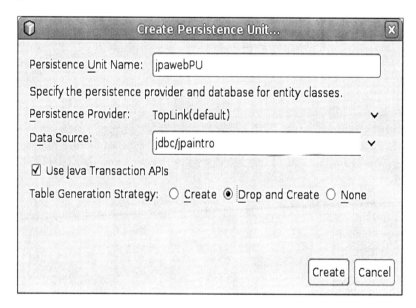

It is a good idea to leave the **Use Java Transaction APIs** checkbox checked. This will instruct our JPA implementation to use the **Java Transaction API (JTA)** to allow the application server to manage transactions. If we uncheck this box, we will need to manually write code to manage transactions.

Most JPA implementations allow us to define a table generation strategy. We can instruct our JPA implementation to create tables for our entities when we deploy our application, to drop the tables then regenerate them when our application is deployed, or not create any tables at all. NetBeans allows us to specify the table generation strategy for our application by clicking the appropriate value in the **Table Generation Strategy** radio button group.

When working with a new application, it is a good idea to select the **Drop and Create** table generation strategy. This will allow us to add, remove, and rename fields in our JPA entity at will without having to make the same changes in the database schema. When selecting this table generation strategy, tables in the database schema will be dropped and recreated, therefore any data previously persisted will be lost.

Once we have created our new data source, database connection and persistence unit, we are ready to create our new JPA entity.

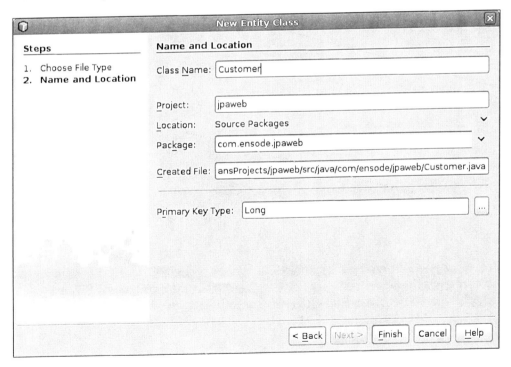

We can do so by simply clicking on the **Finish** button. At this point NetBeans generates the source for our JPA entity.

> JPA allows the primary field of a JPA entity to map to any column type (VARCHAR, NUMBER). It is best practice to have a numeric surrogate primary key, that is, a primary key that serves only as an identifier and has no business meaning in the application. Selecting the default Primary Key type of long will allow for a wide range of values to be available for the primary keys of our entities.

```java
package com.ensode.jpaweb;

import java.io.Serializable;
import javax.persistence.Entity;
import javax.persistence.GeneratedValue;
import javax.persistence.GenerationType;
import javax.persistence.Id;

@Entity
public class Customer implements Serializable {
    private static final long serialVersionUID = 1L;
    private Long id;

    public void setId(Long id) {
        this.id = id;
    }

    @Id
    @GeneratedValue(strategy = GenerationType.AUTO)
    public Long getId() {
        return id;
    }

    //Other generated methods (hashCode(), equals() and
    //toString() omitted for brevity.

}
```

As we can see, a JPA entity is a standard Java object. There is no need to extend any special class or implement any special interface. What differentiates a JPA entity from other Java objects are a few JPA-specific annotations.

The `@Entity` annotation is used to indicate that our class is a JPA entity. Any object we want to persist to a database via JPA must be annotated with this annotation.

The `@Id` annotation is used to indicate what field in our JPA entity is its primary key. The primary key is a unique identifier for our entity. No two entities may have the same value for their primary key field. This annotation can be placed just above the getter method for the primary key class. This is the strategy that the NetBeans wizard follows. It is also correct to specify the annotation right above the field declaration.

The `@Entity` and the `@Id` annotations are the bare minimum two annotations that a class needs in order to be considered a JPA entity. JPA allows primary keys to be automatically generated. In order to take advantage of this functionality, the `@GeneratedValue` annotation can be used. As we can see, the NetBeans generated JPA entity uses this annotation. This annotation is used to indicate the strategy to use to generate primary keys. All possible primary key generation strategies are listed in the following table:

Primary Key Generation Strategy	Description
`GenerationType.AUTO`	Indicates that the persistence provider will automatically select a primary key generation strategy. Used by default if no primary key generation strategy is specified.
`GenerationType.IDENTITY`	Indicates that an identity column in the database table the JPA entity maps to must be used to generate the primary key value.
`GenerationType.SEQUENCE`	Indicates that a database sequence should be used to generate the entity's primary key value.
`GenerationType.TABLE`	Indicates that a database table should be used to generate the entity's primary key value.

In most cases, the `GenerationType.AUTO` strategy works properly, therefore it is almost always used. For this reason the **New Entity Class** wizard uses this strategy.

> When using the sequence or table generation strategies, we might have to indicate the sequence or table used to generate the primary keys. These can be specified by using the `@SequenceGenerator` and `@TableGenerator` annotations, respectively. Consult the Java EE 5 JavaDoc at `http://java.sun.com/javaee/5/docs/api/` for details.

For further knowledge on primary key generation strategies you can refer EJB 3 Developer Guide by **Michael Sikora**, which is another book by Packt Publishing (`http://www.packtpub.com/developer-guide-for-ejb3/book`).

Adding Persistent Fields to Our Entity

At this point, our JPA entity contains a single field, its primary key. Admittedly not very useful, we need to add a few fields to be persisted to the database.

```java
package com.ensode.jpaweb;

import java.io.Serializable;
import javax.persistence.Entity;
import javax.persistence.GeneratedValue;
import javax.persistence.GenerationType;
import javax.persistence.Id;

@Entity
public class Customer implements Serializable {
    private static final long serialVersionUID = 1L;
    private Long id;
    private String firstName;
    private String lastName;

    public void setId(Long id) {
        this.id = id;
    }

    @Id
    @GeneratedValue(strategy = GenerationType.AUTO)
    public Long getId() {
        return id;
    }

    public String getFirstName() {
        return firstName;
    }

    public void setFirstName(String firstName) {
        this.firstName = firstName;
    }

    public String getLastName() {
        return lastName;
    }

    public void setLastName(String lastName) {
        this.lastName = lastName;
    }

    //Additional methods omitted for brevity
}
```

In this modified version of our JPA entity, we added two fields to be persisted to the database; firstName will be used to store the user's first name, lastName will be used to store the user's last name. JPA entities need to follow standard JavaBean coding conventions. This means that they must have a public constructor that takes no arguments (one is automatically generated by the Java compiler if we don't specify any other constuctors), and all fields must be private, and accessed through getter and setter methods.

Automatically Generating Getters and Setters

In NetBeans, getter and setter methods can be generated automatically. Simply declare new fields as usual then use the "insert code" keyboard shortcut (default is *Alt+Insert*), then select **Getter and Setter** from the resulting pop-up window, then click on the check box next to the class name to select all fields, then click on the **Generate** button.

Before we can use JPA persist our entity's fields into our database, we need to write some additional code.

Creating a Data Access Object (DAO)

It is a good idea to follow the DAO design pattern whenever we write code that interacts with a database. The DAO design pattern keeps all database access functionality in DAO classes. This has the benefit of creating a clear separation of concerns, leaving other layers in our application, such as the user interface logic and the business logic, free of any persistence logic.

There is no special procedure in NetBeans to create a DAO. We simply follow the standard procedure to create a new class by selecting **File | New**, then selecting **Java** as the category and the **Java Class** as the file type, then entering a name and a package for the class. In our example, we will name our class CustomerDAO and place it in the com.ensode.jpaweb package.

At this point, NetBeans create a very simple class containing only the package and class declarations.

To take complete advantage of Java EE features such as dependency injection, we need to make our DAO a JSF managed bean. This can be accomplished by simply opening `faces-config.xml`, clicking its **XML** tab, then right-clicking on it and selecting **JavaServer Faces | Add Managed Bean**.

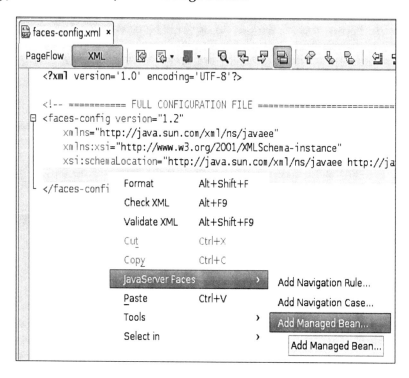

We get the **Add Manged Bean** dialog as seen in the following screenshot:

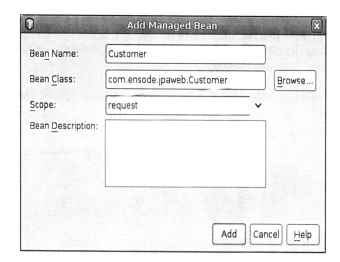

We need to enter a name, fully qualified name, and scope for our managed bean (which, in our case, is our DAO), then click on the **Add** button.

This action results in our DAO being declared as a managed bean in our application's `faces-config.xml` configuration file.

```
<managed-bean>
  <managed-bean-name>CustomerDAO</managed-bean-name>
  <managed-bean-class>
   com.ensode.jpaweb.CustomerDAO
  </managed-bean-class>
  <managed-bean-scope>session</managed-bean-scope>
</managed-bean>
```

We could at this point start writing our JPA code manually, but with NetBeans there is no need to do so, we can simply right-click on our code and select **Persistence | Use Entity Manager**, and most of the work is automatically done for us.

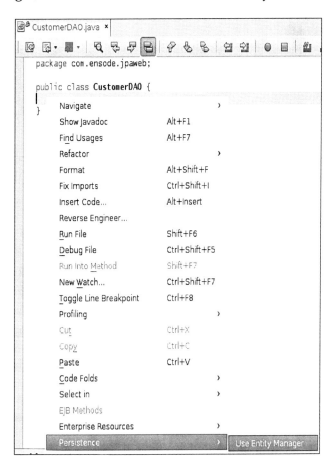

Here is how our code looks like after doing this trivial procedure:

```
package com.ensode.jpaweb;

import javax.annotation.Resource;
import javax.naming.Context;
import javax.persistence.EntityManager;
import javax.persistence.PersistenceContext;

@PersistenceContext(name = "persistence/LogicalName",
        unitName = "jpawebPU")
public class CustomerDAO {
  @Resource
  private javax.transaction.UserTransaction utx;

  protected void persist(Object object) {
    try {
      Context ctx =
        (Context) new javax.naming.InitialContext().
          lookup("java:comp/env");
      utx.begin();
      EntityManager em = (EntityManager)
        ctx.lookup("persistence/LogicalName");
      em.persist(object);
      utx.commit();
    } catch (Exception e) {
      java.util.logging.Logger.getLogger(
        getClass().getName()).log(
        java.util.logging.Level.SEVERE,
        "exception caught", e);
      throw new RuntimeException(e);
    }
  }
}
```

All highlighted code is automatically generated by NetBeans. The main thing NetBeans does here is add a method that will automatically insert a new row in the database, effectively persisting our entity's properties.

As we can see, NetBeans automatically generates all necessary import statements. Additionally, our new class is automatically decorated with the @ PersistenceContext annotation. This annotation allows us to declare that our class depends on an EntityManager (we'll discuss EntityManager in more detail shortly). The value of its name attribute is a logical name we can use when doing a JNDI lookup for our EntityManager. NetBeans by default uses persistence/ LogicalName as the value for this property.

The Java Naming and Directory Interface (JNDI) is an API we can use to obtain resources, such as database connections and JMS queues, from a directory service.

The value of the `unitName` attribute of the `@PersistenceContext` annotation refers to the name we gave our application's Persistence Unit.

 We illustrated how to create a Persistence Unit earlier in the chapter.

NetBeans also creates a new instance variable of type `javax.transaction.UserTransaction`. This variable is needed since all JPA code must be executed in a transaction. `UserTransaction` is part of the Java Transaction API (JTA). This API allows us to write code that is transactional in nature. Notice that the `UserTransaction` instance variable is decorated with the `@Resource` annotation. This annotation is used for **dependency injection**. in this case an instance of a class of type `javax.transaction.UserTransaction` will be instantiated automatically at run-time, without having to do a JNDI lookup or explicitly instantiating the class.

 Dependency injection is a new feature of Java EE 5 not present in previous versions of J2EE, but that was available and made popular in the Spring framework. With standard J2EE code, it was necessary to write boilerplate JNDI lookup code very frequently in order to obtain resources. To alleviate this situation, Java EE 5 made dependency injection part of the standard.

The next thing we see is that NetBeans added a `persist` method that will persist a JPA entity, automatically inserting a new row containing our entity's fields into the database. As we can see, this method takes an instance of `java.lang.Object` as its single parameter. The reason for this is that the method can be used to persist any JPA entity (although in our example, we will use it to persist only instances of our `Customer` entity).

The first thing the generated method does is obtain an instance of `javax.naming.InitialContext` by doing a JNDI lookup on `java:comp/env`. This JNDI name is the root context for all Java EE 5 components.

The next thing the method does is initiate a transaction by invoking `uxt.begin()`. Notice that since the value of the `utx` instance variable was injected via dependency injection (by simply decorating its declaration with the `@Resource` annotation), there is no need to initialize this variable.

Next, the method does a JNDI lookup to obtain an instance of `javax.persistence.EntityManager`. This class contains a number of methods to interact with the database. Notice that the JNDI name used to obtain an `EntityManager` matches the value of the `name` attribute of the `@PersistenceContext` annotation.

Once an instance of `EntityManager` is obtained from the JNDI lookup, we persist our entity's properties by simply invoking the `persist()` method on it, passing the entity as a parameter to this method. At this point, the data in our JPA entity is inserted into the database.

In order for our database insert to take effect, we must commit our transaction, which is done by invoking `utx.commit()`.

It is always a good idea to look for exceptions when dealing with JPA code. The generated method does this, and if an exception is caught, it is logged and a `RuntimeException` is thrown. Throwing a `RuntimeException` has the effect of rolling back our transaction automatically, while letting the invoking code know that something went wrong in our method. The `UserTransaction` class has a `rollback()` method that we can use to roll back our transaction without having to throw a `RunTimeException`.

At this point we have all the code we need to persist our entity's properties in the database. Now we need to write some additional code for the user interface part of our application. NetBeans can generate a rudimentary JSF page that will help us with this task.

Generating the User Interface

To have NetBeans automatically generate the user interface, first we need to create a new JSP as usual, by right-clicking on the project, selecting **New | JSP**, then entering a name for our JSP in the **New JSP File** wizard. At this point, the generated markup for the new JSP will look like this:

```
<%@page contentType="text/html" pageEncoding="UTF-8"%>
<!DOCTYPE HTML PUBLIC "-//W3C//DTD HTML 4.01 Transitional//EN"
    "http://www.w3.org/TR/html4/loose.dtd">
<html>
    <head>
        <meta http-equiv="Content-Type" content="text/html;
charset=UTF-8">
        <title>JSP Page</title>
    </head>
    <body>
        <h1>Hello World!</h1>
    </body>
</html>
```

Once we have our JSP, we can drag the **JSF Form** element from the NetBeans palette into our markup, then select **Form Generated From Entity Class**, enter the fully qualified name for our JPA entity, then select **Editable** in the **Form Fields** radio buttons.

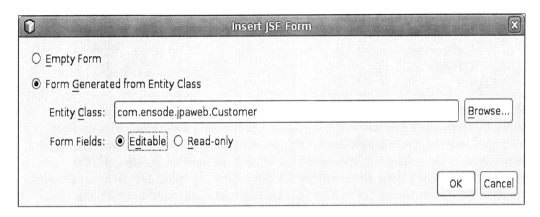

After adding the generated markup, we need to manually add the standard JSF `<%@ taglib%>` elements to our page. After modifying the generated title and deleting the `<h2>` tag generated by the **New JSP File** wizard, our page markup now looks like this:

```
<%@page contentType="text/html" pageEncoding="UTF-8"%>
<!DOCTYPE HTML PUBLIC "-//W3C//DTD HTML 4.01 Transitional//EN"
"http://www.w3.org/TR/html4/loose.dtd">
<%@ taglib prefix="f" uri="http://java.sun.com/jsf/core"  %>
<%@ taglib prefix="h" uri="http://java.sun.com/jsf/html" %>
<html>
    <head>
        <meta http-equiv="Content-Type" content="text/html;
charset=UTF-8">
        <title>Insert Customer</title>
    </head>
    <body>
      <f:view>
        <h2>Create</h2>
        <h:form>
          <h:panelGrid columns="2">
            <h:outputText value="FirstName:"/>
            <h:inputText id="firstName"
              value="#{anInstanceOfcom.ensode.jpaweb.Customer.
                      firstName}"
            title="FirstName" />
```

```
            <h:outputText value="LastName:"/>
            <h:inputText id="lastName"
                value="#{anInstanceOfcom.ensode.jpaweb.
                        Customer.lastName}"
                title="LastName" />
        </h:panelGrid>
      </h:form>
    </f:view>
  </body>
</html>
```

Notice that NetBeans automatically inserts JSF complete with value binding expressions mapping to our entity's properties. It uses a temporary placeholder managed bean name to access our entity. In our example, the generated managed bean name is `anInstanceOfcom.ensode.jpaweb.Customer`. In general, the generated managed bean name will be the fully qualified name of the bean's class, prefixed by `anInstanceOf`. Before this code can work, we need to make our JPA entity a JSF managed bean following the same procedure we used for the DAO.

In order to be able to persist the user-entered data, we need to make a few modifications to the generated markup in our JSP.

```
<h:form>
  <h:panelGrid columns="2">
    <h:outputText value="FirstName:"/>
    <h:inputText id="firstName"
      value="#{Customer.firstName}" title="FirstName" />
    <h:outputText value="LastName:"/>
    <h:inputText id="lastName" value="#{Customer.lastName}"
      title="LastName" />
    <h:panelGroup/>
    <h:commandButton value="Submit"
      action="#{Controller.saveCustomer}"/>
  </h:panelGrid>
</h:form>
```

The first thing we need to do is modify the value binding expression of the generated `<h:inputText>` elements to match the name we gave our JPA entity in `faces-config.xml` (`Customer`, in our case), then we need to add a command button so that our page will be submitted.

Implementing the Controller

At this point, we have the presentation layer (View) of our application ready, as well as the data access layer (Model), the only thing missing is to add a controller to complete the third layer of our application, which will follow the MVC design pattern.

```
package com.ensode.jpaweb;

public class Controller {

    private CustomerDAO customerDAO;
    private Customer customer;

    public CustomerDAO getCustomerDAO() {
        return customerDAO;
    }

    public void setCustomerDAO(CustomerDAO customerDAO) {
        this.customerDAO = customerDAO;
    }

    public Customer getCustomer() {
        return customer;
    }

    public void setCustomer(Customer customer) {
        this.customer = customer;
    }

    public String saveCustomer() {
        String returnVal;
        try {
            customerDAO.persist(customer);
            returnVal = "success";
        } catch (Exception e) {
            returnVal = "failure";
            e.printStackTrace();
        }

        System.out.println(this.getClass().getName() +
                    ".saveCustomer()\nreturnVal = " + returnVal);
        return returnVal;

    }
}
```

Our controller has a `saveCustomer()` method that will be invoked when the user clicks on the **Submit** button on the page, the method simply invokes the `persist()` method on the DAO, then uses standard JSF navigation to go to a confirmation page if everything went fine, or to an error page if an exception was thrown.

> Markup for the confirmation an error pages is not shown, but available from this book's code download.

Notice the `Controller` class has two instance variables for our JPA entity and our DAO. There is no need for us to explicitly instantiate these variables, instead we can use a JSF feature called **managed properties**. Managed properties are injected at runtime by using dependency injection. In order to configure this the application's `faces-config.xml` needs to be modified.

```xml
<managed-bean>
  <managed-bean-name>CustomerDAO</managed-bean-name>
  <managed-bean-class>
    com.ensode.jpaweb.CustomerDAO
  </managed-bean-class>
  <managed-bean-scope>session</managed-bean-scope>
</managed-bean>
<managed-bean>
  <managed-bean-name>Customer</managed-bean-name>
  <managed-bean-class>
    com.ensode.jpaweb.Customer
  </managed-bean-class>
  <managed-bean-scope>request</managed-bean-scope>
</managed-bean>
<managed-bean>
  <managed-bean-name>Controller</managed-bean-name>
  <managed-bean-class>
    com.ensode.jpaweb.Controller
  </managed-bean-class>
  <managed-bean-scope>request</managed-bean-scope>
  <managed-property>
    <property-name>customerDAO</property-name>
    <property-class>
      com.ensode.jpaweb.CustomerDAO
    </property-class>
  <value>#{CustomerDAO}</value>
  </managed-property>
  <managed-property>
    <property-name>customer</property-name>
```

```
<property-class>
  com.ensode.jpaweb.Customer
</property-class>
<value>#{Customer}</value>
    </managed-property>
  </managed-bean>
```

The `<managed-property>` element is used to define our managed properties. The `<property-name>` element is used to indicate the managed property name; the value of this element must match the name of the property in the managed bean's code (in our example, both the `customer` and `customerDAO` properties are managed properties). The value of the `<property-class>` element must be the fully qualified name of the property type, and the value of the `<value>` attribute must match the value of the `<managed-bean-name>` element for managed beans used to populate managed properties. In our example, our JPA entity is declared as a managed bean, using a value of `Customer` as its logical name, which matches the value binding expression of `#{Customer}` used to populate the `customer` managed property of our controller. In order to have the `customerDAO` property populated at runtime, our `CustomerDAO` class needs to be added as a managed bean like we previously did for the `Customer` class.

Trying Out Our Application

At this point, we have a complete, albeit simple, application that will gather input from the user, populate a JPA entity from this input, and save the data to the database. We can execute our application by right-clicking on the project and selecting **Run**.

At this point the application server is started if it wasn't running already, our application is deployed and a new window of the default web browser is automatically opened, pointing to the URL of our application. After entering some data into the input fields, our page looks like the following screenshot.

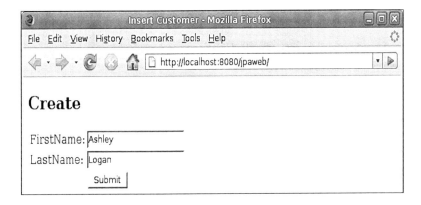

Notice that the labels for the fields aren't very user-friendly. Recall that this page was almost completely generated from our JPA entity bean. By default, NetBeans uses the property name as the label for each field. We are free, of course, to modify these labels to make them more readable for our users.

After clicking the **Submit** button, our data is saved to the database and we are directed to a confirmation screen.

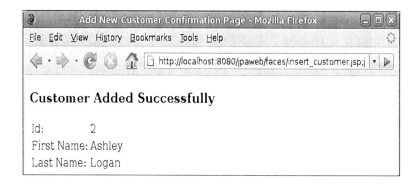

If we inspect our database schema, we can see that a CUSTOMER table was created automatically, since we used the **Drop and Create** Table generation strategy. Additionally, a new row was inserted when we clicked on the **Submit** button.

We can inspect the database schema by going to the **Services** tab, right-clicking on our schema (**jpaintro**), then selecting **Connect**. Expanding the **Tables** node reveals the newly created **CUSTOMER**.

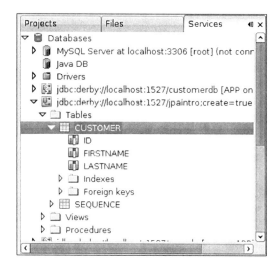

We can view the data in the table by right-clicking on it and selecting **View Data**. At this point a new **SQL Command** window is opened and an SQL query retrieving all the data in our table is automatically executed.

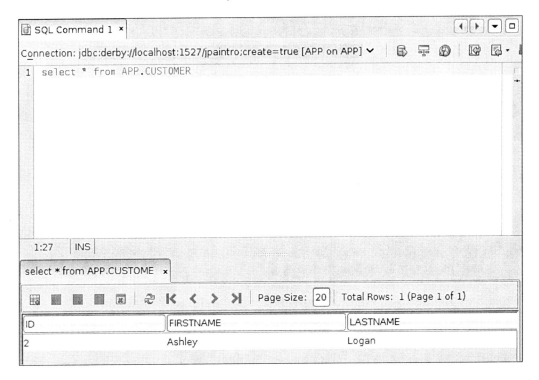

As we have seen, NetBeans makes it easy to write code that inserts rows into a database table by generating JPA code.

If we need to add additional functionality such as retrieving, updating, or deleting data, we would need to write additional methods in our DAO. The DAO would invoke corresponding methods on `EntityManager`. The following table lists some of the most commonly used methods on `EntityManager`.

EntityManager method	Description	Example
`<T> T find(Class<T> entityClass, Object primaryKey)`	Retrieves a row of data matching the supplied primary key from the database table our JPA entity maps to. The first parameter must be the class of our JPA entity, the second parameter must be the primary key.	`customer = em.find(Customer.class, new Long(2));`
`<T> T merge(T entity)`	Updates the data in the database with the values contained in the JPA entity's properties.	`em.merge(customer);`
`remove(Object entity)`	Deletes the row corresponding to the JPA entity from the database table the entity maps to.	`em.remove(customer);`

Just like the `persist()` method, the methods listed on the above table must be invoked inside a transaction, therefore a DAO's method invoking the above `EntityManger` methods should follow the pattern in our DAO's `persist()` method (lookup `EntityManager`, begin a transaction, invoke the method, commit the transaction, look for any exceptions and throw a `RuntimeException` to roll back the transaction, if necessary).

If we are working with a JSF application, such as in our example, we would need to write additional methods on our Controller managed bean that would invoke DAO methods whenever a user submits a form. Additionally we would have to write additional JSP pages to create the user interface.

As we will see later in this chapter, NetBeans can automate most of the steps described in the previous two paragraphs. But before we get there, we will discuss one great feature of NetBeans: automated generation of JPA entities from an existing database schema.

Automated Generation of JPA Entities

In the previous section, we saw how we can automatically create database tables from JPA entities. This is an optional feature of the JPA specification, however most JPA implementations implement it. One feature that is not available from JPA is the converse, generating JPA entities from database tables. Luckily for us, NetBeans provides this functionality.

In this section, we will be using a custom database schema. In order to create the schema, we need to execute an SQL script that will create the schema and populate some of its tables. To do this, we need to go to the **Services** window, right-click on **JavaDB**, then select **Create Database...**.

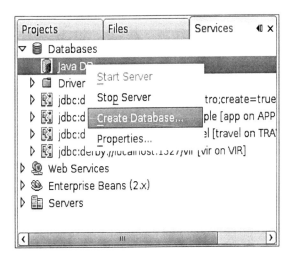

We then need to add the database information in the **Create Java DB Database** wizard.

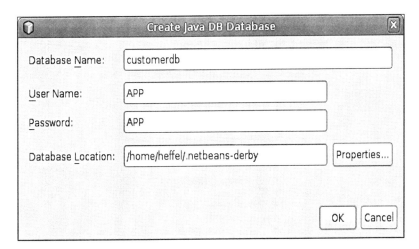

At this point, we can open the SQL script by going to **File | Open File...**, then navigating to its location on our disk and opening it.

The file name of our script is `create_populate_tables.sql`. It is included as part of the source bundle for this chapter.

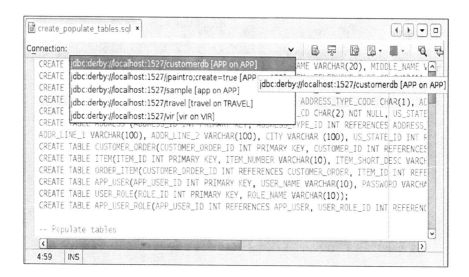

Once we have opened the SQL script, we need to select our newly created connection from the **Connection** combo box, then click on the 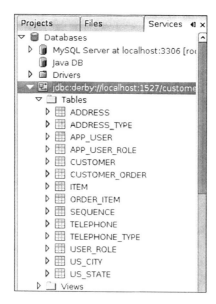 icon to execute it.

Our database will now have a number of tables.

NetBeans allows us to generate JPA entities from an existing schema. To do so we need to create a new project, then right-click on the project, then select **New | Entity Classes from Database...**

 NetBeans allows us to generate JPA entities from pretty much any kind of Java project. In our example we will be using a Web Application project.

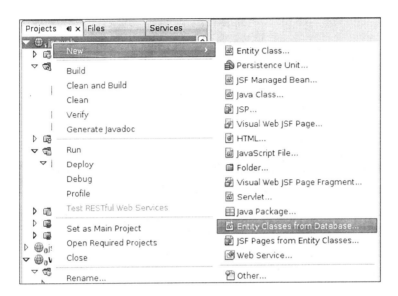

We see a **New Entity Classes from Database** dialog as depicted in the screenshot below:

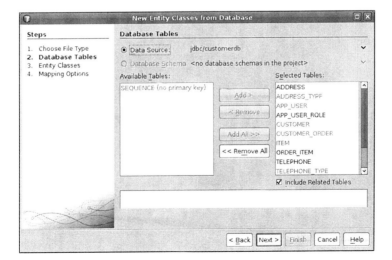

At this point we can either select an existing data source, or, like we did in the previous example, create one "on the fly". In our example we created a new one, then selected the database connection we created earlier in this section.

Once we have created or selected our data source, we need to select one or more tables to use to generate our JPA entities. If we wish to create JPA entities for all tables, we can simply click on the **Add All>>** button.

After clicking **Next>**, NetBeans gives us the opportunity to change the names of the generated classes, although the defaults tend to be sensible. We should also specify a package for our classes, and it is a good idea to check the **Generate Named Query Annotations for Persistent Fields** checkbox.

 Named Queries are explained in detail in the next subsection.

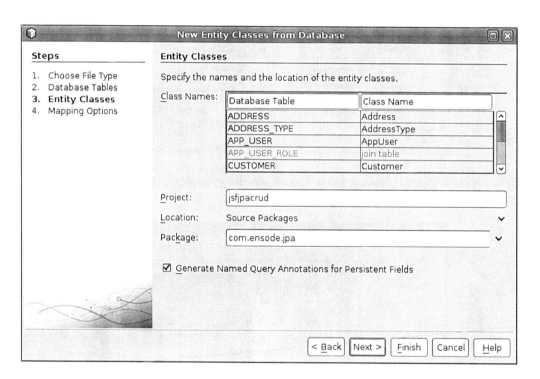

In the next screen in the wizard, we can select how associated entities will be fetched (eagerly or lazily). By default, the default behavior is selected, which is to fetch "one-to-one" and "many-to-one" relationships eagerly, and "one-to-many" and "many-to-many" relationships lazily.

Additionally, we can select what collection type to use for the "many" side of a "one-to-many" or "many-to-many" relationship. The default value is `java.util.Collection`. Other valid values are `java.util.List` and `java.util.Set`.

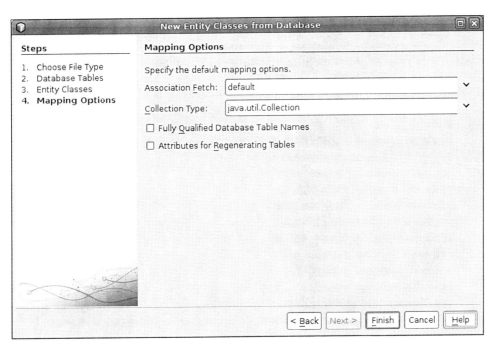

Checking the **Fully Qualified Database Table Names** checkbox results in adding the catalog and schema elements of the table being mapped to the `@Table` annotation for each generated entity.

Checking the **Attributes for Regenerating Tables** results in the generated `@Column` annotations having attributes such as `length`, which specifies the maximum length allowed in the column; `nullable`, which specifies if `null` values are allowed in the column; `precision` and `scale`, which specify the precision and scale of decimal values, respectively. Checking this attribute also adds the `uniqueConstraints` attribute to the generated `@Table` annotation to specify any unique constraints that apply to the table, if necessary. When clicking **Finish**, NetBeans generates JPA entities for all tables in the database. Our database contained a table named CUSTOMER table. Let's take a look at the generated `Customer` JPA entity.

```
package com.ensode.jpa;

//Import statements removed for brevity.

@Entity
@Table(name = "CUSTOMER")
@NamedQueries({@NamedQuery(name = "Customer.findByCustomerId",
```

```
    query = "SELECT c FROM Customer c WHERE c.customerId = :customerId"),
    @NamedQuery(name = "Customer.findByFirstName", query = "SELECT c FROM
    Customer c WHERE c.firstName = :firstName"),
    @NamedQuery(name = "Customer.findByMiddleName", query = "SELECT c FROM
    Customer c WHERE c.middleName = :middleName"),
    @NamedQuery(name = "Customer.findByLastName", query = "SELECT c FROM
    Customer c WHERE c.lastName = :lastName"),
    @NamedQuery(name = "Customer.findByEmail", query = "SELECT c FROM
    Customer c WHERE c.email = :email")})
    public class Customer implements Serializable {

        @Id
        @Column(name = "CUSTOMER_ID", nullable = false)
        private Integer customerId;
        @Column(name = "FIRST_NAME")
        private String firstName;
        @Column(name = "MIDDLE_NAME")
        private String middleName;
        @Column(name = "LAST_NAME")
        private String lastName;
        @Column(name = "EMAIL")
        private String email;
        @OneToMany(mappedBy = "customerId")
        private Collection<CustomerOrder> customerOrderCollection;
        @OneToMany(mappedBy = "customerId")
        private Collection<Address> addressCollection;
        @OneToMany(mappedBy = "customerId")
        private Collection<Telephone> telephoneCollection;

        //Getters, setters and other generated methods and
        //constructors removed for brevity.
    }
```

As we can see, NetBeans generates a class decorated with the @Entity annotation, which marks the class as a JPA entity. Notice that NetBeans automatically decorated one of the fields with the @Id annotation, based on the primary key constraint in the table used to generate the JPA entity. Notice that no primary key generation strategy is used. We either need to populate the primary key ourselves, or add the @GeneratedValue annotation manually.

Also notice the @Table annotation. This is an optional annotation that indicates what table our JPA entity maps to. If the @Table annotation is not used, then our entity will map to a table having the same name as the entity class (case insensitive). In our particular example, the @Table annotation is redundant, but there are cases where it is useful. For example, some database schemas have tables named in plural

(CUSTOMERS), but it makes sense to name our entities in singular (Customer). Additionally, the standard naming convention for database tables containing more than one word is to use underscores to separate words (CUSTOMER_ORDER) where in Java the standard is to use camel case (CustomerOrder). The @Table annotation allows us to follow established naming standards in both the relational database and the Java worlds.

Named Queries and JPQL

Next, we see the @NamedQueries annotation (this annotation is only generated if we click on the **Generate Named Query Annotations for Persistent Fields** checkbox of the **New Entity Classes from Database** wizard). This query contains a value attribute (the attribute name can be omitted from the code since it is the only attribute in this annotation). The value of this attribute is an array of @NamedQuery annotations. The @NamedQuery annotation has a name attribute, which is used to give it a logical name (By convention, the JPA entity name is used as part of the query name. As we can see in the generated code, the **New Entity Classes from Database** wizard follows this convention), and a query attribute, which is used to define a **Java Persistence Query Language (JPQL)** query to be executed by the named query.

JPQL is a JPA-specific query language. Its syntax is similar to SQL. The **New Entity Classes from Database** wizard generates a JPQL query for each field in our entity. When the query is executed, a List containing all instances of our entity that match the criteria in the query will be returned. The following code snippet illustrates this process.

```
import java.util.List;
import javax.persistence.EntityManager;
import javax.persistence.Query;

public class CustomerDAO {

  public List findCustomerByLastName(String someLastName)
  {
    //code to lookup EntityManager omitted for brevity

    Query query =
        em.createNamedQuery("Customer.findByLastName");
    query.setParameter("lastName", someLastName);
    List resultList = query.getResultList();
    return resultList;
  }
}
```

Here we see a DAO object containing a method that will return a list of `Customer` entities for customers whose last name equals the one provided in the method's parameter. In order to implement this, we need to obtain an instance of an object of type `javax.pesistence.Query`. As we can see in the previous code snippet, this can be accomplished by invoking the `createNamedQuery()` method in `EntityManager`, passing the query name (as defined in the `@NamedQuery` annotation) as a parameter. Notice that the named queries generated by the NetBeans wizard contain strings preceded by a colon (`:`), these strings are **named parameters**. Named parameters are "placeholders" we can use to substitute for appropriate values.

In our example, we set the `lastName` named parameter in JPQL query with the `someLastName` argument passed to our method.

Once we have populated all parameters in our query, we can obtain a `List` of all matching entities by invoking the `getResultList()` method in our `Query` object.

Going back to our generated JPA entity, notice the wizard automatically placed the `@Id` annotation in the field mapping to the table's primary key. Additionally, each field is decorated with the `@Column` annotation, which allows us to follow standard naming conventions in both the relational database and Java worlds. In addition to allowing us to specify what column each field maps to, the `@Column` annotation has a `nullable` attribute that allows us to specify if the column accepts null values or not. As we can see, the wizard automatically sets `nullable` to `false` for the entity's primary key field.

Entity Relationships

There are several annotations we can use in JPA entities to define relationships between them. In our `Customer` entity shown above, we can see that the wizard detected several one-to-many relationships in the CUSTOMER table, and automatically added the `@OneToMany` annotation to define these relationships in our entity. Notice that each field annotated with the `@OneToMany` annotation is of type `java.util.Collection`. The `Customer` is the "one" side of the relationship, since a customer can have many orders, many addresses (street, mail), or many telephone numbers (home, work, cell). Notice that the wizard uses generics to specify the type of objects we can add to each collection. Objects in these collections are the JPA entities mapping to the corresponding tables in our database schema.

Notice that `@OneToMany` annotation has a `mappedBy` attribute. This attribute is necessary since each of these relationships is bi-directional (we can access all addresses for a customer, and for a given address, we can obtain what customer it belongs to). The value of this attribute must match the name of the field on the other side of the relationship. Let's take a look at the `Address` entity to illustrate the other side of the customer-address relationship.

```
package com.ensode.jpa;

//imports omitted for brevity.

@Entity
@Table(name = "ADDRESS")

//Named queries omitted for brevity

public class Address implements Serializable {
    private static final long serialVersionUID = 1L;
    @Id
    @Column(name = "ADDRESS_ID", nullable = false)
    private Integer addressId;
    @Column(name = "ADDR_LINE_1")
    private String addrLine1;
    @Column(name = "ADDR_LINE_2")
    private String addrLine2;
    @Column(name = "CITY")
    private String city;
    @Column(name = "ZIP")
    private String zip;
    @JoinColumn(name = "ADDRESS_TYPE_ID",
                referencedColumnName = "ADDRESS_TYPE_ID")
    @ManyToOne
    private AddressType addressTypeId;
    @JoinColumn(name = "CUSTOMER_ID",
                referencedColumnName = "CUSTOMER_ID")
    @ManyToOne
    private Customer customerId;
    @JoinColumn(name = "US_STATE_ID",
                referencedColumnName = "US_STATE_ID")
    @ManyToOne
    private UsState usStateId;

// Getters, setters, constructor and other methods
// omitted for brevity.
}
```

Notice that the `Address` entity has a `customerId` field. This field is of type `Customer`, the entity we were just discussing.

A more appropriate name for this field would have been `customer`, the **New Entity Classes from Database** names the field based on the column name in the database. This is one small disadvantage of using the wizard to generate JPA entities. Of course we are free to rename the field and the corresponding getter and setter methods. Additionally, we would have to change the value of the `mappedBy` attribute of the `@OneToMany` annotation on the other side of the relationship.

Notice that the field is decorated with a `@ManyToOne` annotation. This annotation marks the "many" side of the one-to-many relationship between `Customer` and `Address`. Notice that the field is also decorated with the `@JoinColumn` annotation. The `name` attribute of this annotation indicates the column in the database our entity maps to that defines the foreign key constraint between the `ADDRESS` and `CUSTOMER` tables. The `referencedColumnName` attribute of `@JoinColumn` is use to indicate the primary key column of the table on the "one" side of the relationship (`CUSTOMER`, in our case).

In addition to one-to-many and many-to-one relationships, JPA provides annotations to denote many-to-many, and one-to-one relationships. In our schema, we have many-to-many relationships between the `CUSTOMER_ORDER` and `ITEM` tables, since an order can have many items, and an item can belong to many orders.

The table to hold orders was named `CUSTOMER_ORDER` since the word `ORDER` is a reserved word in SQL.

Let's take a look at the `CustomerOrder` JPA entity to see how the many-to-many relationship is defined.

```
package com.ensode.jpa;

//imports deleted for brevity

@Entity
@Table(name = "CUSTOMER_ORDER")

//Named queries deleted for brevity
public class CustomerOrder implements Serializable {
    private static final long serialVersionUID = 1L;
    @Id
    @Column(name = "CUSTOMER_ORDER_ID", nullable = false)
    private Integer customerOrderId;
    @Column(name = "ORDER_NUMBER")
```

```
    private String orderNumber;
    @Column(name = "ORDER_DESCRIPTION")
    private String orderDescription;
    @JoinTable(name = "ORDER_ITEM", joinColumns =
    {@JoinColumn(name = "CUSTOMER_ORDER_ID",
                 referencedColumnName =
                 "CUSTOMER_ORDER_ID")},
    inverseJoinColumns = {@JoinColumn(name = "ITEM_ID",
                          referencedColumnName = "ITEM_ID")})
    @ManyToMany
    private Collection<Item> itemIdCollection;
    @JoinColumn(name = "CUSTOMER_ID",
                referencedColumnName = "CUSTOMER_ID")
    @ManyToOne
    private Customer customerId;

//Constructor, getters, setters and other methods deleted for
//brevity

}
```

Notice that the CustomerOrder entity has a property of type java.util.Collection named itemIdCollection.

> Again, the property name generated by the wizard could be improved. A better name would have been itemCollection.

This property holds all items for the order. Notice that the field is decorated with the @ManyToMany annotation. This annotation is used to declare a many-to-many relationship between the CustomerOrder and Item JPA entities. Notice that the field is also annotated with the @JoinTable annotation. This annotation is necessary since a join table is necessary in a database schema whenever there is a many-to-many relationship between tables. Using a join table allows us to keep the data in the database normalized.

The @JoinTable annotation allows us to specify the table in the schema that is used to denote the many-to-many relationship in the schema. The value of the name attribute of @JoinTable must match the name of the join table in the schema. The value of the joinColumns attribute of @JoinColumn must be the foreign key relationship between the join table and the owning side of the relationship. We already looked at the @JoinColumn annotation when looking at one-to-many relationships. In this case, its name attribute must match the name of the column in the join table that has the foreign key relationship, and its referencedColumnName attribute must indicate the name of the primary key column on the owning side of the relationship. The value of the inverseJoinColumns attribute of @JoinTable has a similar role as its joinColumns attribute, except it indicates the corresponding columns for the non-owning side of the relationship.

The side of the many-to-many relationship containing the above annotations is said to be the **owning side** of the relationship, let's look at how the many-to-many relationship is defined in the non-owning side of the relationship, which, in our case is the Item JPA entity.

```
package com.ensode.jpa;

//Imports deleted for brevity

@Entity
@Table(name = "ITEM")

//Named queries deleted for brevity

public class Item implements Serializable {
    private static final long serialVersionUID = 1L;
    @Id
    @Column(name = "ITEM_ID", nullable = false)
    private Integer itemId;
    @Column(name = "ITEM_NUMBER")
    private String itemNumber;
    @Column(name = "ITEM_SHORT_DESC")
    private String itemShortDesc;
    @Column(name = "ITEM_LONG_DESC")
    private String itemLongDesc;
    @ManyToMany(mappedBy = "itemIdCollection")
    private Collection<CustomerOrder> customerOrderIdCollection;

    //Constructors, getters, setters and other methods
    //deleted for brevity.
}
```

As we can see, the only thing we need to do on this side of the relationship is to create a Collection property, decorate it with the @ManyToMany annotation and specify the property name in the other side of the relationship as the value of its mappedBy attribute.

In addition to one-to-many and many-to-many relationships, it is possible to create one-to-one relationships between JPA entities.

The annotation to use to indicate a one-to-one relationship between two JPA entities is @OneToOne. Our schema doesn't have any one-to-one relationship between tables, therefore this annotation was not added to any of the entities generated by the wizard.

 One-to-one relationships are not very popular in database schemas, since all data in a single entity is kept in a single table. Nevertheless JPA supports one-to-one relationships in case it is needed.

The procedure to indicate a one-to-one relationship between two entities is similar to what we have already seen, the owning side of the relationship must have a field of the type of the JPA entity at the other side of the relationship. This field must be decorated with the @OneToOne and @JoinColumn annotations.

Suppose we had a schema in which a one-to-one relationship was defined between two tables named PERSON and BELLY_BUTTON. This is a one-to-one relationship since each person has one belly button and each belly button belongs to only one person. (The reason the schema was modeled this way instead of having the columns relating to the BELLY_BUTTON table in the PERSON table escapes me, but bear with me, I'm having a hard time coming up with a good example!).

```
@Entity
public class Person implements Serializable {
    @JoinColumn(name="BELLY_BUTTON_ID")
    @OneToOne
    private BellyButton bellyButton;

    public BellyButton getBellyButton(){
      return bellyButton;
    }

    public void setBellyButton(BellyButton bellyButton){
      this.bellyButton = bellyButton;
    }
}
```

If the one-to-one relationship is **unidirectional** (we can only get the belly button from the person), this would be all we had to do. If the relationship is **bidirectional**, then we need to add the @OneToOne annotation on the other side of the relationship, and use its mappedBy attribute to indicate the other side of the relationship.

```
@Entity
@Table(name="BELLY_BUTTON")
public class BellyButton implements Serializable(
```

```
{
  @OneToOne(mappedBy="bellyButton")
  private Person person;

  public Person getPerson(){
    return person;
  }
  public void getPerson(Person person){
    this.person=person;
  }
}
}
```

As we can see, the procedure to establish one-to-one relationships is very similar to the procedure used to establish one-to-many and many-to-many relationships.

Once we have generated JPA entities from a database, we need to write additional code containing business and presentation logic. Alternatively, we can use NetBeans to generate code for these two layers.

Generating JSF Applications from JPA Entities

One very nice feature of NetBeans is that it allows us to generate JSF applications that will perform create, read, update, and delete (CRUD) operations from existing JPA entities. This feature, combined with the ability to create JPA entities from an existing database schema, as described in the previous section, allows us to write web applications that interact with a database in record time.

To generate JSF pages from existing JPA entities, we need to right-click on the project and select **New | JSF Pages from Entity Classes...**.

 In order for us generate JSF pages from existing JPA entities, the current project must be a Web application project.

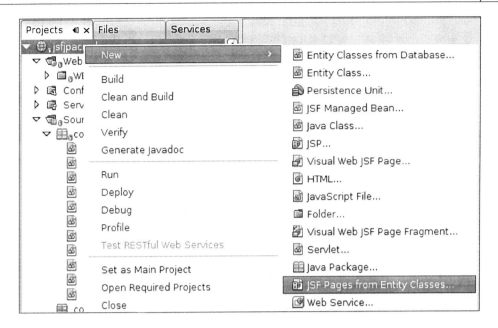

At this point we are presented with the **New JSF Pages from Entity Classes** wizard.

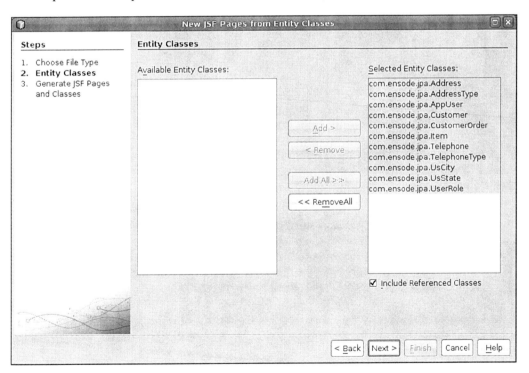

We need to select one or more JPA entities. We would typically want to select all of them. They can easily be selected by clicking on the **Add All>>** button.

The next page in the wizard allows us to specify a package for newly created JSF managed beans. Two types of classes are generated by the wizard: **JPA Controllers** and **JSF Classes**. We can specify packages for both of these individually.

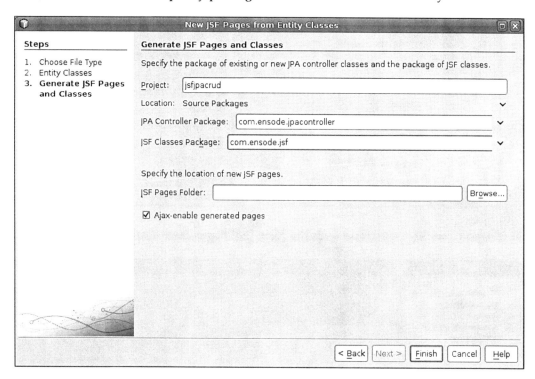

We are also given the opportunity to specify a folder for the JSF pages to be created. If we leave this field blank, pages will be created in our project's **Web Pages** folder.

 The value of the **JPA Controller Package** and **JSF Classes Package** text fields default to the package where our JPA entities reside. It is a good idea to modify this default, since placing the JSF managed beans in a different package separates the data access layer classes from the user interface and controller layers of our application.

At this point in the wizard we can specify if we would like the generated pages to be Ajax enabled. This can be done by simply checking the **Ajax-enable generated pages** checkbox.

After clicking **Finish**, a complete web application that can perform CRUD operations will be created.

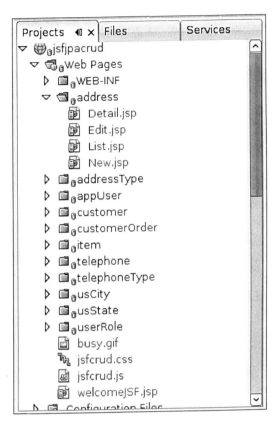

As we can see, NetBeans generates a folder for each of our entities under the **Web Pages** folder of our application. Each of the folders has a **Detail**, **Edit**, **List**, and **New** JSP files. The **Detail** JSP will display all properties for a JPA entity, the **Edit** JSP will allow users to update information for a specific entity, the **List** JSP will display all instances of a specific entity in the database, and the **New** JSP will provide functionality to create new entities.

The generated application is a standard JSF application; we can execute it by simply right-clicking on the project and selecting **Run**. At that point the usual things happen: the application server is started if it wasn't already up, the application is deployed and a web browser window is opened displaying the welcome page for our application.

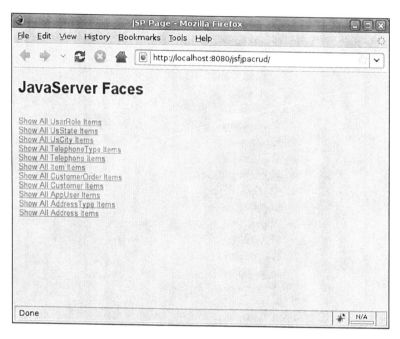

As we can see, the welcome page contains a link corresponding to each of our JPA entities. The links will display a table displaying all existing instances of our entity in the database. Then we click on the **Show All Customer Items.**

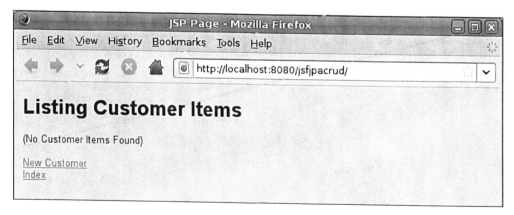

Since we haven't inserted any data to the database yet, the page displays the message **(No Customer Items Found)**. We can insert a customer into the database by clicking on the **New Customer** link.

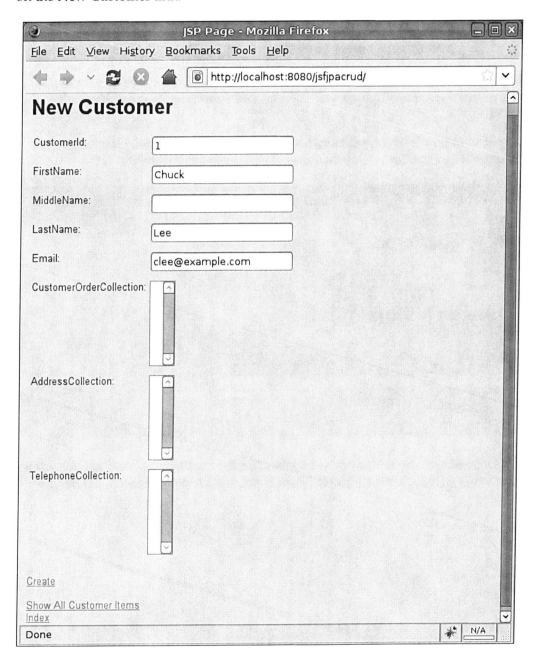

Notice how an input field is generated for each property in our entity, which in turn corresponds to each column in the database table.

 As we can see, an input field was generated for the primary key field of our entity. This field is only generated if the JPA entity does not use a primary key generation strategy.

For properties in which there is a one-to-many relationship, a multiple select box is generated (in our example they are empty, since we haven't added any to the database yet).

After entering some information on the page and clicking on the **Create** link, a new customer is inserted into the database and we are directed to the **List** JSP.

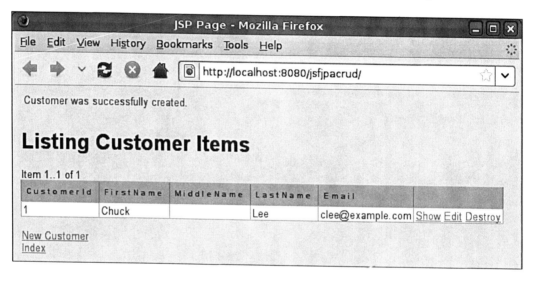

At this point we can see our newly created customer in the list of customers on this JSP. Notice that the JSP has links to **Show**, **Edit**, and **Destroy** (delete) the entity.

Let's say we would want to add an address for our customer. We could do so by clicking on the **Index** link, then clicking on **Show All Address Items**, then on **New Address**.

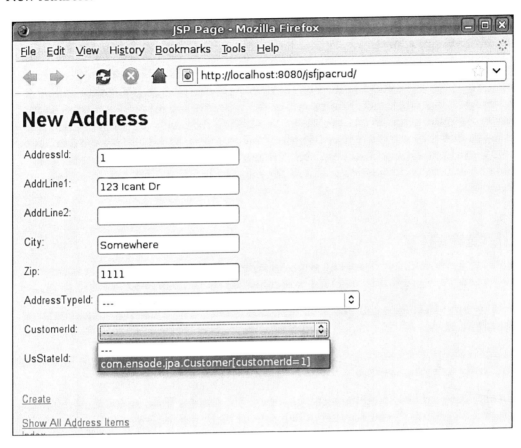

The `Address` entity is at the "one" end of several one-to-many relationships, notice how a combo box is generated for each one of the entities at the "many" end. Since we wish to assign this address to the customer we just added, we attempt to select a customer from the **CustomerId** combo box.

A better name could be used for the **CustomerId** field. The reason this is the label for the combo box is because it matches the property name on the `Address` JPA entity, which in turn could have a better name, such as `customer`. Recall that all entities on this project were automatically generated from an existing database schema.

Clicking on the combo box reveals a cryptic, almost undecipherable (from the users point of view anyway), label for our customer. The reason we see this label is because the labels generated for each item in the combo box come from the `toString()` method of the entities used to populate it. We can work around this issue by modifying the `toString()` method so that it returns a user-friendly `String` suitable to use as a label.

As we can see, the generated code from NetBeans wizards could certainly use some tweaking, such as modifying the `toString()` methods of each JPA entity so that it can be used as a label, modifying some of the property names on the entities so that they make more sense to us developers, modifying the labels on the generated JSF pages so that they are more user friendly. Nevertheless, as we can see we can have a fully working application completely created by a few clicks of the mouse. This functionality certainly saves us a lot of time and effort (just don't tell your boss about it).

Summary

In this chapter, we saw the many ways in which NetBeans can help us speed up development of applications taking advantage of the Java Persistence API (JPA).

We saw how NetBeans can generate new JPA classes with all required annotations already in place.

Additionally, we covered how NetBeans can automatically generate code to persist a JPA entity to a database table.

We also covered how NetBeans can generate JPA entities from an existing database schema, including the automated generation of JPQL named queries.

Finally, we saw how NetBeans can generate a complete JSF application from existing JPA entities.

6
Visual Web JSF Development

One very nice NetBeans feature is that it allows development of web applications by simply dragging-and-dropping components from a palette into a design window. In addition to allowing us to easily develop web applications this way, the NetBeans Visual Web functionality also allows us to easily display data from a database by simply dragging a database table into a visual JSF component on the design window.

The following topics will be covered in this chapter:

- Writing our first Visual Web application
- Populating components with database data
- Ajax-enabling Visual Web applications

Writing Our first Visual Web Application

To create a new web application taking advantage of NetBeans Visual Web functionality, we need to create a new web application project and add the Visual Web JavaServer Faces framework to it.

 Consult Chapter 2 *Developing Web Applications with Servlets and JSPs* for detailed instructions on creating a new web application.

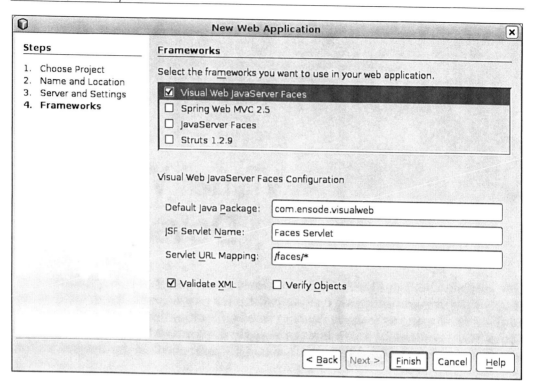

 The **Default Java Package** field defaults to the project name. It is a good idea to modify this field.

After creating the project NetBeans should look something like the following screenshot.

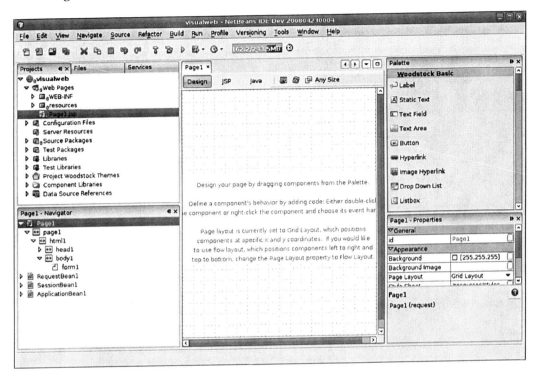

NetBeans automatically creates a new JSP, named **Page1.jsp**. Additionally, NetBeans automatically generates a request scoped managed bean named `Page1.java` that can be used to programmatically manipulate components on the page. An additional request scoped managed bean, a session scoped, and an application scoped managed bean named `RequestBean1.java`, `SessionBean1.java`, and `ApplicationBean1.java`, respectively, are also created. All of these managed beans are automatically added to the application's `faces-config.xml` configuration file.

We can add components to **Page1.jsp** by simply dragging components from the palette into the design window. For example, if we wish to add a text field to the page, all we need to do is drag the **Text Field** component from the palette into the design window.

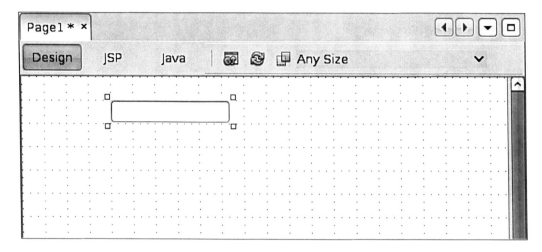

We can customize our text field by modifying its attributes on the **Properties** window.

 We can gain screen real estate in the **Properties** window by either detaching it (keyboard shortcut *Alt+Shift+D*) then resizing it or by minimizing the **Palette** window.

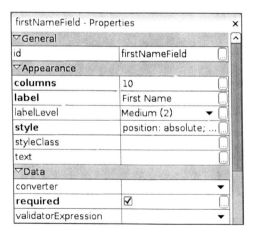

As can be seen in the above screenshot, in this example, we modified the **id** attribute from its default value of **textField1** to **firstNameField**. We also modified the **columns** attribute to **10** from its default value of **20**. The **columns** attribute dictates how many characters are visible in the text field without scrolling. Additionally, we modified the **label** attribute to **First Name**. This attribute adds a label to our text field. The **style** attribute is meant to add CSS styles to our component; NetBeans automatically sets this value to a style that will place the text field component in the correct location on the page. Lastly, we made our text field required by checking the **required** check box.

As we modify these attributes, the design window changes to reflect our changes.

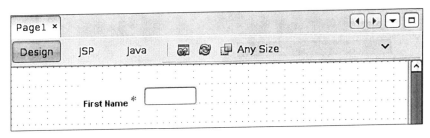

Notice that the label was automatically added to our page, as well as a red asterisk indicating that the field is required. The size of the text field was also modified to reflect the value we gave to its **columns** attribute.

Visual JSF applications are standard JSF applications, therefore while we are graphically manipulating the page, a JSP is being created behind the scenes. We can view the source of the JSP by clicking on the **JSP** tab.

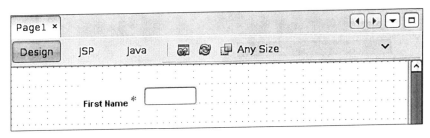

Notice that this JSP markup is a bit different to what we have seen before. The reason for this is that there are two ways JSPs can be coded. The first way is to use "traditional" JSP tags, which is what we have seen so far. The second method is to use XML syntax to write our JSPs. JSPs generated by the NetBeans Visual Web editor use the second approach.

When using XML syntax, instead of using a `<%@ taglib%>` directive, we use XML namespaces to include tag libraries in the JSP. Notice that the generated JSP markup uses the standard HTML JSF tag library. Additionally, it uses a custom JSF library with a URI of `http://www.sun.com/webui/webuijsf`. This tag library contains all the custom components see in the **Palette** window.

The custom tag library used by NetBeans Visual Web is known as the **Woodstock Tag Library**, more information about this library can be found at `https://woodstock.dev.java.net/`.

We can add markup directly into the JSP, and when we go back to the design view it should update accordingly. As we can see from the markup above, the attributes we set in the **Properties** window are attributes of the custom JSP tags used by visual web.

Sometimes it is faster to set the attributes directly in the markup rather than using the properties window, since we can use NetBeans code completion (*Ctrl+Space*) this way, saving us from scrolling up and down the properties window in order to find a property we wish to modify.

By clicking on the **Java** tab we can see the generated `Page1.java` request scoped managed bean.

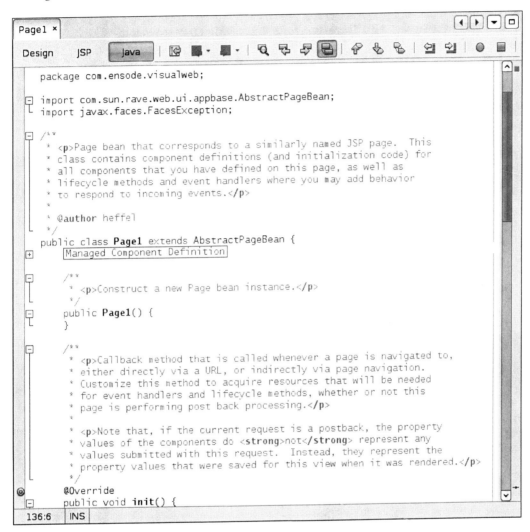

Like with most JSF applications, we need to bind the value of our text field to a managed bean property. When using Visual Web we can simply add a property to the generated session scoped managed bean named `SessionBean1.java`. For our example, we simply add a private instance variable of type `String` named `page1FirstName`, and the corresponding getter and setter methods.

A quick way to add an instance variable and the corresponding getter and setter methods is to hit the "insert code" keyboard shortcut (*Alt+Insert*), then select **Add Property...** from the resulting pop-up menu.

```java
 * @return reference to the scoped data bean
 */
protected ApplicationBean1 getApplicationBean1() {
    return (ApplicationBean1) getBean("ApplicationBean1");
}

private String page1FirstName;

/**
 * Get the value of page1FirstName
 *
 * @return the value of page1FirstName
 */
public String getPage1FirstName() {
    return page1FirstName;
}

/**
 * Set the value of page1FirstName
 *
 * @param page1FirstName new value of page1FirstName
 */
public void setPage1FirstName(String page1FirstName) {
    this.page1FirstName = page1FirstName;
}
}
```

Once we have added the property to our managed bean, we can bind our text field to it by right-clicking on it on the design window and selecting **Bind To Data....** Binding the text field to a managed bean property results in the property being automatically updated with the user-entered data in the field. Additionally when the page is loaded the value of the text field is populated with the value of the managed bean property.

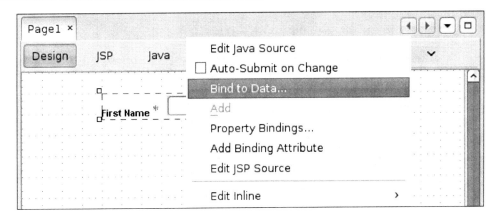

At this point the **Bind to Data** window opens, we need to click on the **Bind to an Object** tab then select the appropriate property from the managed bean.

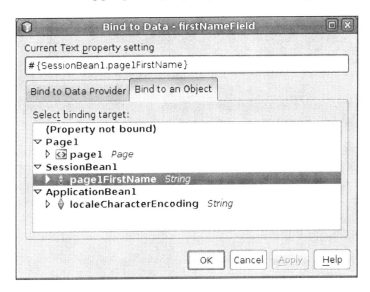

Notice that the value of the **Current Text property setting** field (#{SessionBean1.page1FirstName}) in the window contains the JSF property notation that will be added to the JSP markup.

After clicking on the **OK** button, the value of the text property of our text field will be bound to the page1FirstName property in the managed bean, therefore when the form is submitted the value of this property will be populated with the user-entered value in the field.

In order to submit the form, we need to add a submit button to the page. We can simply drag the button component from the palette into our page.

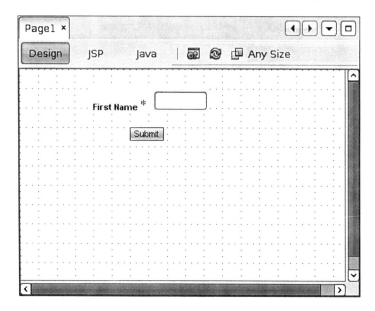

When we drop the button component into the page, its label turns editable. In our example we changed the label to read **Submit**.

Like standard JSF command buttons, for visual web JSF application buttons we need to specify an action to be performed when the button is pressed. This action can either be a String constant or a method binding expression bound to a method that takes no arguments and returns a String. We can simply double-click on the button and an action method will automatically be created in the page's request scoped bean (Page1.java, in our example).

```java
public String button1_action() {
    return "success";
}
```

The button's `action` property will automatically be set to this new method.

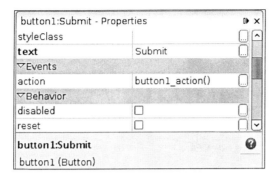

In our example we replaced the default body of the method with a single statement, returning the string `success`.

In a real application, we would add some business logic here, more than likely saving the user-entered data into a database, then returning a value if the operation was successful or a different value if there was a problem.

Now we need to add a page to land when the user submits the form, to do this we need to go to **File | New File...**, select the **Java Server Faces** category, and the **Visual Web JSF Page** file type.

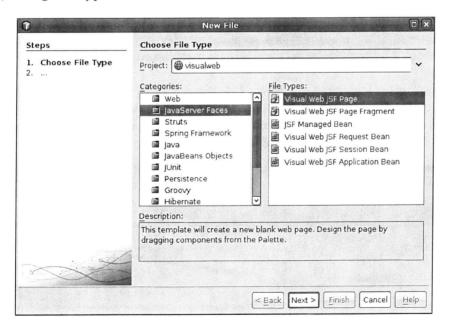

Then we need to select a name and a package for the generated managed bean.

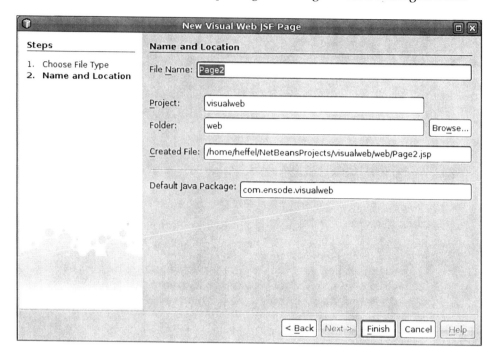

In our example, we simply keep the default values and click **Finish**.

Generated request scoped managed beans have the same name as the name we choose for our page, therefore it is a good idea to name our visual web JSF pages using standard Java class naming conventions

After creating our new page, we drag a **Label** and a **Static Text** component from the palette into its design window. We then change the label text to read **First Name**, and bind the static text component to the firstName property of SessionBean1, which is the same value the text field in the previous page was bound to.

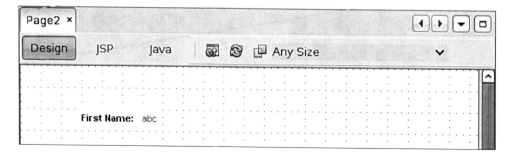

At this point we need to connect our two pages so that the second page is displayed after submitting the first. The easiest way to do this is through the NetBeans page flow editor, which we can access by opening the application's `faces-config.xml` configuration file and clicking on the **PageFlow** tab.

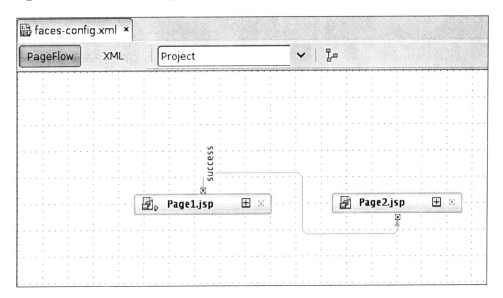

 Refer to Chapter 4 *Developing Web Applications using JavaServer Faces* for a detailed explanation on how to use the page flow editor.

At this point we have a complete (albeit simple) Visual JSF application. We can deploy and execute it in one step by right-clicking on the project and selecting **Run** (alternatively, if our project is the main project, we can simply hit *F6*). At this point the application server is started if it wasn't up already, our application is deployed and its welcome page is loaded in the browser.

After entering a value on the text field and submitting the form, the second page will be displayed in the browser.

Since we bound the static text component to the same managed bean property as the text field on the first page, it displayed the user-entered value from the previous page.

Adding Additional Components to Our Application

Now that we have a fully functional, but very basic application, it is time to add some additional components to it.

Adding Additional Text Fields

We will now add two more text fields for our application, in addition; to capturing the user's first name, we will now capture his/her middle name and last name as well.

After adding two more text fields for middle name and last name to our application, setting their **label** and **required** attributes as appropriate, we can align the components by clicking *Ctrl* on them then right-clicking on one of the components and selecting **Align | Left**.

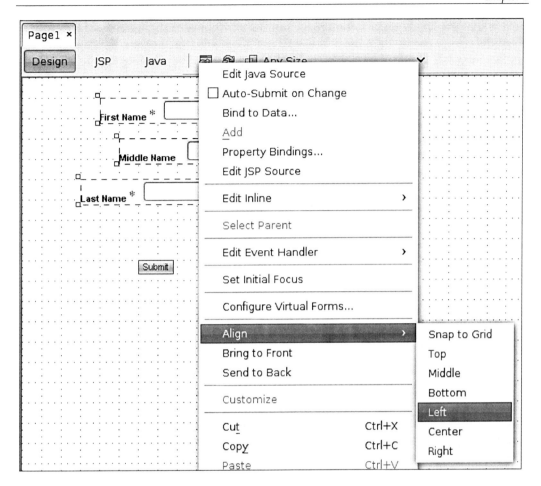

After aligning our components, our design window now looks like this:

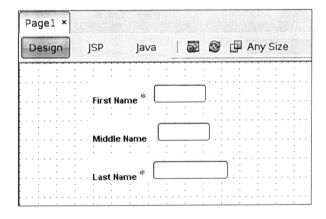

Notice that the labels were left aligned, not the components themselves. If we right align the components, then the labels will not align with each other. Most web applications left align input fields and right align the corresponding labels. If we wish to use this layout in our application, then we can't use the **label** attribute of our components. Instead, we need to add label components individually from the palette into the appropriate location in the design window.

After adding the labels, middle aligning them with their respective text fields, then right aligning them to each other, and re-arranging the vertical space between fields so that it takes less space, our design window now looks like this:

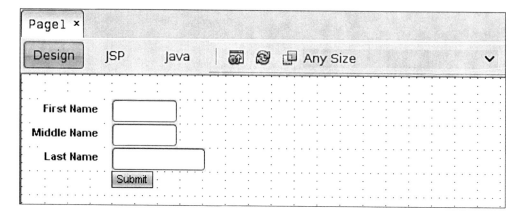

Notice that the asterisks indicating required fields disappeared. The reason for this is that the labels are not yet related to their respective components. To do this, we need to set their **for** property in the **Properties** window.

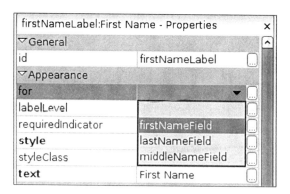

After doing this for each label in our page, the appropriate required indicators are displayed.

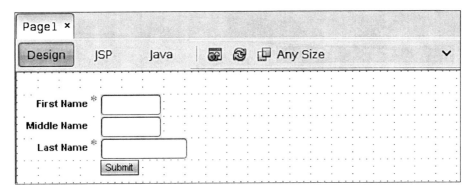

At this point we need to bind the new fields to new properties in our session scoped managed bean.

 The procedure to bind the new fields is identical to what we saw when we bound the first name text field to the `firstName` property in the managed bean, therefore it is not shown.

Adding a Drop-Down List Component

We will now add a drop-down list to our page, in order to capture the user's salutation when sending him/her correspondence. All we need to do is drag the **Drop Down List** component from the palette into the appropriate location on the page.

After dropping our drop-down list component into page and adding a corresponding label component our page now looks like this:

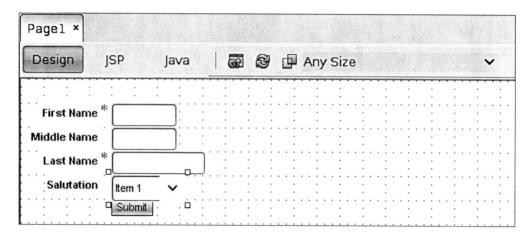

NetBeans automatically assigns some default items to our drop-down list. We need to modify them to suit our needs. We can accomplish this by right-clicking on the drop-down list and selecting **Configure Default Options...**

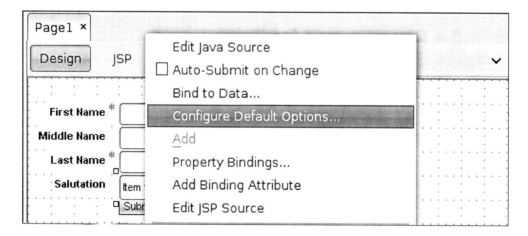

At this point a window pops up allowing us to enter options for our drop-down. By default we should see three options labeled: **Item 1**, **Item 2**, and **Item 3**, with values of **item1**, **item2**, and **item3**, respectively. Clicking on each value makes the field editable; we can modify each one to fit our needs.

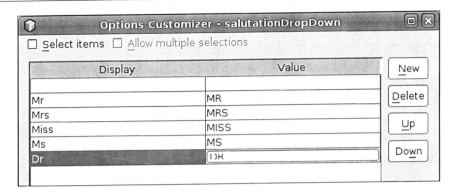

 All components that can display multiple options, such as **Checkbox Group** and **Radio Button Group**, can be configured this way.

Notice we added an "empty" selection at the top of the list. This allows the users not to enter any value for our drop-down.

 We can add, delete, and move items as necessary by using the buttons to the right of the window.

We now need to bind the user-selected value to a property in one of the managed beans. To do this we need to assign a value binding expression to the **selected** property of the drop-down component by clicking on the ellipsis (...) button next to it on the **Properties** window. At this point we can select a property from the managed beans and assign it to this attribute.

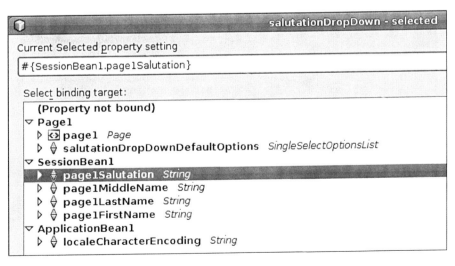

Now our design window should look like this:

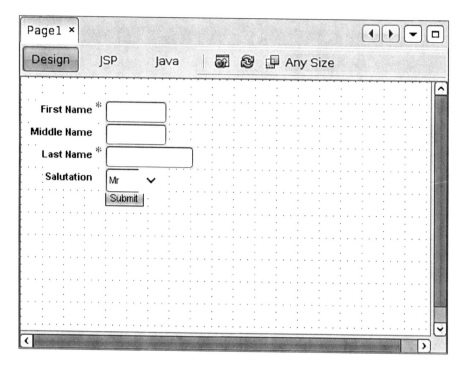

At this point we should modify our confirmation page (Page2.jsp in our example), to display all user-entered values. We can do so by following the same procedure we used earlier, adding static text components to the page and binding them to the same values the input fields are bound to. After doing so we are ready to run this new version of the application.

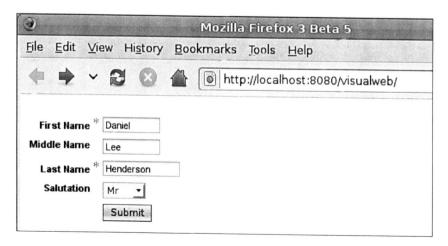

After entering data for all fields and submitting the form, we see our confirmation page displayed in the browser.

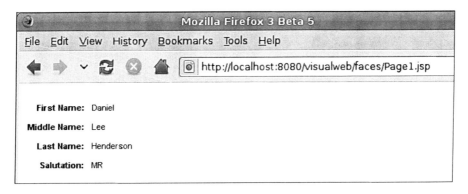

Notice that our form has a couple of required fields. If a user attempts to submit the form without entering any data in the required fields, the labels for the fields will turn red, indicating that there is a problem with the data input for those fields. Although it is nice that we get that functionality with no effort on our part, we should display an error message explaining the problem to the user. There are several ways to do this; we will explain three of the most common methods.

Adding a Message Component to Each Input Field

The first approach we can use to add descriptive error messages to the page is to drop **Message** components next to each input field in the page.

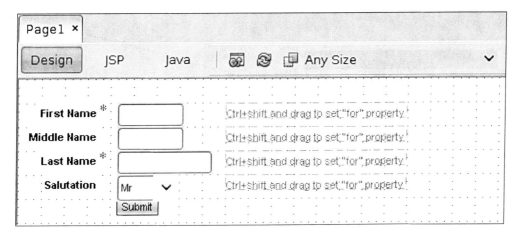

At this point we are prompted to hit *Ctrl + Shift*, then drag the mouse from the message component to the field the message will be associated to. After doing so, our page now looks like this:

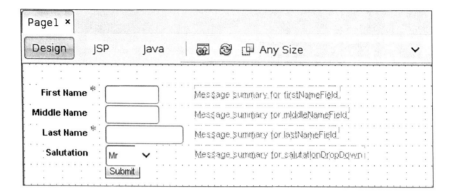

 An alternate way of assigning message components to their corresponding input fields is to set the **for** property to the field's component id in the **Properties** window.

After executing our application and attempting to submit the form with required values missing, we will see an error message next to each field with failed validation.

Notice that the field id's are shown in the error message. This default behavior is not very user friendly, since field id's are not known to the user. We can override this default behavior by setting the **label** property of each input field; the value of this property should match each component's label text.

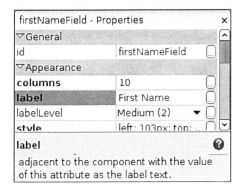

As we discussed earlier in the chapter, setting the **label** property for each input field also has the effect of adding a label to each field, therefore at this point each of our fields will have two labels: the one generated by the **label** attribute, and the one we added to the page. Since we need the **label** attribute to make our error messages user friendly, we need to remove the **label** components from the page.

Recall from earlier in the chapter that using the **label** attribute resulted in difficulty aligning our components the way a web application's input fields are usually aligned. In order to work around this issue, we can hold down the *Shift* key of our keyboard while pressing the right or left arrows of our keyboard, this has the effect of allowing us to move the components one pixel at a time, instead of left aligning the components like we were doing earlier.

After setting the label attribute of each input field, and vertically aligning the components by hitting *Shift + left arrow/right* arrow, our design page now looks like this:

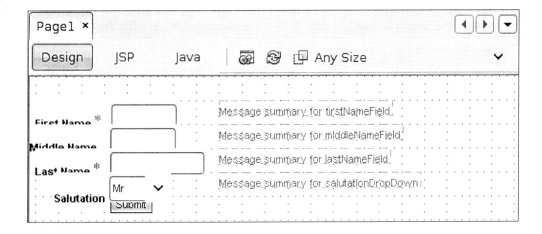

Notice some of the labels and components are not completely visible in the design window. This shouldn't be a concern since they will be displayed properly in the rendered page.

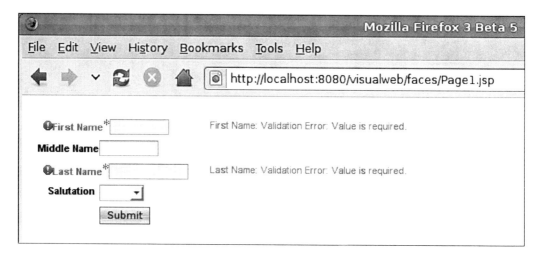

Notice how now each error message matches the label of the appropriate component. Also notice that since visual web JSF automatically adds an icon to each label corresponding to a component that failed validation, vertical alignment is temporarily lost whenever there are validation errors.

Grouping Error Messages with the Message Group Component

Sometimes it is desirable to display all error messages together (usually at the top or bottom of the page), instead of next to each component. Visual JSF includes the **Message Group** component, which can be used for this purpose.

Using this component is very simple, we only need to drop it into the appropriate location on our page. After doing this and removing individual **Message** components, our design window now looks like this:

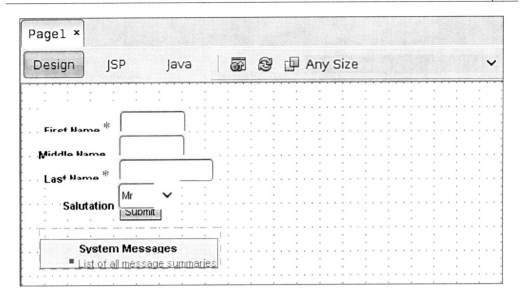

After deploying our application and attempting to submit the page with required field values missing, we can see the **Message Group** component in action.

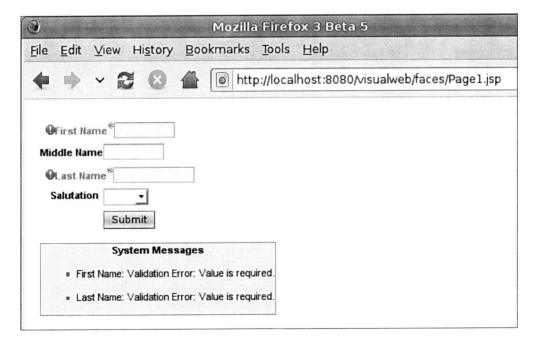

At the time of writing, there was an issue which caused the **Drop Down List** and **Button** components not to align properly with other components in some situations (they align properly in the design window, but don't align properly on the rendered page). We confess, we moved these components as appropriate before taking each screenshot. We expect the issue to be fixed before publication.

Ajax Autovalidation

Another way we can validate our text fields is by using the built-in Ajax enabled autovalidation. This approach allows us to validate user input as soon as the text field loses focus, providing instant feedback to the user. In order to do this, we need to set the **autoValidate** attribute of the text field to "true". The easiest way to do this is to click on the checkbox next to this attribute in the **Properties** window.

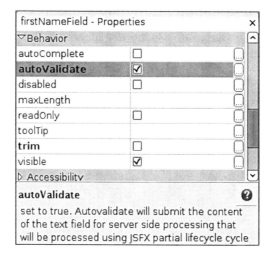

At this point, the text field will be validated as soon as it loses focus by triggering an Ajax request to the server. If validation fails, the text field's component will turn red, but no error message will be displayed. In order to display an error message, we need to add an **Alert** component to the page.

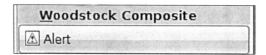

Once we have the **Alert** component on the page, we need to set the `notify` attribute of the text field to be validated to be the component id of the alert component. In our example, we modified the default `id` attribute of the alert component to be `autoValidateAlert`. Since it is placed inside a **Form** component with an id of `form1`, and **Form** is a naming container, the full id of our alert is `form1:autoValidateAlert`.

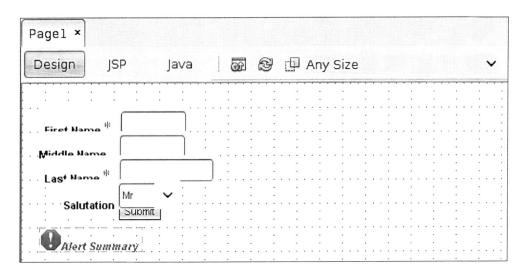

The `notify` attribute of the **Text Field** component is not shown on the **Properties** window; we need to modify the JSP source to add it. In the JSP source, we should look for a `<webuijsf:textField>` component with an `id` attribute of `firstNameField`, and add the full id of the alert component as its value.

```
<webuijsf:textField autoValidate="true" columns="10"
                    id="firstNameField" label="First Name"
                    required="true"
                    notify="form1:autoValidateAlert"/>
```

 For clarity, additional attributes that are irrelevant to the discussion at hand were removed from the above code snippet.

We need to go through this procedure for each text field we wish to autovalidate. In our example, we need to do it for both required fields in our page (First Name and Last Name). Once we have set up autovalidation, our fields will be validated via an Ajax request as soon as they lose focus. If validation fails, the alert component will display an error message, without doing a full page request.

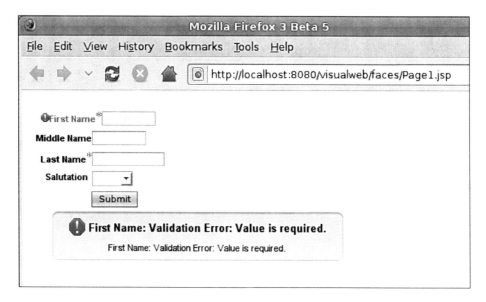

Notice that the alert's title (summary) and body (detail) messages are exactly the same. This behavior is not exactly user friendly and can be improved. The solution is to use the standard JSF error message customization technique. We need to add a resource bundle (property file) to our application, define some keys that JSF assigns to standard error messages, and give them custom values to be used as custom error messages.

When creating Visual JSF projects, a resource bundle is created by default. The file name is `Bundle.properties`, and it is located in the default Java package selected when creating the project. In our project, the file is located in the `com.ensode.visualweb` package. We need to add two properties to our resource bundle; one will set the summary error message to be displayed as the header of the alert, and the other one will set the detailed error message to be displayed as its body.

We can see the keys for standard JSF error messages by expanding the **Libraries** node in the **Projects** window, then expanding the **GlassFish V2** node and **jsf-impl. jar**. Inside the **javax.faces** package we will see a `Messages.properties` file; this file contains all standard error message keys (and values).

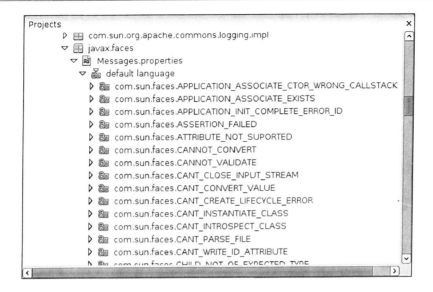

Error message keys follow the pattern `keyname` for summary errors and `keyname_detail` for detailed errors. If there is no detailed error message for a specific error, the default is to use the summary message for the detailed message as well. This is exactly what is happening in our case. `Messages.properties` only specifies a summary error message for required validation errors.

Looking at `Messages.properties`, we can infer that the key for the required validation error is `javax.faces.component.UIInput.REQUIRED`, therefore we need to add a `javax.faces.component.UIInput.REQUIRED_detail` key to our property file. While we are at it, we can add a user-friendlier summary validation message.

To modify our property file, we can either right-click on it and select **Edit** to open it in a text editor, or right-click on it and select **Open** to open it in NetBeans' property file editor. After choosing the second approach and adding the appropriate keys and values, the property file editor should look something like this:

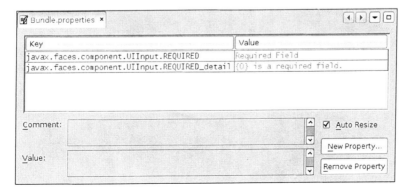

We need to do one more thing before our application picks up our customized error messages; we need to add our property file to the application's `faces-config.xml` configuration file. Near the top of the file, right after the opening `<faces-config>` tag, we need to add an `<application>` tag. Nested inside this tag, we need to add a `<message-bundle>` tag. The value of this tag must be the fully qualified name of our resource bundle (`com.ensode.visualweb.Bundle`, in our case).

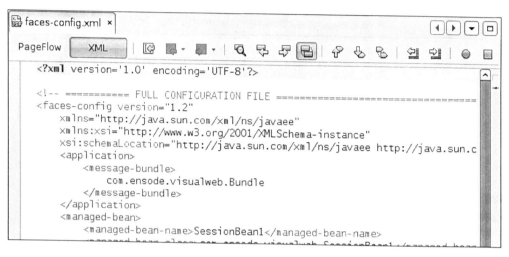

Our application will now display user friendly error messages when autovalidation is triggered.

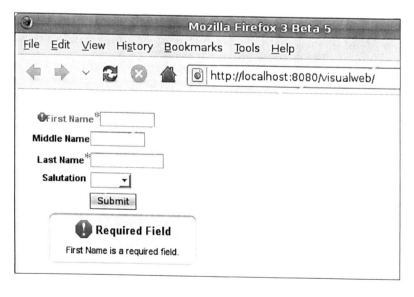

Organizing Our Page into Tabs

One fairly common problem encountered when developing web applications is that sometimes input forms become overwhelmingly long. One common way of addressing this issue is to separate input fields into tabs. Traditionally, creating tabs involved some fairly advanced knowledge of HTML, JavaScript, and CSS. However, NetBeans Visual Web includes built-in support for tabs, allowing us to easily create them without having to be intimately familiar with these technologies.

We can add a **tabSet** component by dragging it from the **Palette** window to the **Navigator**, just inside the page's **Form** component.

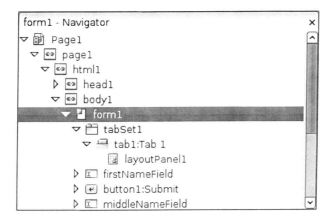

When dropping the **tabSet** component into the **Navigator** window, a **Tab** and **Layout Panel** components are automatically added. We now need to move our components into the newly created tab. We can do so in the **Navigator** window by simply dragging them onto the **layoutPanel** component.

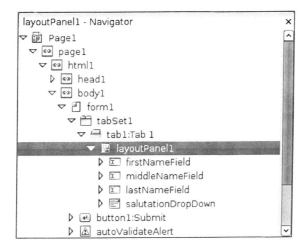

In most situations we would like to have some components that apply to the whole page and are not specific to one particular tab. These components should be left out of the tab. In our example, the submit button and alert fit the bill, therefore we leave them out of the tab.

At this point our components will have lost alignment. We can align them as usual by dragging them in the **Design** window.

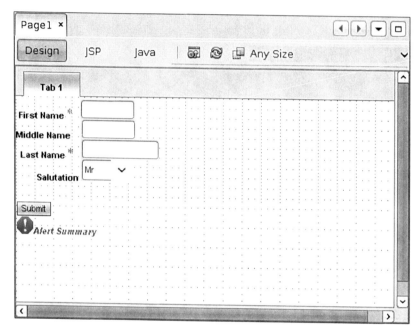

In the above screenshot, in addition to rearranging the components inside the tab, we removed the `style` attribute of the **Submit** button and the alert, since this attribute was being used to place these components in a specific location in the page (CSS absolute positioning). By removing the attribute, the button is placed just under the tab, and the alert is placed just under the button.

Dragging components into the **Navigator** window (as opposed to directly in the **Design** window) has the effect of generating JSP source that better resembles manually coded markup.

When executing our application we can see our newly created tab in action.

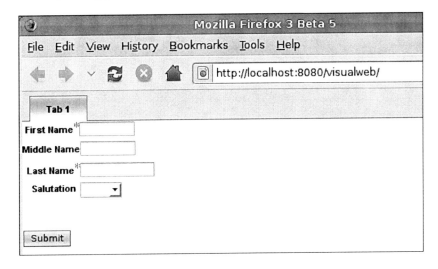

Of course adding a single tab to the page doesn't make a whole lot of sense. In order to take advantage of tabs, we need at least one additional tab in our page. Doing so is very simple; we simply need to drag a **Tab** component from the **Palette** to the **Navigator** window, inside our **Tab Set** component, alternatively, we can right-click either on the **tabSet** or one of the **Tab** components in our page and select **Add Tab**.

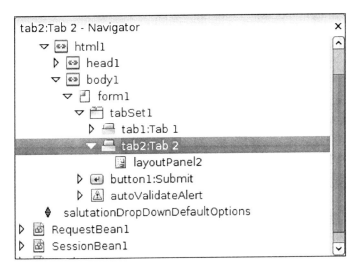

A **Layout Panel** component is automatically added to the new tab. We can add components to the new tab by either dragging them from the **Palette** into the design window or to the **Layout Component** in the **Navigator** window.

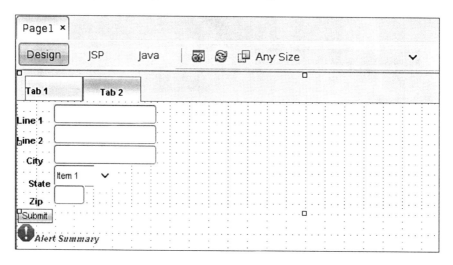

It is a good idea to give our tabs meaningful names. We can do so by simply right-clicking on the tab in the **Design** window and selecting **Edit Text**.

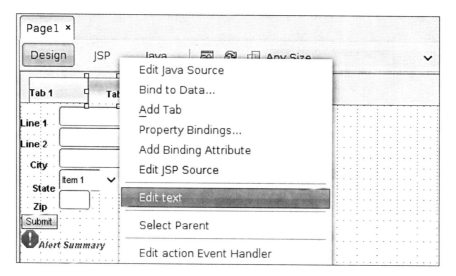

After renaming both of our tabs, and executing our application, we can see our new tab in action.

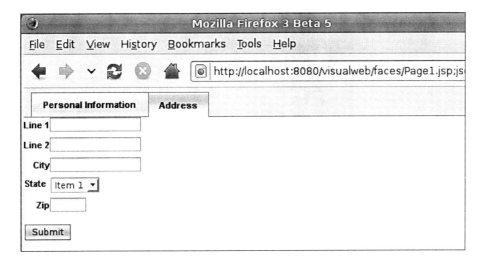

Binding a Drop-Down List to a Database Table

Notice that our new tab has, among other components, a **Drop Down List** component used to allow the user to select a state. We of course need to add the correct options to this drop-down. We could add the options by hand like we discussed earlier, or we could use a very nice Visual Web feature, populating drop-down options from a database table.

 This section assumes that the `customerdb` database has been already created, as described in the previous chapter.

Populating a **Drop Down List** component from a database table is very simple, we simply need to drag the table from the **Services** window to our **Drop Down List** component in the **Design** window.

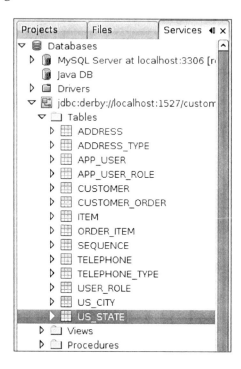

After dropping the database table into our drop-down list, the text inside it in the **Design** window changes to indicate its options are bound to existing data.

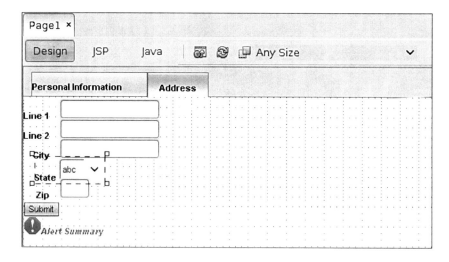

When we execute our application we can see the binding in action.

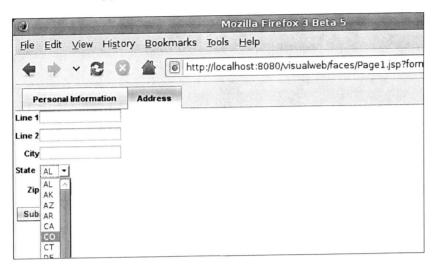

Notice that by default the state codes are being shown to the user. NetBeans Visual Web attempts to make a best guess on what value to display and what value to send to the server. Although certainly the state code is a reasonable value to show to the user, we may want to display the state name instead of its code. In order to do this, we need to right-click on the **Drop Down List** component and select **Bind to Data...**, then select the appropriate value to display from the **Display field** list.

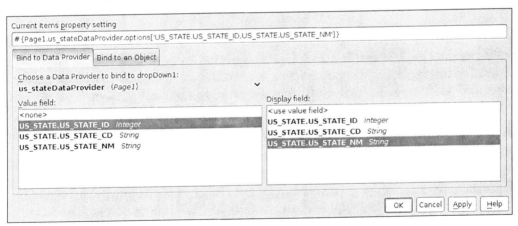

The **Value Field** list allows us to select what value will be sent to the server when the form is submitted, we can select any of the columns in the table we bound to our drop-down component. Similarly, the **Display** list allows us to specify what value to display to the user for each option on the drop-down; again we can select any of the columns in the bound table.

We could have also selected a different value to be sent to the server by selecting a different value from the **Value field** list. However, in this particular case we are happy with the default selection.

After making this modification and executing our code, we can see our changes in action.

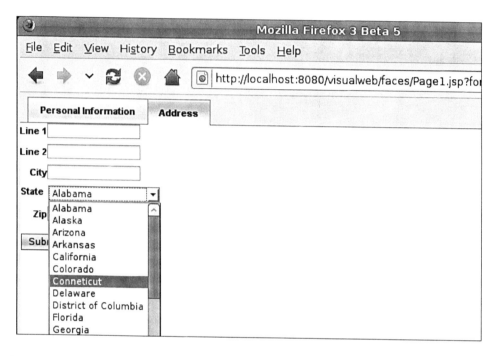

Before moving on, it is worth noting that the technique explained in this section can be used with several other components where the user has the ability to pick one or more options from a list, such as checkboxes, radio buttons, and others.

Ajax-Enabling Visual Web Applications

Woodstock JSF components include JavaScript functions that allow us to very easily Ajax-enable our Visual Web applications. By far, the easiest JavaScript function to use and understand is the `refresh()` function. This function is present in most JSF components. It allows us to dynamically modify the component on the page based on an action performed on another component.

 Consult the Woodstock Tag Library Descriptor Documents at `http://webdev2.sun.com/woodstock-tlddocs/` to see all components that support the `refresh()` function.

For example, using the `refresh()` function, we could dynamically modify the options on a drop-down component based on the selection on another drop-down component, or we could modify the text on a static text component based on values that are entered in a text field. These tasks would be done by making an Ajax request to the server and updating the component without refreshing the whole page.

The `refresh()` JavaScript function needs to be invoked whenever a JavaScript event such as `onChange`, `onBlur`, `onMouseOver`, and so on is triggered.

In the following example, we will illustrate how to update a static text component based on selections made on various drop-down components. In this example, we simulate an application in which a laptop computer can be customized and ordered. As the user selects different options for the laptop, its price changes accordingly.

After creating a visual web project as usual, the first thing we need to do is to create some properties in a session scoped managed bean to hold the values selected by the user, and the value to be displayed in the static text component. The easiest way to go here is to modify the generated `SessionBean1.java` managed bean.

```java
package com.ensode.ajaxlaptoporder;

import com.sun.rave.web.ui.appbase.AbstractSessionBean;
import javax.faces.FacesException;

public class SessionBean1 extends AbstractSessionBean {

    private int price;
    private String selectedScreenSize = "12";
    private String selectedMemory = "1";
    private String selectedHardDiskSize = "60";

    public SessionBean1() {
    }

    //Automatically generated methods removed for brevity

    public int getPrice() {
        return price;
    }

    public void setPrice(int price) {
        this.price = price;
    }

    public String getSelectedHardDiskSize() {
```

```
            return selectedHardDiskSize;
    }

    public void setSelectedHardDiskSize(
      String selectedHardDiskSize) {
        this.selectedHardDiskSize = selectedHardDiskSize;
        calculatePrice();
    }

    public String getSelectedMemory() {
        return selectedMemory;
    }

    public void setSelectedMemory(String selectedMemory) {
        this.selectedMemory = selectedMemory;
        calculatePrice();
    }

    public String getSelectedScreenSize() {
        return selectedScreenSize;
    }

    public void setSelectedScreenSize(
      String selectedScreenSize) {
        this.selectedScreenSize = selectedScreenSize;
        calculatePrice();
    }

    public void calculatePrice() {

        Integer selectedScreenSizeInteger =
          new Integer(selectedScreenSize);
        Integer selectedMemoryInteger =
          new Integer(selectedMemory);
        Integer selectedHardDiskSizeIntegcr =
          new Inleger(selectedHardDiskSize);

        setPrice(selectedScreenSizeInteger *
          ApplicationBean1.PRICE_PER_INCH +
          selectedMemoryInteger *
          ApplicationBean1.PRICE_PER_RAM_GB +
          selectedHardDiskSizeInteger *
          ApplicationBean1.PRICE_PER_HD_GB);
    }
}
```

Notice that we added a method called `calculatePrice()` at the end of the class. This method will calculate a new price based on user selections. Also notice that each setter method invokes this method. This will have the effect of updating the price every time a user makes a selection on one of the drop-down components. We also defined some constants in the `ApplicationBean1.java` application scoped JSF managed bean. These constants are used to calculate the new price. We placed these constants in an application scoped bean since they will be the same for every user in the application. Had we put them in a session scoped bean, then there would be a separate copy of these constants for each user, which wouldn't use the server memory efficiently.

The constants defined in `ApplicationBean1.java` are very simple and straightforward, therefore they are not shown. The full source for the example can be found in the book's source code download.

Next, we need to place the appropriate components into the design window of the page, add the options for each drop-down as usual, and bind the values of each component to the appropriate property in `SessionBean1.java`.

It is important to bind the properties to be used in an Ajax call to properties to a JSF managed bean with a scope of session, since binding them to a request scoped managed bean may result in values being lost between Ajax requests.

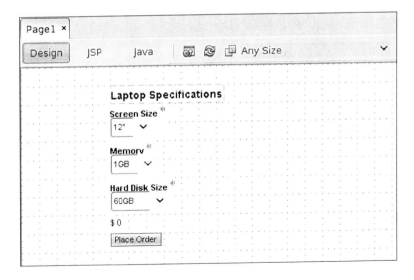

In the previous example, we set the `labelOnTop` attribute of each drop down component to `true`. This has the effect of having the label for the component be rendered right above it.

Once we have placed the components in the page, we need to invoke the `refresh()` JavaScript function on the text field, displaying the price every time a user changes the value of one of the drop-down components. In order to do this we need to set the `onChange` attribute of each drop-down component to invoke the `refresh()` function on the text field.

In order to do this, we need to select the drop-down in the design window, then go to the **Properties** window and click on the ellipsis (...) button next to the **onChange** property.

We then need to add the JavaScript call as the value for this property.

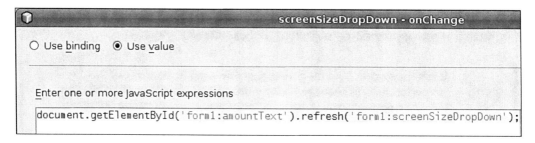

Notice from the screenshot that we first need to get a reference to the component to be updated (a static field in this example). We do this by invoking `document.getElementById()`, and passing the client side ID of the component.

 In JSF, form components are **naming** components, which means that the client side id of any of their child components consist of the value of the form's `id` attribute, followed by a colon, followed by the value of the child component's `id` attribute. For this reason the client side id of the static text field is `form1:amountText`, which is composed of the form's `id` attribute and the component's `id` attribute.

Once we have a reference to the component to be updated, we invoke the `refresh()` JavaScript function on it, passing the client id of the component firing the event as an attribute.

In our example, we need to go through these steps for each drop-down component in the page. Once we have added all the appropriate JavaScript calls, we are ready to deploy and test our application.

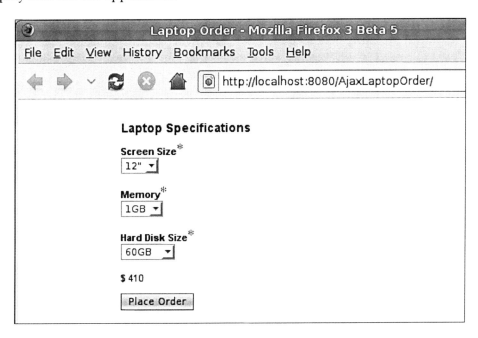

Modifying the selected values in each drop-down will have the effect of making an Ajax call to the server. The setter method for the appropriate property will be invoked, resulting in the `calculatePrice()` method being invoked as well. This method updates the value for which the static text field is bound, resulting in this field being updated dynamically.

Summary

In this chapter, we explored the visual web features of NetBeans, which allow us to develop JSF web applications by simply dragging and dropping components into a page.

We saw how to use some of the most commonly used visual web components, such as drop-down and text field components, as well as some more elaborate components, such as the tab component.

Additionally, we covered how to bind components to database data; specifically how to populate a drop-down component's options from a database table.

Finally, we also saw how easy it is to incorporate Ajax functionality into visual web applications by taking advantage of JavaScript functions provided by the Woodstock JSF library.

We certainly didn't cover each and every component provided by visual JSF, since doing so would probably take a whole book, however we did provide the general workflow to be used when working with visual JSF, and this knowledge can be used when using each and every one of the components.

7
Implementing the Business Tier with Session Beans

Most enterprise applications have a number of common requirements such as transactions, security, scalability, and so forth. Enterprise JavaBeans (EJBs) allow application developers to focus on implementing business logic, while not having to worry about implementing these requirements. There are two types of EJBs: session beans, and message driven beans. In this chapter we will be discussing session beans, which greatly simplify server side business logic implementation. In the next chapter we will discuss message driven beans, which allow us to easily implement messaging functionality in our applications.

 Previous versions of J2EE included Entity Beans as well. As of Java EE 5, Entity Beans have been deprecated in favor of the Java Persistence API.

The following topics will be covered in this chapter:

- Introduction to session beans
- Creating a session bean with NetBeans
- EJB transaction management
- Implementing aspect-oriented programming with interceptors
- EJB timer service
- Generating session beans from JPA entities

Introduction to Session Beans

Session beans encapsulate business logic for enterprise applications. It's a good idea to use session beans when developing enterprise applications, since we as application developers can focus on developing business logic, not having to worry about other enterprise application requirements such as scalability, security, transactions, so on and so forth.

 Even though we as application developers don't directly implement common enterprise application requirements, such as transactions and security, we can configure these services via annotations.

There are two types of session beans: **stateless** and **stateful**. The difference between the two of them is that stateful session beans maintain conversational state with their client between method invocations, whereas stateless session beans do not.

Creating a Session Bean in NetBeans

Session Beans can be created in two types of NetBeans projects: **Enterprise Application** or **EJB Module**. EJB Module projects can contain only EJBs, whereas Enterprise Application project can contain EJBs along with their clients, which can be web applications or "standalone" Java applications.

When deploying enterprise applications to the GlassFish application server included with NetBeans, it is possible to deploy standalone clients as part of the application to the application server. These standalone clients are then available via Java Web Start (http://java.sun.com/products/javawebstart/). This feature also allows us to easily access more EJBs from the client code by using annotations, since with "true" standalone clients executing outside the application server require JNDI lookups to obtain a reference to the EJB.

As creating an Enterprise Application project results in a simpler programming model, that is the type of project we will use for this example.

To create an Enterprise Application project, go to **File | New Project**, select the **Enterprise** category, then **Enterprise Application**.

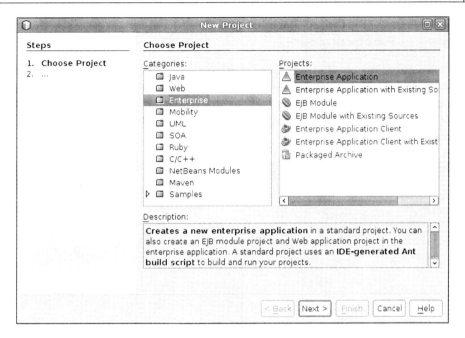

After clicking **Next>**, we need to enter a **Project Name,** as shown in the following screenshot:.

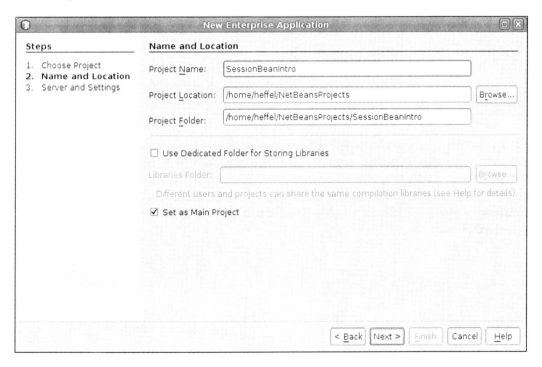

Usually the defaults for **Project Location** and **Project Folder** are sensible, therefore it makes sense to leave them alone.

In the next screen, we need to select the modules to be included in our enterprise application. **Create EJB Module** and **Create Web Application Module** are selected by default. In our example we will create an application client module and won't be creating a web application module, therefore we need to uncheck and check the corresponding checkboxes.

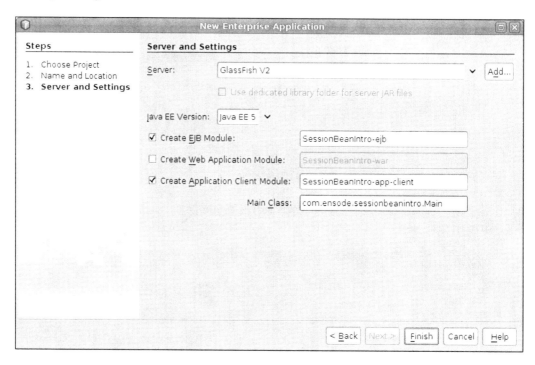

When choosing to create an application client module, the package of the main class defaults to the project name, in lowercase. This package name does not conform to standard Java package naming conventions, which by default start with a domain name "backwards" (**com.companyname** for a domain name of **companyname.com**), therefore it is a good idea to modify this default to a value that does conform to the standard convention.

Once we click **Finish**, we should see three new projects in our **Project** window.

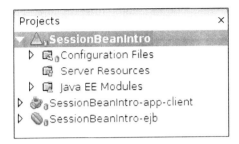

In our example, **SessionBeanIntro** is our enterprise application project, **SessionBeanIntro-app-client** is our application client module, and **SessionBeanIntro-ejb** is our EJB module.

Now that we have created our project, it is time to create our first session bean. We can do so by right-clicking on the EJB module and selecting **New** | **Session Bean**.

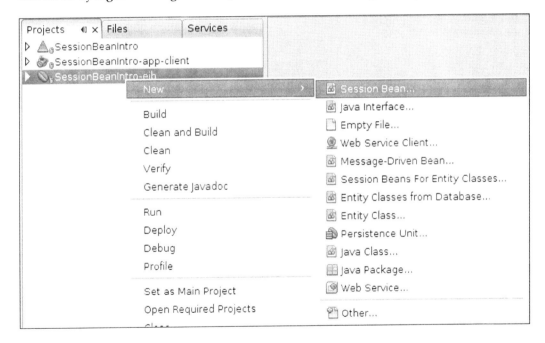

We now need to select from a number of options:

1. It is a good idea to override the default name given to our session bean.

2. We need to specify the package for our session bean.

3. We need to specify the session bean type: stateless or stateful. Stateful session beans maintain conversational state with the client (which simply means that the values of any of their member variables are in a consistent state between method calls). Stateless session beans don't maintain conversational state, for this reason they perform better than stateful session beans.

4. We need to specify if our session bean will have a remote interface, which is used for clients executing in a different JVM than our bean, a local interface, which is meant for clients running in the same JVM as our bean, or both a remote and a local interface.

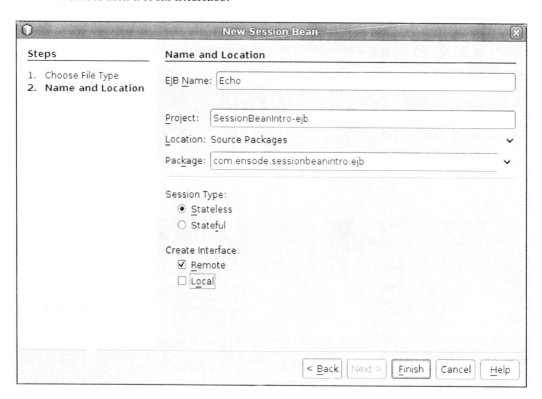

Our example bean does not need to maintain conversational state with its clients, therefore we should make it a stateless session bean. Its only client will be executing in a different JVM, therefore we need to create a remote interface, and don't need to create a local interface.

NetBeans automatically appends the suffix **Bean** to whatever name we choose for our session bean, therefore we shouldn't explicitly use this suffix in our bean names. For instance, in our example, we created a session bean named `Echo`, therefore the generated class name for it will be `EchoBean`.

After selecting all the appropriate options and clicking **Finish**, our session bean and remote interface are created.

The generated code for our session bean is simply an empty class with the `@Stateless` annotation already added.

```java
/*
 * To change this template, choose Tools | Templates
 * and open the template in the editor.
 */

package com.ensode.sessionbeanintro.ejb;

import javax.ejb.Stateless;

/**
 *
 * @author heffel
 */
@Stateless
public class EchoBean implements EchoRemote {

    // Add business logic below. (Right-click in editor and choose
    // "EJB Methods > Add Business Method" or "Web Service > Add Operation")

}
```

Notice that our bean implements the remote interface, which at this point is an empty interface with the @Remote annotation added. This annotation was added because we chose to create only a remote interface. Had our interface been a local interface, it would have been decorated with the @Local interface instead.

The reason we need to have a remote and/or local interface is because session bean clients never invoke the bean's methods directly. Instead they obtain a reference of a class implementing their remote and/or local interface and invoke the methods on this class.

The remote and/or local interface implementation is created automatically by the EJB container when we deploy our bean. This implementation does some processing before invoking our session bean's method. Since the methods need to be defined both on the interface and our bean, typically we would need to add the method signature to both the bean and its remote and/or local interface. However, when working with session beans in NetBeans, we can simply right-click on the bean's source code and select **EJB Methods | Add Business Method**. This will result in the method being added to both the bean and the remote/local interface. Doing this results in a window popping up, prompting us for the method name, return type, parameters, and the interface(s) where the method should be added (remote and/or local).

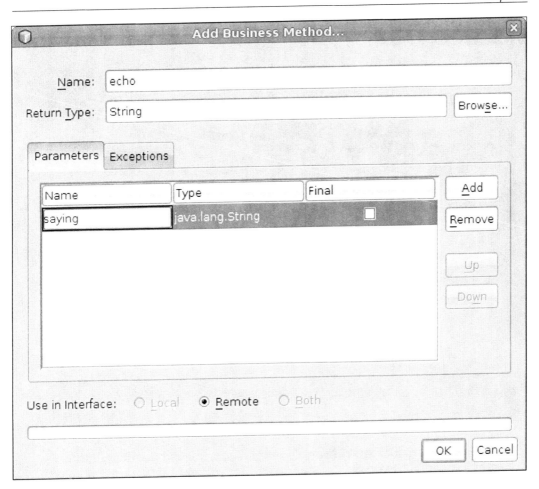

In our example we will add a method named echo that takes a String as a
parameter and returns a String. Since our bean only has a remote interface, the
radio buttons for **Local** and **Both** are grayed out.

After entering the appropriate information, the method is added both to the bean and its remote interface.

```java
/*
 * To change this template, choose Tools | Templates
 * and open the template in the editor.
 */

package com.ensode.sessionbeanintro.ejb;

import javax.ejb.Stateless;

/**
 *
 * @author heffel
 */
@Stateless
public class EchoBean implements EchoRemote {

    public String echo(String saying) {
        return null;
    }

    // Add business logic below. (Right-click in editor and choose
    // "EJB Methods > Add Business Method" or "Web Service > Add Operation")

}
```

The default implementation will simply return `null`. For this simple example we will simply modify it to return the parameter that was passed, prepending it with the string `"echoing: "`.

```java
    public String echo(String saying) {
        return "echoing: " + saying;
    }
```

At this point we have a simple, but complete, stateless session bean.

Accessing the Bean from a Client

Now it is time to focus our attention on the client. The client needs to obtain a reference to an instance of a class implementing the remote interface for our bean. When using NetBeans, this is very easy. We simply need to right-click on the client code (`com.ensode.sessionbeanintro.Main` in the application client project in our example) and select **Enterprise Resources | Call Enterprise Bean**.

At this point we are shown a list of all open projects that have EJBs in them. We need to select the bean we wish to access from one of these projects.

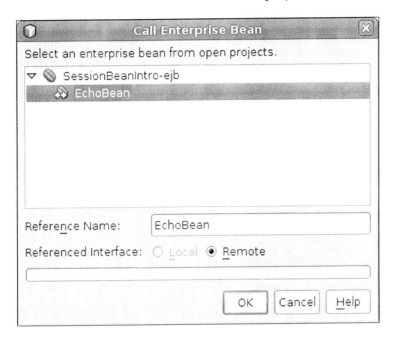

Had our bean had both a local and remote interface, we would have been given the choice to select the appropriate one. However, since it only has a remote interface, the option to select a local interface is disabled. In our particular example, even if we had the option of selecting a local interface, the correct option would have been to select the remote interface since our client will be executing in a different JVM from the server, and local interfaces are not accessible across JVMs.

At this point a member variable of type `EchoBeanRemote` (our bean's remote interface) is added to the client. This variable is annotated with the `@EJB` annotation. This annotation is used to inject the instance of the remote interface at runtime.

In previous versions of J2EE, it was necessary to perform a JNDI lookup to obtain a reference to the home interface of the bean, then use the home interface to obtain a reference to the remote or local interface. As we can see, the procedure to obtain a reference to an EJB has been greatly simplified in Java EE 5.

```
Main.java ×

1   /*
2    * To change this template, choose Tools | Templates
3    * and open the template in the editor.
4    */
5
6   package com.ensode.sessionbeanintro;
7
8   import com.ensode.sessionbeanintro.ejb.EchoRemote;
9   import javax.ejb.EJB;
10
11  /**
12   *
13   * @author heffel
14   */
15  public class Main {
16      @EJB
17      private static EchoRemote echoBean;
18
19      /**
20       * @param args the command line arguments
21       */
22      public static void main(String[] args) {
23          // TODO code application logic here
24          |   }
25
26
```

Now we simply need to add a call to the echo() method on the remote interface, and our client will be complete.

```
    public static void main(String[] args) {
        // TODO code application logic here
        JOptionPane.showMessageDialog(null, echoBean.echo(
                "I hate hello world examples!"));
    }
```

Executing the Client

The easiest way to execute the client from inside NetBeans is to add the class in the Enterprise Application Client project containing the main() method we wish to execute as the **Main** class of the Enterprise Application project. In our example, the fully qualified name of this class is com.ensode.sessionbeanintro.Main.

In order to do this, we need to right-click on the project, select **Properties**, then select the **Run** category.

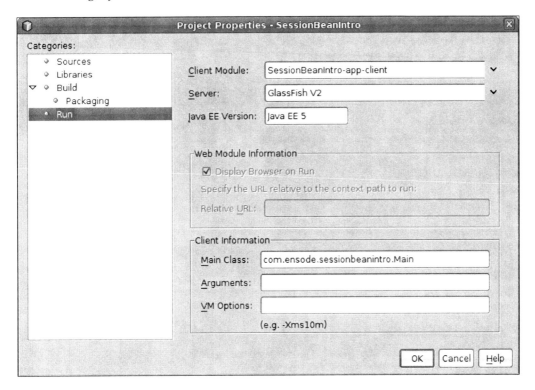

Then we need to enter the fully qualified name of the class to execute as the value of the **Main Class** field under the **Client Information** section.

 The fully qualified name of the main class in the Enterprise Application Client project can be found by right-clicking on the project, selecting **Properties**, then **Run**.

Once we have done this, we can execute our client by simply right-clicking on the Enterprise Application Project and selecting **Run**. After a few seconds, we should see an information dialog displaying the output of the session bean's method.

Clients deployed this way take advantage of Java Web Start technology. Java Web Start Applications run on the client workstation, however, they can be executed from a URL. When deploying to GlassFish, we can find out the URL of our application client, by opening the GlassFish Admin Console, expanding **Applications | Enterprise Applications**, clicking on our project, then clicking on the **Launch** link next to our application client module.

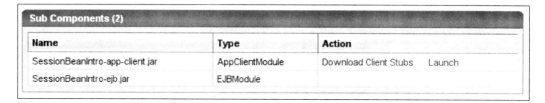

The URL will be displayed in the main browser window.

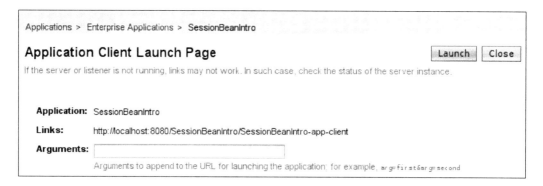

Session Bean Transaction Management

As previously mentioned, one of the advantages of Enterprise JavaBeans is that they automatically take care of transactions. However, there is still some configuration that we need to do in order to better control transaction management.

Transactions allow us to execute all the steps in a method or, if one of the steps fails (for instance, an exception is thrown), roll back the changes made in that method.

Primarily what we need to configure is our bean's behavior if one of its methods is called while a transaction is in progress. Should the bean's method become part of the existing transaction? Should the existing transaction be suspended, and a new transaction created just for the bean's method? We can configure this behavior via the `@TransactionAttribute` annotation.

The `@TransactionAttribute` annotation allows us to control how an EJB's methods will behave both when invoked while a transaction is in progress, and when invoked when no transaction is in progress. This annotation has a single `value` attribute that we can use to indicate how the bean's method will behave in both of these circumstances.

The following table summarizes the different values that we can assign to the `@TransactionAtttibute` annotation.

@TransactionAttribute value	Method Invoked while a Transaction is in Progress	Method Invoked while no Transaction is in Progress
`TransactionAttributeType.MANDATORY`	Method becomes part of the existing transaction.	`TransactionRequiredException` is thrown.
`TransactionAttributeType.NEVER`	`RemoteException` is thrown.	Method is executed without any transaction support.
`TransactionAttributeType.NOT_SUPPORTED`	Client transaction is temporarily suspended, the method is executed without transaction support, then the client transaction is resumed.	Method is executed without any transaction support.
`TransactionAttributeType.REQUIRED`	Method becomes part of the existing transaction.	A new transaction is created for the method.
`TransactionAttributeType.REQUIRES_NEW`	Client transaction is temporarily suspended, a new transaction is created for the method, then the client transaction is resumed.	A new transaction is created for the method.
`TransactionAttributeType.SUPPORTS`	Method becomes part of the existing transaction.	Method is executed without any transaction support.

The @TransactionAttribute annotation can be used to decorate the class declaration of our Enterprise JavaBean, or it can be used to decorate a single method. If used to decorate the class declaration, then the declared transaction behavior will apply to all methods in the bean. When used to decorate a single method, the declared behavior will affect only the decorated method. If a bean has a @TransactionAttribute annotation both at the class level and at the method level, the method level annotation takes precedence. If no transaction attribute is specified for a method, then TransactionAttributeType.REQUIRED attribute is used by default.

The following example illustrates how to use this annotation.

```
package com.ensode.sessionbeanintro.ejb;

import javax.ejb.Stateless;
import javax.ejb.TransactionAttribute;
import javax.ejb.TransactionAttributeType;

@Stateless
public class EchoBean implements EchoRemote {

    @TransactionAttribute(
        TransactionAttributeType.REQUIRES_NEW)
    public String echo(String saying) {
        return "echoing: " + saying;
    }

}
```

As we can see, we simply need to decorate the method to be configured with the @TransactionAttribute annotation with the appropriate TransactionAttributeType enumeration constant as a parameter to configure transactions for a single method. As mentioned before, if we wish all of our methods to use the same transaction strategy, we can place the @TransactionAttribute annotation at the class level.

Implementing Aspect-Oriented Programming with Interceptors

Sometimes we wish to execute some logic just before and/or just after a method's main logic executes. For example, we might want to measure the execution time of a method to track down performance problems, or we might want to send a message to a log every time we enter and leave a method, to make it easier to track down bugs or exceptions.

The most common solution to these kind of problems is to add a little bit of code at the beginning and end of every method. This approach has several problems: the logic needs to be implemented several times, if we later wish to modify or remove the functionality, we need to modify several methods.

Aspect-oriented programming is a paradigm that solves the above problems by providing a way to implement the logic to be executed just before and/or just after a method's main logic in a separate class. EJB 3.0 introduced the ability to implement aspect oriented programming via **interceptors**.

Implementing aspect-oriented programming via interceptors consists of two steps: coding the interceptor class and decorating the EJBs to be intercepted with the @ Interceptors annotation.

Implementing the Interceptor Class

An interceptor is a standard Java class. It must have a single method with the following signature:

```
@AroundInvoke
public Object methodName(InvocationContext invocationContext)
  throws Exception
```

Notice that the method must be decorated with the @AroundInvoke annotation, which marks the method as an interceptor method. The InvocationContext parameter can be used to obtain information from the intercepted method, such as its name, parameters, the class that declares it and more. It also has a proceed() method that is used to indicate when to execute the method logic.

The following table summarizes some of the most useful InvocationContext methods, refer to the Java EE 5 JavaDoc (accessible within NetBeans by going to **Help | JavaDoc References | Java EE 5 SDK**) for more information.

Method Name	Description
getMethod()	Returns an instance of java.lang.reflect.Method that can be used to introspect the intercepted method.
getParameters()	Returns an array of objects containing the parameters passed to the intercepted method.
getTarget()	Returns the object containing the method being invoked, return value is java.lang.Object.
proceed()	Invokes the method being intercepted.

The following illustrates a simple interceptor class.

```
package com.ensode.sessionbeanintro.ejb;

import java.lang.reflect.Method;
import javax.interceptor.AroundInvoke;
import javax.interceptor.InvocationContext;

public class LoggingInterceptor {

    @AroundInvoke
    public Object logMethodCall(
            InvocationContext invocationContext)
            throws Exception {
        Object interceptedObject =
            invocationContext.getTarget();
        Method interceptedMethod =
            invocationContext.getMethod();

        System.out.println("Entering " +
                interceptedObject.getClass().getName() + "." +
                interceptedMethod.getName() + "()");

        Object o = invocationContext.proceed();

        System.out.println("Leaving   " +
                interceptedObject.getClass().getName() + "." +
                interceptedMethod.getName() + "()");

        return o;
    }
}
```

The above example logs a message to the application server log just before and just after an intercepted method is executed. The purpose of implementing something like this would be to aid in debugging applications.

 For simplicity, the above example simply uses `System.out.println` to output messages to the application server log. A real application more than likely would use a logging API such as the Java Logging API or Log4j.

The first thing we do in our interceptor method is to obtain a reference to the object and method being intercepted. We then output a message to the log indicating the class and method being invoked. This code is executed just before we let the intercepted method execute, which we do by invoking `invocationContext.proceed()`. We store the return value of this method in a variable, then add some additional logic to be executed just after the method finishes. In our example, we simply send an additional line of text to the application server log. Finally our method returns the return value of `invocationContext.proceed()`.

Decorating the EJB with the @Interceptors Annotations

In order for an EJB's method to be intercepted, it must be decorated with the `@Interceptors` annotation. This annotation has a single class array attribute. This attribute contains all the interceptors to be executed before and/or after the method call.

The `@Interceptors` annotation can be used at the method level, in which case it applies only to the method it decorates, or at the class level, in which it applies to every method in the bean.

The following example is a new version of our `EchoBean` session bean, slightly modified to have its `echo()` method intercepted by the `LoggingInterceptor` we wrote in the previous section.

```
package com.ensode.sessionbeanintro.ejb;

import javax.ejb.Stateless;
import javax.ejb.TransactionAttribute;
import javax.ejb.TransactionAttributeType;
import javax.interceptor.Interceptors;

@Stateless
public class EchoBean implements EchoRemote {

    @Interceptors({LoggingInterceptor.class})
    @TransactionAttribute(
        TransactionAttributeType.REQUIRES_NEW)
    public String echo(String saying) {
        return "echoing: " + saying;
    }
}
```

Notice that the only change we had to make to our session bean was to add the `@Interceptors` annotation to its `echo()` method. In this particular case, the class array attribute has a single value, which is the `LoggingInterceptor` class we defined above. This has the effect of executing all the code in the interceptor's `logMethodCall()` method before the `invocationContext.proceed()` call just before the method is executed, and all the code after the `invocationContext.proceed()` call just after the method ends. In our example, we are using a single interceptor for our bean's method. If we need our method to be intercepted by more than one interceptor, we can do that by adding additional interceptor classes between the curly braces in the `@Interceptors` annotation, the list of interceptors between the curly braces must be separated by commas.

At this point we are ready to test our interceptor. In NetBeans, we can simply right-click on the project in the **Projects** window and select **Run**. After doing so, we should see the output of the interceptor's `logMethodCall()` in NetBean's GlassFish output window.

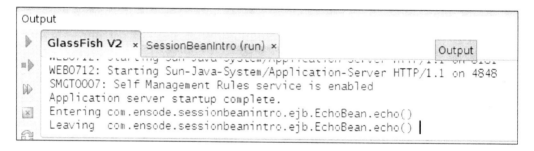

EJB Timer Service

Stateless session beans and message-driven beans (another type of EJB discussed in the next chapter) can have a method that is executed automatically at regular intervals. This functionality is useful in case we want to execute some logic periodically (once a week, every day, every hour, etc.) without having to explicitly call any methods. This functionality is achieved by the **EJB timer service**.

In order to use the EJB timer service, an instance of `javax.ejb.TimerService` must be injected into the EJB via the `@Resource` annotation. This object will be used to create and cancel timers in two different methods in the EJB. Finally, the EJB must have a method to be invoked when the timer expires. This method must be decorated with the `@Timeout` annotation. The following example illustrates how to use the EJB timer service.

```
package com.ensode.ejbtimer.ejb;

import java.io.Serializable;
import java.util.Collection;
import java.util.Date;
import javax.annotation.Resource;
import javax.ejb.Stateless;
import javax.ejb.Timeout;
import javax.ejb.Timer;
import javax.ejb.TimerService;

@Stateless
public class EJBTimerDemoBean implements EJBTimerDemoRemote {

    @Resource
    TimerService timerService;

    public void startTimer(Serializable info) {
        System.out.println("Starting timer " + info);
        timerService.createTimer(0, 5000, info);
    }

    public void stopTimer(Serializable info) {
        System.out.println("Stopping timer " + info);

Collection<Timer> timers = timerService.getTimers();
        for (Timer timer : timers) {
            if (timer.getInfo().equals(info)) {
                timer.cancel();
                break;
            }
        }
    }

    @Timeout
    public void executeOnTimeout(Timer timer) {
        System.out.println(this.getClass().getName() +
                ".executeOnTimeout() invoked at" +
                new Date() +
                "by timer " + timer.getInfo());
    }
}
```

In this example, we injected an instance of `javax.ejb.TimerService`. This class has methods that allow us to create timers and to obtain a collection of existing timers for a particular EJB.

We then implemented a method called `startTimer()`. This method invokes the `createTimer()` method in the `TimerService` instance that was injected into our EJB. The `createTimer()` method creates a new timer; there are several overloaded versions of this method. The one we used in our example has three parameters: the first parameter is a `long` value indicating how many milliseconds from the time the method is invoked should the timer start counting; the second parameter indicates how many milliseconds before the timer expires; the third parameter is an instance of `java.io.Serializable`, which is used as a unique identifier for the created timer.

 Consult the Java EE 5 JavaDoc documentation for information on other versions of the `createTimer()` method.

Additionally, we created a method called `stopTimer()`. This method is used to cancel a specific timer and has a single parameter of `java.io.Serializable`. Clients are expected to pass the unique identifier of the timer to cancel as the value of this parameter. In order to cancel the timer, we first need to obtain all timers for our EJB via the `getTimers()` method of `TimerService`. This method returns a `Collection` of `javax.ejb.Timer` objects. We then need to iterate through this `Collection`, obtain the unique identifier of each `Timer` object via its `getInfo()` method, and compare it to the value of our method's parameter. If they match, we have found the timer to cancel, and we do so by invoking its `cancel()` method.

Finally, we defined a method to be invoked when a timer times out. Methods to be executed when the timer times out must be decorated with the `@Timeout` annotation, must be public, return void, and have a single parameter of type `Timer`. In our example we simply send some output to the application server log. Notice that part of the output is the unique identifier for the timer that expired when the method was invoked, which we can obtain by invoking it's `getInfo()` method.

Implementing the Client

There is nothing special we need to do to implement a client for an EJB taking advantage of the EJB timer service. We simply need a client to invoke the methods that create and cancel the timers. These methods are invoked just like any other EJB methods defined in a local and/or remote interface.

The following example illustrates a simple client for our EJB.

```
package com.ensode.ejbtimerservice;

import com.ensode.ejbtimer.ejb.EJBTimerDemoRemote;
import javax.ejb.EJB;

public class Main {

    @EJB
    private static EJBTimerDemoRemote eJBTimerDemoBean;

    public static void main(String[] args)
            throws InterruptedException {
        eJBTimerDemoBean.startTimer("first");
        Thread.sleep(2000);
        eJBTimerDemoBean.startTimer("second");
        Thread.sleep(15000);
        eJBTimerDemoBean.stopTimer("first");
        Thread.sleep(10000);
        eJBTimerDemoBean.stopTimer("second");
    }
}
```

In this client, we simply create two timers by invoking the startTimer() method we implemented in our session bean a couple of times, sleeping for two seconds between method calls. We then have the timer sleep for fifteen seconds before stopping both timers by invoking the stopTimer() method in the session bean, waiting ten seconds between each method call.

After deploying and executing our project in NetBeans, we should see the following output in the GlassFish output console.

Generating Session Beans from JPA Entities

One very nice NetBeans feature is that it allows generation of stateless session beans from existing JPA entities. The generated session beans act as DAO's (Data Access Objects). This feature, combined with the ability to generate JPA entities from an existing database schema, allows us to completely generate the data access layers of our application without having to write a single line of Java code.

To take advantage of this functionality, we need to create an EJB project (**File | New Project**, select **Enterprise** from the **Categories** list, then select **EJB Module** from the **Projects** list), or use the EJB project from an **Enterprise Application** project, and add some JPA entities to it, either by manually coding them or by generating them from an existing schema, as discussed in Chapter 5.

Once we have some JPA entities in the project, we need to go to **File | New**, select **Persistence** from the categories list, and **Session Beans For Entity Classes** from the **File Types** list.

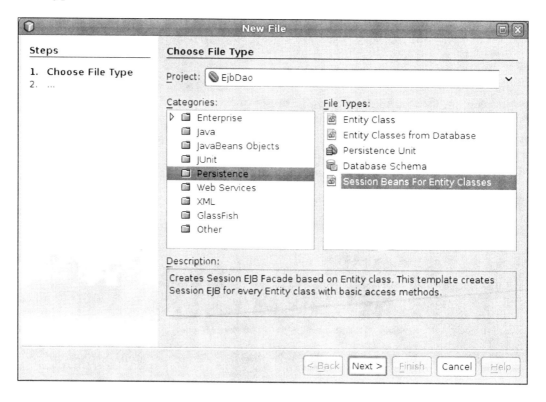

The next screen in the wizard allows us to select for which of the existing JPA entity classes in the project we want to generate session beans. In most cases, they should be generated for all of them by simply clicking on the **Add All** button.

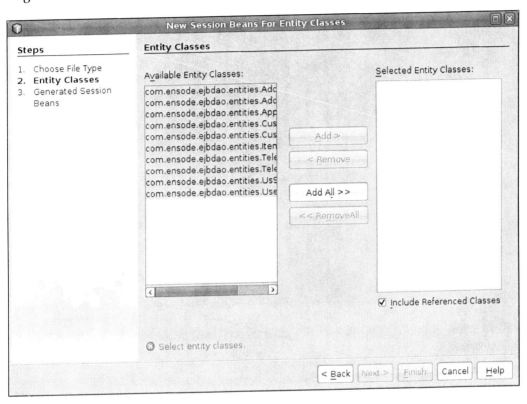

The last screen in the wizard allows us to specify the project, package, and whether we want to generate local and/or remote interfaces.

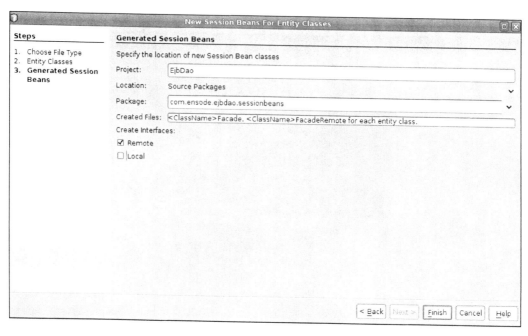

After clicking **Finish**, the session beans are created and placed in the package we specified.

The generated session beans contain a number of methods that allow us to perform CRUD (create, read, update, delete) operations on our entities. Let's now take a look at one of the generated session beans.

```java
package com.ensode.ejbdao.sessionbeans;

import com.ensode.ejbdao.entities.Customer;
import java.util.List;
import javax.ejb.Stateless;
import javax.persistence.EntityManager;
import javax.persistence.PersistenceContext;

@Stateless
public class CustomerFacade implements CustomerFacadeRemote {
    @PersistenceContext
    private EntityManager em;

    public void create(Customer customer) {
        em.persist(customer);
```

```
        }

    public void edit(Customer customer) {
        em.merge(customer);
    }

    public void remove(Customer customer) {
        em.remove(em.merge(customer));
    }

    public Customer find(Object id) {
        return
            em.find(
            com.ensode.ejbdao.entities.Customer.class, id);
    }

    public List<Customer> findAll() {
        return em.createQuery(
            "select object(o) from Customer as " +
            "o").getResultList();
    }
}
```

As we can see, the generated session bean is not much more than a facade to EntityManager. Wrapping its calls inside a session bean gives us all of its advantages, such as transaction management and distributed code. The generated create() method is used to create new entities, the edit() method updates an existing entity, the remove() method deletes an existing entities. The find() method finds an entity with the given primary key, and the findAll() method returns a List of all entities in the database.

We are, of course, free to add additional methods to the generated session bean. For example, sometimes it is necessary to add a method to find all entities that meet a specific criteria, such as finding all customers with the same last name.

 One disadvantage of adding methods to the generated session bean is that if for any reason they need to be regenerated, we will lose our custom methods and they will need to be re-added. In order to avoid this situation, it is a good idea to extend the generated session beans and add additional methods in the child classes (as of Java EE 5, session beans can extend one another). This will prevent our methods from being "wiped out" if we ever need to regenerate our session beans.

Summary

In this chapter, were introduced to session beans, and it was explained how NetBeans can help us speed up session bean development. We covered how Enterprise JavaBeans in general, and session beans in particular, allow us to easily implement transaction strategies in our enterprise applications. We also covered how we can implement Aspect-Oriented Programming (AOP) with session beans via interceptors. Additionally, we looked at how session beans can have one of their methods invoked periodically by the EJB container, by taking advantage of the EJB Timer Service. Lastly, we covered how NetBeans can help speed up the implementation of the data access layer of our applications by generating session beans implementing the Data Access Object (DAO) design pattern automatically.

8

Messaging with JMS and Message Driven Beans

The **Java Messaging Service (JMS)** is a standard Java EE messaging API that allows loosely coupled, asynchronous communication between Java EE components.

NetBeans includes good support to aid us in creating applications that take advantage of the JMS API, generating a lot of necessary boilerplate code, allowing us to focus on the business logic of our application.

We will cover the following topics in this chapter:

- Introduction to JMS
- Creating an enterprise project to take advantage of JMS
- Creating JMS resources from NetBeans
- Implementing a JMS message producer
- Implementing a JMS message consumer
- Processing JMS messages with message driven beans

Introduction to JMS

JMS is a standard Java EE 5 API that allows loosely coupled, asynchronous communication between Java EE components. Applications taking advantage of JMS do not interact directly with each other, instead JMS message producers send messages to a message destination (JMS Queue or Topic), and JMS message consumers receive messages from said destinations.

There are two messaging domains that can be used when working with JMS: the Point To Point (PTP) messaging, in which a JMS message is processed by only one message receiver; and Publish/Subscribe (pub/sub) messaging, in which all message receivers subscribed to a specific topic receive and process each message for said topic. JMS applications using the PTP messaging domains use message queues as their JMS destinations, whereas applications using pub/sub use message topics.

The following diagram illustrates the JMS architecture.

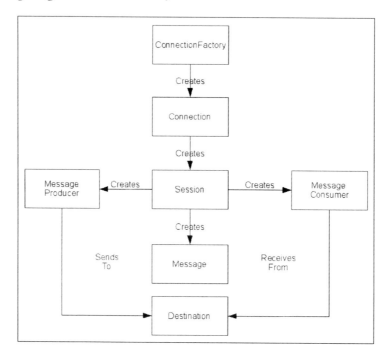

When working with JMS we need to obtain a reference to a connection factory, either via JNDI or via dependency injection. From this connection factory we can create a JMS session, which in turn can be used to create JMS messages.

When developing code to send messages to a JMS destination, we need to create a JMS message producer from the JMS session. In turn, we use this message producer to send messages to the destination.

When developing code to receive messages from a JMS destination, we need to create a message consumer from the JMS session. We can then use this message consumer to retrieve messages from our JMS destination.

When working with JMS in NetBeans, we need to create an Enterprise Application project. Additionally, when using GlassFish, the necessary JMS resources such as JMS destinations and connection factories can be created directly in NetBeans.

Creating the Project and JMS Resources

In order to take advantage of JMS, we need to create an Enterprise Application project, as usual.

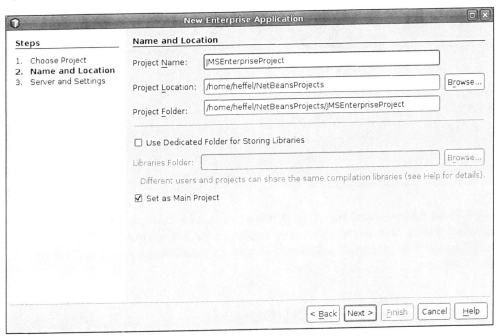

In our example, we will be adding an EJB module and an Application Client module.

Any type of Java EE module can be a JMS message producer and/or consumer by simply invoking methods from the JMS API. We chose to create an EJB module, since, later in the chapter, we will be creating a Message Driven Bean (MDB), which is a type of EJB. We chose an application client since it is one of the simplest modules that can be added to an enterprise application, allowing us to focus on JMS code without having to worry about writing lots of extraneous code. However, in real applications, it is common to have web applications or Session Beans act as JMS message producers, with an MDB acting as the consumer.

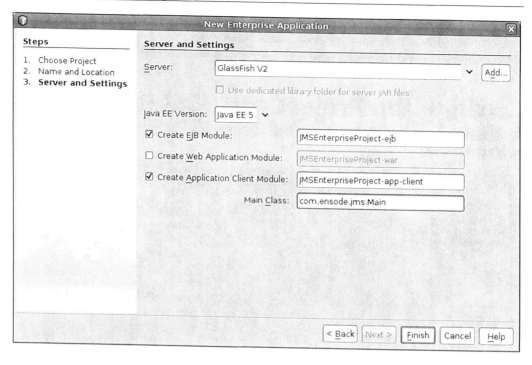

Now that we have created our project, we need to add a couple of necessary JMS resources, a JMS destination (Queue or Topic) and a JMS connection factory. When using GlassFish as our application server, we can create these resources directly from NetBeans.

Creating a JMS Destination

JMS Destinations are an intermediate location where JMS producers place messages, and JMS consumers retrieve them. When using the Point To Point (PTP) messaging domain, JMS destinations are message queues, where with the Publish/Subscribe messaging domain, the destination is a message topic.

In our example we will be using the PTP messaging domain, therefore we need to create a message queue. The procedure to create a message topic is almost identical.

In order to create a message queue, we need to click on **File | New File**, select **GlassFish** from the **Categories** list, and **JMS Resource** from the **File Types** list.

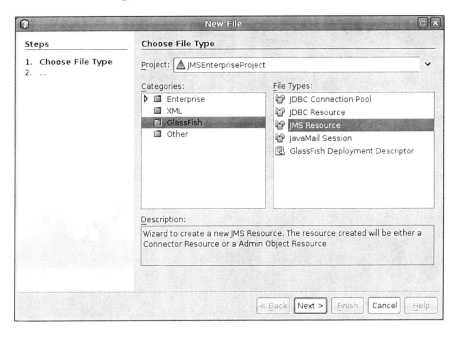

We then need to enter a **JNDI Name** for our queue. In our example, we simply picked the default name **jms/MyQueue**, and accept the default resource type of **javax.jms.Queue**.

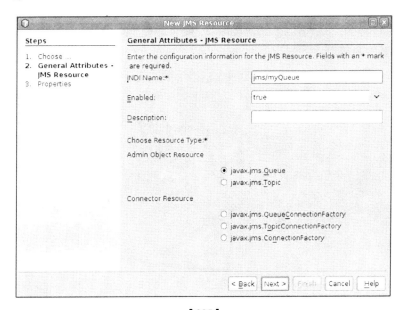

JMS message queues require a `Name` property. In our example we simply chose to use the **JNDI Name** of our queue (minus the `jms/` prefix) as the value of this property.

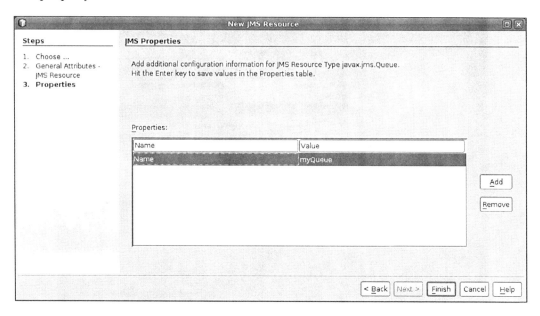

At this point we have created a JMS queue to act as a JMS destination for our application. We also need to create a JMS connection factory. The JMS queue and connection factory will not actually be created until we deploy our project.

The first few steps in creating a connection factory are exactly the same as the ones we used for creating the queue (**File | New File**, select **GlassFish** and **JMS Resource**, then click **Next>**).

At this point we simply need to select **javax.jms.ConnectionFactory** as the resource type and enter a suitable **JNDI Name** for our connection factory.

Selecting **javax.jms.ConnectionFactory** as the resource type has the
advantage of allowing us to use this resource to create connections for
both queues and topics. If we don't need to create one or the other, we can
select to create a resource of type **javax.jms.TopicConnectionFactory** or
javax.jms.QueueConnectionFactory as appropriate, however choosing
javax.jms.ConnectionFactory allows more flexibility.

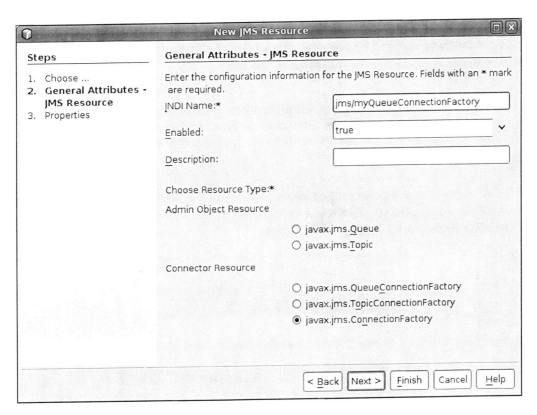

At this point we can simply click **Finish**, or we can click **Next** to assign additional
properties to our connection factory. However, this step is not necessary for
connection factories.

Sending Messages to a Message Destination

Once we have created our connection factory and destination (queue or topic), we need to write some code to send messages to it.

In our example, we will use the application client to send messages to the queue. NetBeans can generate a lot of the necessary boilerplate code automatically. In order to generate this code, the connection factory and destination to be used need to be created in the server. Recall we mentioned in the previous section that GlassFish JMS resources created with NetBeans aren't actually created until we deploy our project. In order for these resources to be available to our application client, we need to deploy the project to have these resources created.

 Deploying the project at this point might generate a `java.util.zip.ZipException` for the EJB module in the GlassFish output window. The reason for this is that we haven't yet added any EJBs to the module. This error can be safely ignored.

After we have deployed our project, we can generate the JMS code opening the main class for the application client project by right-clicking on its source, and selecting **Enterprise Resources | Send JMS Message**.

At this point we need to select a message destination and connection factory.

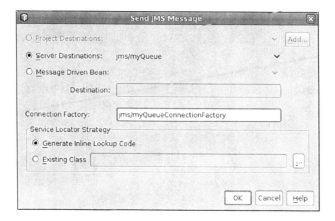

NetBeans detects the different destinations in the server, and provides them in a drop-down list. It also makes a best guess at the JNDI name of the connection factory, which, in our case, turns out not to be correct. The previous screenshot shows the corrected connection factory JNDI name.

At this point NetBeans generates two methods in our code: a method to send a JMS message to our destination, and another method to create it. Additionally, it injects the necessary resources, the messaging destination, and connection factory into our code via the @Resource annotation.

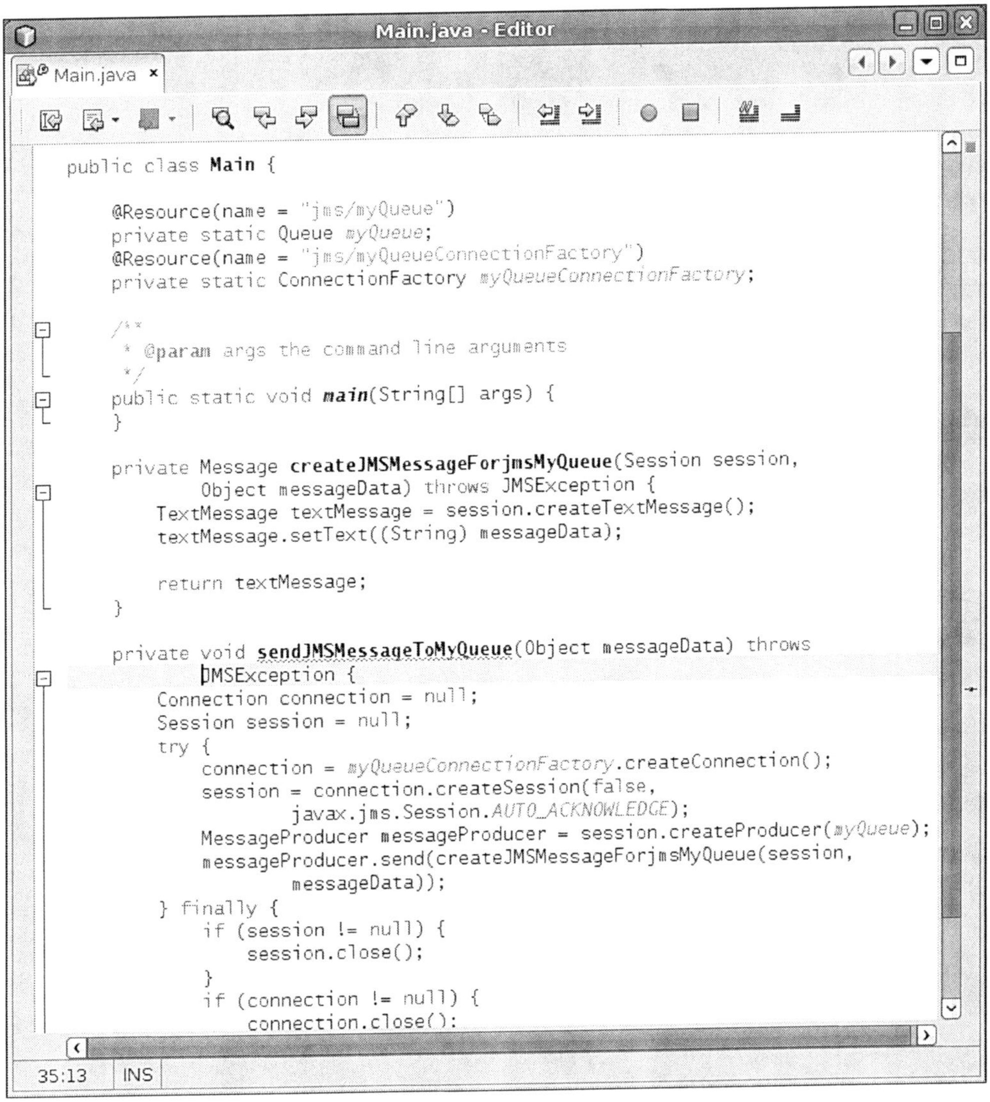

```java
public class Main {

    @Resource(name = "jms/myQueue")
    private static Queue myQueue;
    @Resource(name = "jms/myQueueConnectionFactory")
    private static ConnectionFactory myQueueConnectionFactory;

    /**
     * @param args the command line arguments
     */
    public static void main(String[] args) {
    }

    private Message createJMSMessageForjmsMyQueue(Session session,
            Object messageData) throws JMSException {
        TextMessage textMessage = session.createTextMessage();
        textMessage.setText((String) messageData);

        return textMessage;
    }

    private void sendJMSMessageToMyQueue(Object messageData) throws
            JMSException {
        Connection connection = null;
        Session session = null;
        try {
            connection = myQueueConnectionFactory.createConnection();
            session = connection.createSession(false,
                    javax.jms.Session.AUTO_ACKNOWLEDGE);
            MessageProducer messageProducer = session.createProducer(myQueue);
            messageProducer.send(createJMSMessageForjmsMyQueue(session,
                    messageData));
        } finally {
            if (session != null) {
                session.close();
            }
            if (connection != null) {
                connection.close();
```

In the generated code, the `@Resource` annotation uses its `name` attribute to locate the injected resources. This annotation uses the JNDI name of the injected resources to locate them. In some cases, this JNDI lookup may fail even if the value of the annotation is correct. This situation can be corrected by replacing the `name` attribute with `mappedName`, and using the same value we were using for the `name` attribute.

Initially, the method to create the message does not compile, we are expected to provide the body for this method.

In our example, the name of the method is `createJMSMessageForjmsMyQueue()` (the exact method name will vary depending on the name of our JMS destination). It returns an instance of a class implementing `javax.jms.Message`, which all JMS message types must implement, and takes two parameters: an instance of a class implementing `javax.jms.Session`, and an object containing the message data.

The package `javax.jms.Message` has several sub-interfaces which are part of the standard Java EE 5 API. In most cases, we use one of the sub-interfaces to send messages, instead of using a direct implementation of `javax.jms.Message`. The following table summarizes all of the standard Java EE 5 subinterfaces:

Subinterface	Description
BytesMessage	Used to send an array of bytes as a message.
MapMessage	Used to send name-value pairs as messages. The names must be String objects; the values must be either primitive types or Java objects.
ObjectMessage	Used to send serializable objects as messages. A serializable object is an instance of any class that implements `java.io.Serializable`.
StreamMessage	Used to send a stream of Java primitive types as a message.
TextMessage	Used to send a String as a message.

Of the above message types, `TextMessage` and `ObjectMessage` are the most frequently used. We will use `TextMessage` for our example. Using other message types is very similar.

Consult the Java EE 5 JavaDoc for details on the APIs for each of the message types. Java EE 5 JavaDoc can be found at `http://java.sun.com/javaee/5/docs/api/` or directly from NetBeans by going to **Help | Javadoc References | Java EE 5 SDK**

The first thing we need to do is to add the body of the generated
`createJMSMessageForjmsMyqueue()`. In our example, we create a text message by
invoking the `createTextMessage()` method of the instance of `javax.jms.Session`
that is passed as a parameter to this method. We then populate this text message
with the `messageData` object that was passed as a parameter.

 In addition to having a method for creating text messages, `javax.jms.Session` contains methods for creating all standard message types listed in the table above.

Notice that this method is invoked by the generated `sendJMSMessageToMyQueue()`,
we are expected to invoke `sendJMSMessageToMyQueue()`, as opposed to invoking
`createJMSMessageForjmsMyqueue()` directly. In our example, we do this in the
main method of our application.

After all of our modifications, our `main()` and `createJMSMessageForjmsMyqueue()`
methods look like the following screenshot:

```java
public static void main(String[] args) throws JMSException {
    new Main().sendJMSMessageToMyQueue("NetBeans makes JMS trivial!");
}

private Message createJMSMessageForjmsMyQueue(Session session,
        Object messageData) throws JMSException {
    TextMessage textMessage = session.createTextMessage();
    textMessage.setText((String) messageData);

    return textMessage;
}
```

At this point we have a complete application that will send messages to our message
queue. We can deploy the project and execute it, however, we haven't written any
code to retrieve messages yet, which is the next step we need to take. However,
before moving on, let's go through the generated `sendJMSMessageToMyQueue()`
method so that we can better understand how it works.

The first thing the method does is obtain a JMS connection by invoking
the `createConnection()` method on the injected instance of `javax.jms.`
`ConnectionFactory`, and assign it to a local variable of type
`javax.jms.Connection`.

After the JMS connection is created, the method obtains a JMS session by invoking
the `createSession()` method on the `Connection` object. The `createSession()`
method has two parameters; the first parameter is a boolean indicating if the created
session is transacted. Transacted sessions allow the code sending messages to a

JMS destination to send several messages as part of a transaction. To send several messages as part of a transaction, the JMS client sends messages to the queue as usual, then invokes the `commit()` method on the JMS session. By default, the code generated by NetBeans does not create a transacted JMS session, but we can override this by simply changing the value of the first parameter in `createSession()` to `true`.

The second parameter of the `createSession()` method indicates how JMS messages will be acknowledged by the message receiver. There are three valid values for this parameter; all three are defined as constants in the `javax.jms.Session` interface.

[The value of the second parameter to `createSession()` is ignored when creating a transacted session.]

Acknowledge Mode	Description
`Session.AUTO_ACKNOWLEDGE`	When using this mode, the JMS session will auto acknowledge message receipt for the client.
`Session.CLIENT_ACKNOWLEDGE`	When using this mode, message receivers must explicitly invoke the `acknowledge()` method defined in `javax.jms.Message` in order to acknowledge receipt of a message.
`Session.DUPS_OK_ACKNOWLEDGE`	When using this mode, the JMS session will lazily acknowledge message receipts on behalf of the JMS client. Using this acknowledge mode may result in some messages being delivered more than once, but it can improve performance by eliminating some of the work the session must do in order to avoid duplicate message deliveries.

Of the three acknowledge modes, `Session.AUTO_ACKNOWLEDGE` is the most commonly used, since it slightly reduces the amount of work to be done by application developers. NetBeans uses this mode by default in the generated code, but we are free to modify the generated code as necessary to meet our requirements.

After creating a JMS session, the next thing the generated code does is to create a JMS message producer by invoking the `createProducer()` method on the JMS session object. This method takes a JMS destination as its sole parameter. Unsurprisingly, in the generated code the injected message queue is sent as a parameter to this method.

The last thing this method does is to actually send the message to the message queue. This is done by invoking the `send()` method on the `javax.jms.MessageProducer` instance obtained in the previous line. This method takes an instance of a class implementing `javax.jms.Message` or one of its subinterfaces as a parameter. In the generated code, the generated method to create the message (`createJMSMessageForjmsMyQueue()` in our example) is invoked inline, since this method's return value is of the appropriate type.

Notice that most of the body of the generated method to send JMS messages is enclosed in a `try`/`finally` block. Most of the lines inside the `try` block have the potential of throwing a `JMSException`. If this happens, the code attempts to close the JMS session and connection, which is the exact same thing that needs to be done if the code ends normally, therefore it makes sense to put this code in the `finally` block.

Although it is possible to write standalone applications that can retrieve messages from a messaging destination, most Java EE 5 applications rely on message driven beans for this task, and NetBeans makes it very easy to generate message driven beans.

Processing JMS Messages with Message Driven Beans

In order to create a message driven bean, we need to right-click on our EJB project and select **New | Message Driven Bean**. In the resulting dialog window, we need to enter a name, package, and select a JMS destination for the message driven bean.

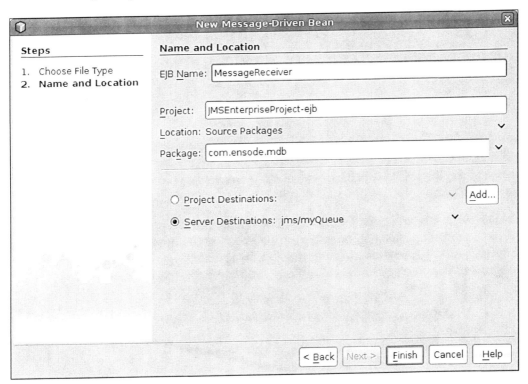

Once we have entered all the required information, our message driven bean is created in the specified package.

```
package com.ensode.mdb;

import javax.ejb.ActivationConfigProperty;
import javax.ejb.MessageDriven;
import javax.jms.Message;
import javax.jms.MessageListener;

@MessageDriven(mappedName = "jms/myQueue", activationConfig =  {
        @ActivationConfigProperty(
            propertyName = "acknowledgeMode",
            propertyValue = "Auto-acknowledge"),
        @ActivationConfigProperty(
            propertyName = "destinationType",
            propertyValue = "javax.jms.Queue")
    })
public class MessageReceiverBean implements MessageListener {

    public MessageReceiverBean() {
    }

    public void onMessage(Message message) {
    }

}
```

In the generated code, all we need to do is implement the body of the onMessage() method, and deploy our project. The onMessage() method will process any messages on the JMS destination our message driven bean is receiving messages from.

We can write any arbitrary code in the onMessage() method. The possibilities are endless. However, this method is typically used to save data from the message into a database, or to write some output into a log. In our example, we will simply send the contents of the message to the stdout log of our application server.

```
public void onMessage(Message message) {
    TextMessage textMessage = (TextMessage) message;
    try {
        System.out.println("Received message:" +
            textMessage.getText());
    } catch (JMSException ex) {
        Logger.getLogger(
```

```
                    MessageReceiverBean.class.getName()).log(
                    Level.SEVERE, null, ex);
        }
    }
```

Notice that we had to cast the message parameter to the actual sub-interface that was sent to the message destination, which in our case is `javax.jms.TextMessage`. To obtain the message contents, we invoked the `getText()` method of `TextMessage`. This method throws `JMSException`; because of this, we had to wrap its invocation in a `try`/`catch` block.

 NetBeans will remind us that we need to catch `JMSException` by underlining the offending code with a wiggly red line. By hitting *Alt+Enter* at the offending line we can have NetBeans generate the `try`/`catch` block automatically.

At this point we are ready to try our application. We can do so by simply right-clicking on our Enterprise Application Project and selecting **Run**. At this point the application will be deployed, and the application client project will be executed, sending a message to our message queue. Our EJBs will also be deployed, and the application server will automatically assign one to process the message sent to the queue. We can see the output of the message driven bean in the application server log.

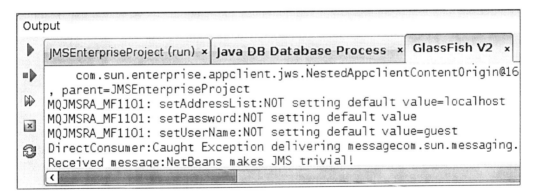

 You might notice an exception in the screenshot above. This is due to a known GlassFish issue and can safely be ignored.

As we can see, NetBeans automates most of the "grunt work" needed to write applications taking advantage of the JMS API, leaving us to only write the business logic part that is specific to our application.

Before moving on, let's discuss the code that NetBeans generates in our Message Driven Beans. Notice that the generated class is decorated with the `@MessageDriven` annotation. This annotation marks our class as a Message Driven Enterprise JavaBean.

The `mappedName` attribute of the `@MessageDriven` annotation should contain the JNDI name of the JMS destination (queue or topic) that our message driven bean will be assigned to.

The value of the `activationConfig` property must be an array of `@ActivationConfigProperty` annotations. The `@ActivationConfigProperty` annotation is used to specify values for certain properties. It has a `propertyName` attribute used to specify the property name, and a `propertyValue` attribute used to specify the property value.

When developing message driven beans, we use `@ActivationConfigProperty` annotations to specify the acknowledge mode of the bean (see explanation in the previous section), and the destination type of the JMS destination the bean is assigned to, which can be `javax.jms.Queue` when using point to point messaging domain, or `javax.jms.Topic` when using the publish/subscribe messaging domain.

In addition to the annotations, we should also notice that the generated message driven bean implements `javax.jms.MessageListener`, which has a single method, `onMessage()`. All message driven beans must implement this interface.

Summary

In this chapter we covered how to develop messaging applications using the JMS API with NetBeans. We looked at how to configure the application server by adding JMS resources directly from NetBeans. We also covered how NetBeans can generate most of the code necessary to send a JMS message, leaving us application developers to simply "fill in the blanks", and write only the business logic part that is specific to our application. Similarly, we covered how NetBeans can generate most of the code necessary to receive a JMS message from a Message Driven Bean, again leaving only the business logic part of our application to be written by hand.

9
Web Services

Web services allow us to develop functionality that can be accessed across a network. What makes web services different from other similar technologies such as EJBs is that they are language and platform independent, which is to say, for example, a web service developed in Java may be accessed by clients written in other languages, and vice versa.

In this chapter, we will cover the following topics:

- Introduction to web services
- Creating a simple web service
- Creating a web service client
- Exposing EJBs as web services

Introduction to Web Services

Web services allow us to write functionality that can be accessed across a network in a language and platform independent way.

There are two different approaches that are frequently used to develop web services: the first approach is to use the **Simple Object Access Protocol (SOAP)**, the second approach is to use the **Representational State Transfer (REST)** protocol. NetBeans supports creating web services using either approach.

In this chapter, we will focus on creating web services and web service clients using the SOAP protocol. For more information regarding RESTful web service development in NetBeans refer to the RESTful web services tutorials at http://www.netbeans.org/kb/trails/java-ee.html.

When using the SOAP protocol, web service operations are defined in an XML document called a **Web Services Definition Language (WSDL)** file. After creating the WSDL, implementation of web services is done in a proper programming language such as Java. The process of creating a WSDL is complex and error prone. Fortunately, when working with Java EE 5, a WSDL can be automatically generated from a web service written in Java when this web service is deployed to the application server. Additionally, if we have a WSDL file available, and need to implement the web service operations in Java, NetBeans can automatically generate most of the Java code for the implementation, creating a class with method stubs for each web service operation. All we need to do is implement the actual logic for each method; all the "plumbing" code is automatically generated.

Building web services using the REST protocol, sometimes referred to as RESTful web services, is simpler to using the traditional SOAP protocol. When developing RESTful web services, all that is done is the exchange of messaging through the HTTP protocol in any format we wish to use, such as HTML, XML, or JSON.

Creating a Simple Web Service

In this section, we will develop a web service that performs conversion of units of length. Our web service will have an operation that will convert inches to centimeters, and another operation to do the opposite conversion (centimeters to inches).

In order to create a web service, we need to create a new web application project. In our example, the project name is **UnitConversion.** We can create the web service by right-clicking on it and selecting **New | Web Service....** In the resulting wizard, we need to enter a name and package for our web service.

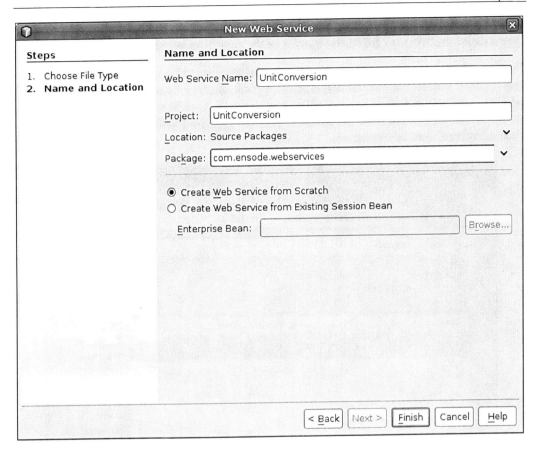

After clicking **Finish**, our web service is created, and the web services visual designer window is automatically opened.

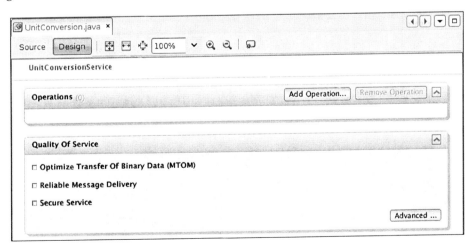

To add a web service operation, we simply need to click on the **Add Operation...** button and fill in the blanks in the resulting window.

Our web service will have two operations; one to convert from inches to centimeters and another one to convert centimeters to inches. Both of these operations will take a single parameter of type double, and return a double value. After clicking on the **Add Operation...** button we can enter the required information for the **inchesToCentimeters** operation.

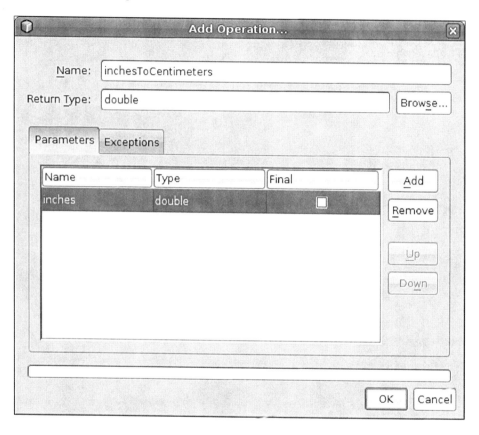

We then need to do the same for the **centimetersToInches** operation (not shown). After doing so our design window will show the newly added operations.

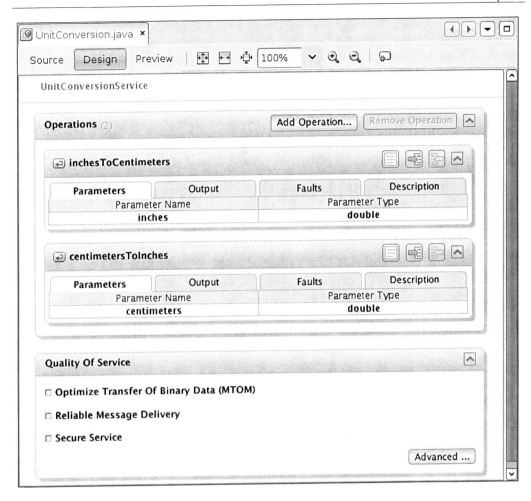

In addition to adding operations to our web service, we can control quality of service settings for it by simply selecting or unselecting checkboxes in the design window.

Web services transmit data as XML text messages between the web service and its client. Sometimes, it is necessary to transmit binary data, such as images. Binary data is normally inlined in the SOAP message, by using **Message Transmission Optimization Mechanism (MTOM)**. Binary data is sent as an attachment to the message, making the transmission of binary data more efficient. When using NetBeans, we can indicate that we wish to use MTOM by simply checking the **Optimize Transfer Of Binary Data (MTOM)** checkbox in the design window.

Checking the **Reliable Message Delivery** checkbox allows us to indicate that we want to make sure that messages are delivered, and they are not delivered more than once. Enabling reliable message delivery allows our applications to recover from situations where our messages may have been lost in transit.

Clicking on the **Secure Service** checkbox results in security features, such as encrypting messages between the client and server and requiring client authentication, to be enabled for our web service.

 Web service security can be configured by clicking on the **Advanced ...** button and selecting the appropriate security options in the resulting window.

When we add web services operations to our service in the design window, NetBeans adds method stubs in the implementation class, we can see these stubs by clicking on the **Source** tab.

```java
package com.ensode.webservices;

import javax.jws.WebMethod;
import javax.jws.WebParam;
import javax.jws.WebService;

/**
 *
 * @author heffel
 */
@WebService()
public class UnitConversion {

    /**
     * Web service operation
     */
    @WebMethod(operationName = "inchesToCentimeters")
    public double inchesToCentimeters(@WebParam(name = "inches")
    double inches) {
        //TODO write your implementation code here:
        return 0.0;
    }

    /**
     * Web service operation
     */
    @WebMethod(operationName = "centimetersToInches")
    public double centimetersToInches(@WebParam(name = "centimeters")
    double centimeters) {
        //TODO write your implementation code here:
        return 0.0;
    }

}
```

Now all we need to do is to replace the generated body of the methods in the class with the "real" bodies, deploy our application, and our web service will be good to go. In our case, all we need to do is divide the inches by 2.54 to convert from inches to centimeters, and multiply the centimeters by 2.54 to convert them to inches.

Notice that the generated web service class is a **Plain Old Java Object (POJO)** using some annotations. The @WebService annotation at the class level is used to indicate that our class is a web service. Each method in the class that is exposed as a web service operation must be annotated with the @WebMethod annotation. The operationName attribute of this annotation is used to map the method to an operation defined in the web service's WSDL.

 When developing web services with NetBeans, we don't need to worry about creating a WSDL file; one will automatically be generated upon deployment of our application.

Additionally, each parameter in each method is decorated with the @WebParam annotation, which maps the method's parameter to a type definition in the service's WSDL schema.

 The WSDL and it's schema can be generated by right-clicking on the web service and selecting **Generate and Copy WSDL...**

Once we have replaced the method bodies with the actual required functionality, we are ready to deploy our web service, which can be done by right-clicking on our project and selecting **Undeploy and Deploy**.

Testing Our Web Service

If we deployed our web service to GlassFish, we can test it by simply right-clicking on it in the **Projects** window and selecting **Test Web Service**.

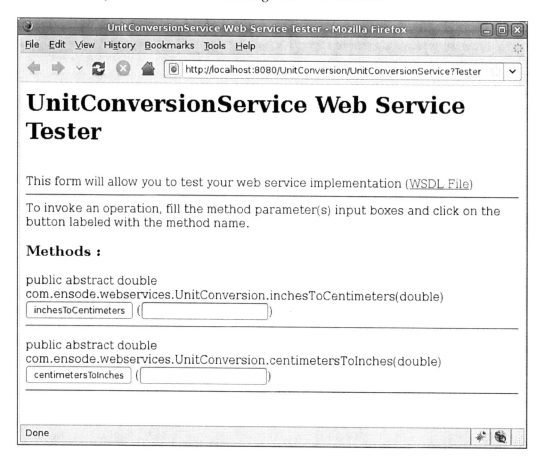

Here we can test our web service's methods by simply entering some values in the text fields and clicking on the appropriate button. For example, entering **2.54** in the second text field and clicking on the button labeled **centimetersToInches** results in the following page being displayed in the browser.

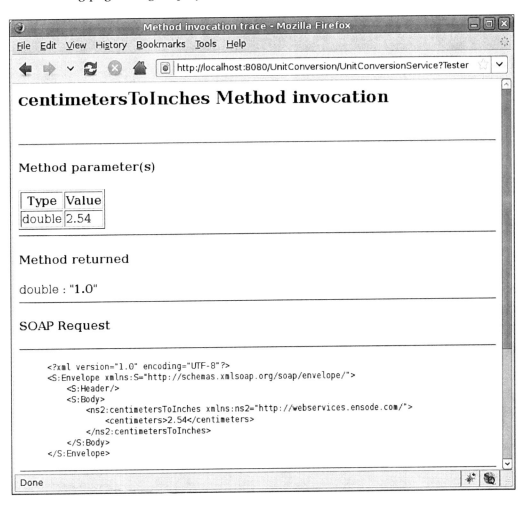

At the top of the page we can see the parameters that were passed to the method, along with the return value. At the bottom of the page we can see the "raw" SOAP request and response.

Developing a Client for Our Web Service

Now that we have developed our web service and tested it to verify that it works properly, we are going to create a simple client that will invoke our web service. A web services client can be any kind of Java project, such as a standard Java application, a Java ME application, a web application, or an enterprise project. To keep our client code simple we will create a Java Application project for our client.

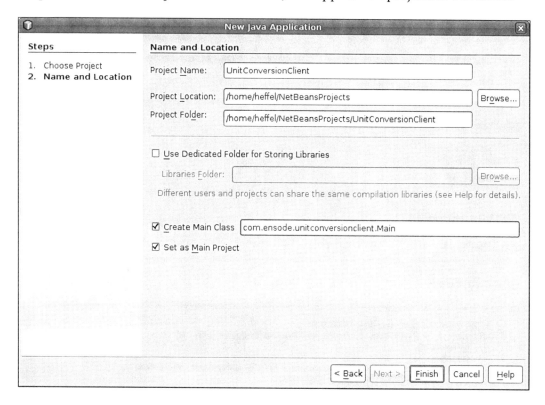

Once we have created our project, we need to create a new web service client by right-clicking on our project in the **Projects** window, then selecting **New | Web Service Client**.

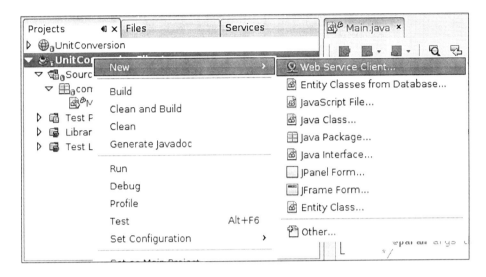

We need to make sure our web services project is open before performing this step. In the resulting window, we need to select the radio button labeled **Project** if it is not selected already, then click **Browse** and select one of the web services we created in our web services project. The URL for the generated WSDL file for the web service we selected will automatically be added to the corresponding text field.

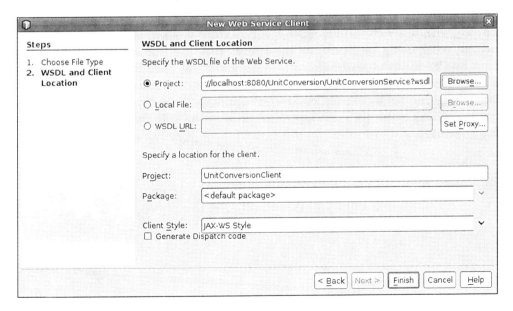

Notice that we can develop web service clients for web services we didn't develop ourselves. In order to do this we simply select the **Local File** radio button to use a WSDL file in our hard drive, or the **WSDL URL** radio button to use a WSDL that is published online.

At this point, a new node labeled **Web Service References** is added to our project. Expanding this node all the way reveals the operations we defined in our web services project.

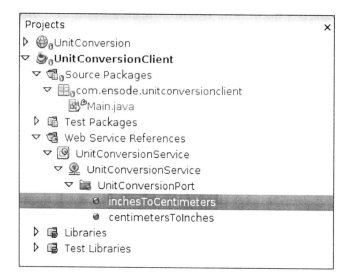

Typically, writing a web service client involves some amount of "boilerplate" code. However, when using NetBeans, we can simply drag the web service operation we wish to invoke to our code. This results in generating all necessary boilerplate code, and leaving us to simply specify which parameters we want to send to the web service. Dragging the **inchesToCentimeters** operation from the **Projects** window to the `main` method of our web services client project results in the following code being generated.

```
package com.ensode.unitconversionclient;

public class Main {

    /**
     * @param args the command line arguments
     */
    public static void main(String[] args) {
        try { // Call Web Service Operation
            com.ensode.webservices.UnitConversionService service =
                    new com.ensode.webservices.UnitConversionService();
            com.ensode.webservices.UnitConversion port =
                    service.getUnitConversionPort();
            // TODO initialize WS operation arguments here
            double inches = 0.0d;
            // TODO process result here
            double result = port.inchesToCentimeters(inches);
            System.out.println("Result = " + result);
        } catch (Exception ex) {
            // TODO handle custom exceptions here
        }
    }
}
```

At this point what we need to do is replace the generated `0.0d` value for the inches parameter and execute our web service client. For our example, we will replace that value with `1.0d`, which should convert to exactly `2.54` centimeters. Although not absolutely necessary, it is good practice to handle any potential exceptions that might be thrown, therefore it is a good idea to write some code inside the generated catch block, at least an invocation to `printStackTrace()` so that we know an exceptions occurred.

If the web service operation implementation we are invoking throws an exception, the exception will be nested inside a `SoapFaultException`. By examining the stack trace of this exception, we will be able to see the nested exception, along with the exact line number in the web service code that threw the exception

At this point, we are ready to execute our web service client code. We should see the following output in the console:

```
Output - UnitConversionClient (run)
  deps-jar:
  wsimport-init:
  wsimport-client-check-UnitConversionService:
  wsimport-client-UnitConversionService:
  wsimport-client-generate:
  wsimport-client-compile:
  Compiling 1 source file to /home/heffel/NetBeansProjects/UnitConversionClient/build/classes
  compile:
  run:
  Result = 2.54
  BUILD SUCCESSFUL (total time: 1 second)
```

Exposing EJBs as Web Services

In our previous web service example, we saw how we can expose a Plain Old Java Object (POJO) as a web service by packaging it in a web application and adding a few annotations to it. This makes it very easy to create web services deployed in a web application.

When working with an EJB module project, we can have stateless session beans exposed as web services. This way they can be accessed by clients written in languages other than Java. Exposing stateless session beans as web services has the effect of allowing our web services to take advantage of all the features available to EJBs, such as transaction management and aspect oriented programming.

There are two ways we can expose a session bean as a web service. When creating a new web service in an EJB module project, the web service will automatically be implemented as a stateless session bean. Additionally, existing session beans in an EJB module project can be exposed as a web service.

Implementing New Web Services as EJBs

In order to implement a new web service as an EJB, we simply need to create the
web service in an EJB module project by right-clicking on the project and selecting
New | Web Service.

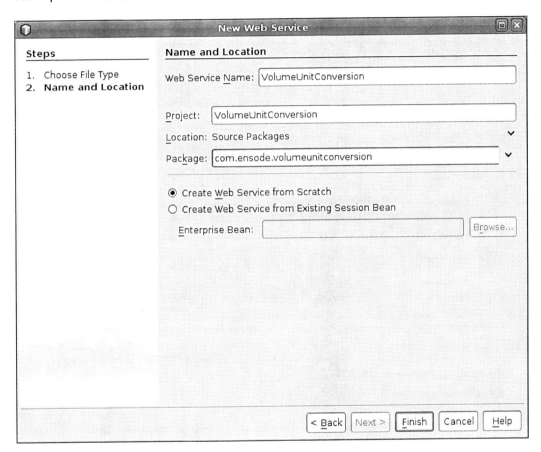

In the web services wizard, we need to enter a name for our web service, a package where our web service implementation code will be created, and select the **Create Web Service from Scratch** radio button, then click **Finish** to generate our web service. At this point we should see the web service visual designer, which we can use to add web services operations as usual. In our example, after adding two operations, our web service visual designer looks like this:

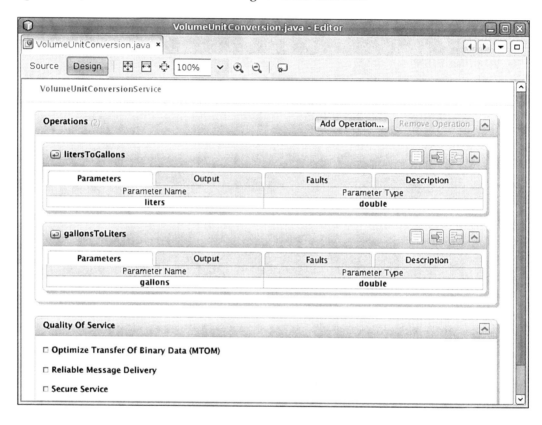

Clicking on the **Source** tab reveals that our web service was implemented as a stateless session bean.

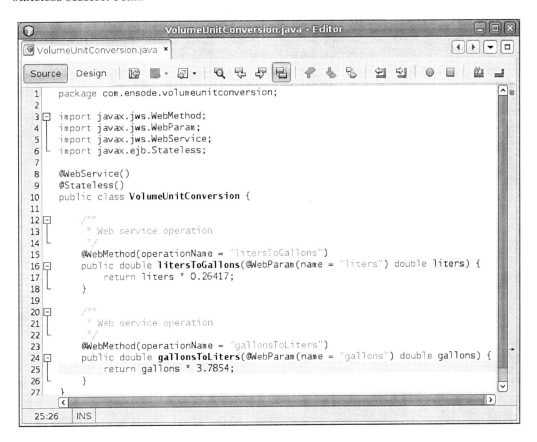

Notice that the generated session bean does not implement neither a local nor remote business interface. It simply is decorated with the @WebService annotation, its methods are decorated with the @WebMethod annotation, and each parameter is decorated with the @WebParam annotation. The only difference between the generated code for this web service and the one for the previous example is that the generated class is a stateless session bean, therefore it can take advantage of EJB transaction management, aspect oriented programming, and other EJB features.

Exposing Existing EJBs as Web Services

The second way we can expose EJBs as web services is to expose an existing EJB as a web service. In order to do this, we need to create a web service as usual by going to **File | New | Web Service**, then entering a name and a package for our web service and select the **Create Web Service from Existing Session Bean** radio button. Then we need to select the session bean to expose as a web service by clicking on the **Browse...** button and selecting the appropriate bean.

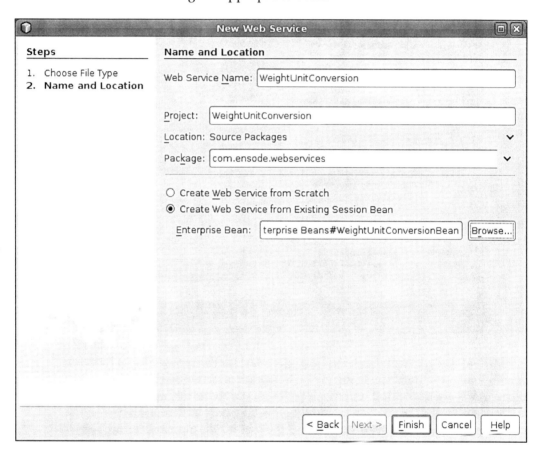

When we click **Finish**, our new web service is created and its web services visual designer window is opened. As we can see, all public methods in the EJB we are exposing as a web service are already added as operations to our web service.

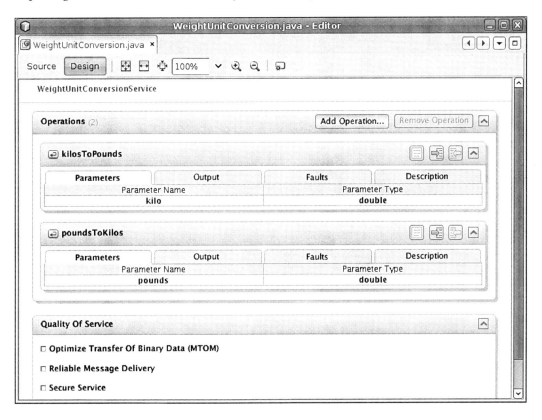

Clicking on the **Source** tab of the web services visual designer, we can see how our new web service is implemented.

As we can see, creating a web service from an existing session bean results in a new stateless session bean being created. This new session bean acts as a client for our existing EJB (as evidenced by the `ejbRef` instance variable in our example, which is annotated with the `@EJB` annotation).

EJBs can also be exposed as web services from a web application project; in which case the generated web service will be a Plain Old Java Object (POJO) annotated with the `@WebService`, `@WebMethod`, and `@WebParam` annotations, with pass-through methods invoking the corresponding methods on the EJB being exposed as a web service.

Creating a Web Service from an Existing WSDL

Normally, creating SOAP web services requires the creation of a WSDL file. The process of creating a WSDL is complex and error prone, but thankfully Java EE frees us from having to create a WSDL file by hand, since it gets generated automatically whenever we deploy a web service into our application server.

[NetBeans can help with the creation of WSDL files, see
`http://www.netbeans.org/kb/60/websvc/wsdl-guide.html`
for more information.]

However, sometimes we have a WSDL file available, and we need to implement its operations in Java code. For these cases, NetBeans provides a wizard that creates a Java class with method stubs from an existing WSDL.

In order to do so, we need to right-click on a Web Application project, then select **New | Other | Web Service from WSDL**. We then need to enter a name, package, and existing WSDL for our web service.

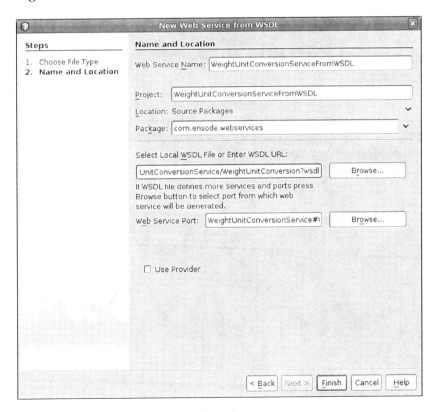

A web service will then be generated with method stubs for all operations defined in the WSDL.

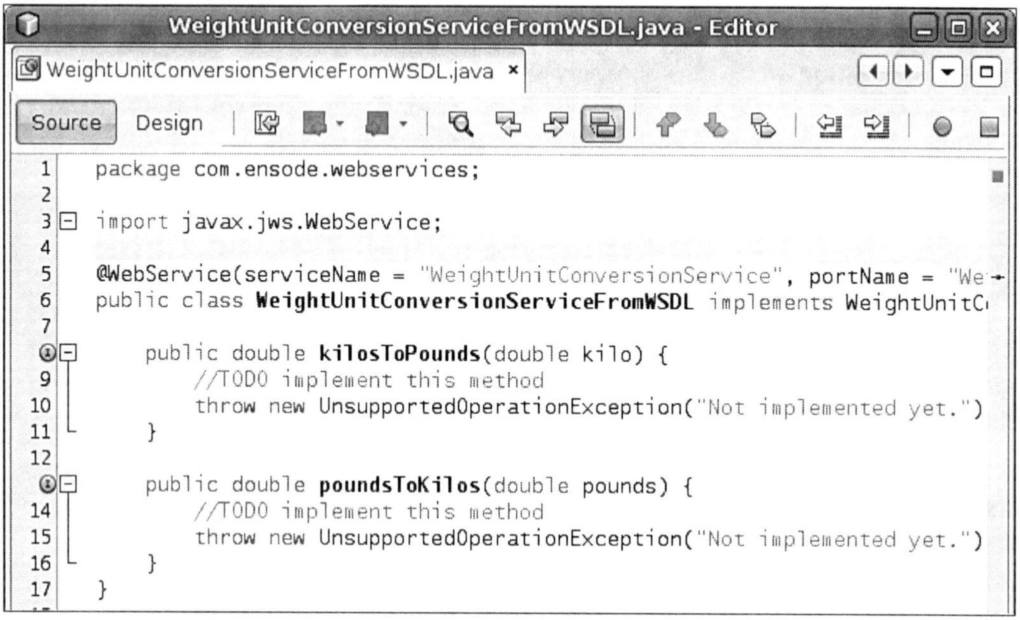

At this point we simply need to add the method bodies for all the generated methods.

In this example, we used the WSDL that was generated from our previous example, which is redundant since we already have implementations for all the operations. However, the procedure illustrated here applies to any WSDL file, either in the local file system or deployed in a server.

Summary

In this chapter, we explored NetBeans support for Web Service development, including how to expose a Plain Old Java Object's (POJO's) methods as web services and how NetBeans automatically adds the required annotations to our web services.

We covered how NetBeans aids us in creating web service clients by generating most of the required boilerplate code, leaving us to simply initialize any parameters to be passed to our web service's operations.

Additionally we covered how to expose EJB methods as web service operations, and how NetBeans supports and makes it easy to expose both new and existing EJBs as web services.

Finally, we saw how NetBeans can help us implement a web service from an existing Web Services Definition Language (WSDL) file, located either on our local file system or deployed on a server, by generating method stubs from said WSDL.

10
Putting it all Together

Previous chapters have discussed NetBeans support for individual Java EE technologies and APIs. In this chapter we will develop a complete enterprise application taking advantage of most of the technologies discussed in the book, including Enterprise Java Beans, Visual Web JavaServer Faces, and the Java Persistence API.

Creating Our Enterprise Project

The first thing we need to do to create our application is to create a new Enterprise Application project. Enterprise Application projects encapsulate any number of Web Application projects, EJB projects, and Application Client projects. Behind the scenes, Enterprise Application projects are deployed in an Enterprise Archive (EAR) file, which NetBeans generates automatically for us.

In order to create an Enterprise Application project, we need to go to **File | New Project**, select the **Java EE** category and the **Enterprise Application** project type.

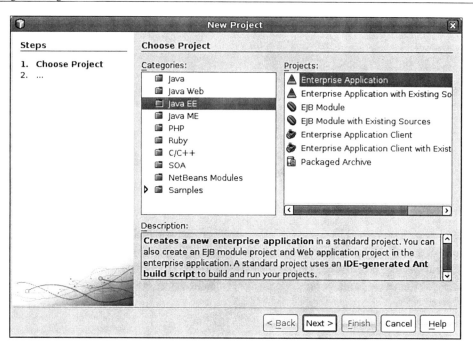

We will develop an application that will manage customer information in a database, therefore, we give our application the name of **CustomerManagement**.

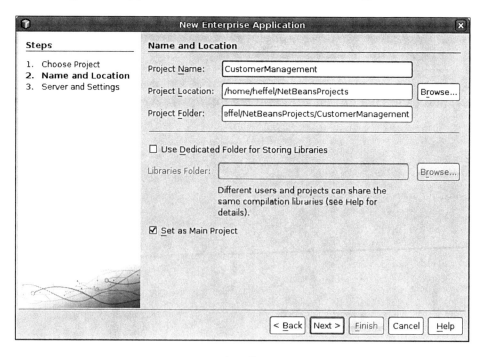

After entering the **Project Name** and clicking **Next>**, we need to make sure that the **Create EJB Module** and **Create Web Application Module** checkboxes are both checked. Default names for these modules are usually reasonable, therefore there is little reason to change them. In our EJB module we will implement our data access layer and business logic. In the web application module we will implement the user interface logic of our application.

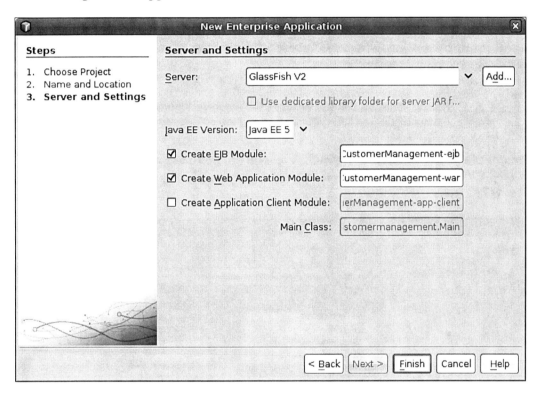

After clicking **Finish**, we should see our newly created project along with the generated EJB module and Web Application module in the **Projects** window.

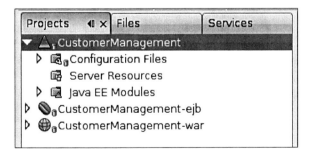

At this point we are ready to start developing our application. The data access layer will be implemented in the EJB module and the user interface layer will be implemented in the web application module.

Implementing the Data Access Layer

Now we are ready to start developing our application. In this project we will be generating JPA entities from an existing database, mimicking the typical situation in a real enterprise project, where a database administrator is in charge of creating the database schema for the application.

 For our example, we will be using the database schema we created in the *Automated Generation of JPA Entities* section of Chapter 5.

In order to do so, we need to right-click on our EJB module project and select **New | Other**, then select the **Persistence** category and **Entity Classes from Database**.

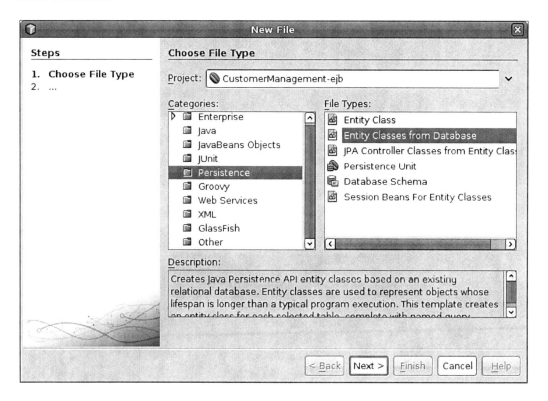

After clicking **Next>**, we need to select the appropriate datasource. In this example we will use the datasource we created in Chapter 5. After selecting the appropriate datasource (**jdbc/customerdb** in our case), verifying the connection information and entering the password, we need to select the tables we will be generating JPA entities for. Although we will be working primarily with one table, it doesn't hurt to generate entities for all tables.

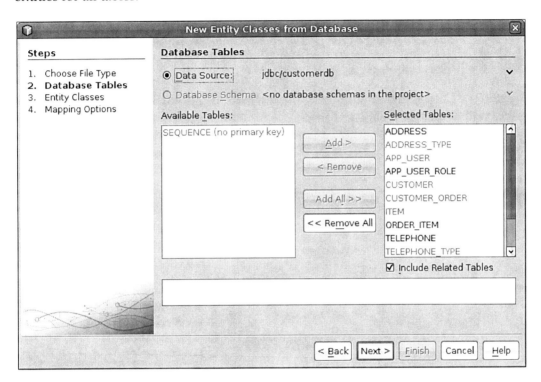

At this point we have all the JPA entities for our project. The generated JPA entities by default do not use a primary key generation strategy. In order to have primary keys generated automatically, we need to decorate the getter method for the primary key field in our entities with the @GeneratedValue annotation; the default generation strategy is AUTO. If we need to override the generation strategy then we can use one of the generation strategies discussed in Chapter 5 *Interacting with Databases through the Java Persistence API.*

The previous screenshot shows a table named SEQUENCE with no primary key. The reason this table exists in our schema is because Toplink Essentials, the default JPA implementation included with GlassFish, by default uses a primary key generation strategy of TABLE, and it requires this table to be present in the schema for primary key generation to work properly. The table default table name and column names for the table used to generate primary keys can be overridden by explicitly specifying a primary key generation of TABLE and using the @TableGenerator annotation on the primary key of our entity. See http://java. sun.com/javaee/5/docs/api/javax/persistence/ TableGenerator.html for details.

Recall from Chapter 5 that in order to interact with JPA entities, we need to write some code to interact with EntityManager. When using NetBeans, it isn't necessary to write this code directly, as NetBeans can generate **Data Access Objects (DAOs)** from existing JPA entities. These DAO's can be implemented as stateless session beans; this way they can take advantage of EJB features, especially transactions.

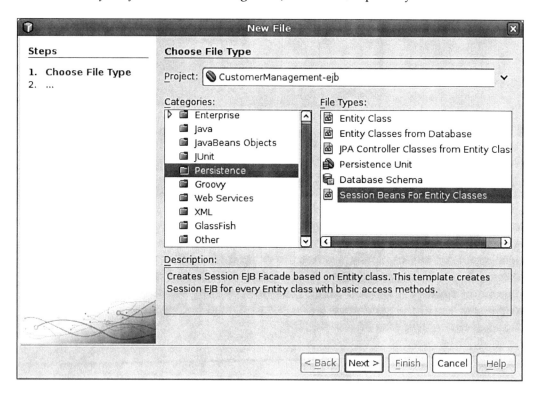

After clicking **Next>**, we need to enter a suitable package name where our session beans will be created.

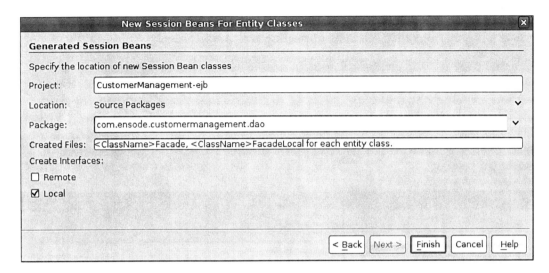

In our particular example, our session beans will only need to be accessed from inside the application server, therefore generating only **Local** business interfaces will suffice.

After clicking **Finish**, session beans are generated with methods to create, update, delete and find each of the JPA entities in the project.

We have now finished implementing the data access layer of our application, without having to write a single line of code!

For more complex applications, we may have to add additional logic to the generated code. For example, we might have to add methods in the session beans to invoke some of the generated named queries in the JPA entities. Similarly we might have to add additional named queries to the entities for retrieving objects meeting additional criteria (for example, where `field1='value1'` and/or `field2='value2'`). For our example, the generated code can be used as it is.

Implementing the User Interface Layer

Now that we have the data access layer ready, it is time to implement the user interface layer. We will be using NetBean's visual web JSF so that we can easily create a highly functional, visually appealing web application.

The first page we will create will contain a table listing all existing customers in the database, it will also have controls to add, update, and delete customers. Since we will be using visual web JSF, we need to create a new visual web page by right-clicking on the **CustomerManagement-war** web module and selecting **New | Visual Web JSF Page...**. At this point the **New Visual Web JSF Page** wizard pops up. We need to enter a name for our JSP, and add a suitable package for the generated managed bean.

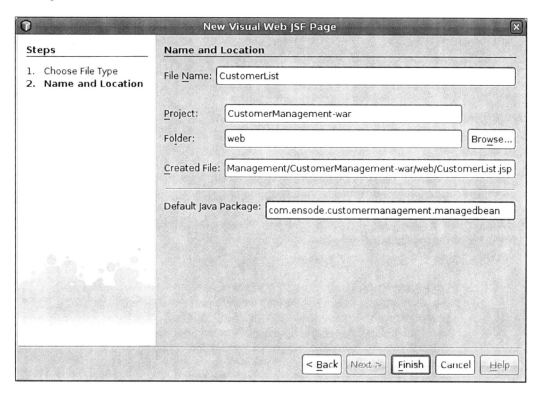

 For each visual web JSF page we create, an identically named JSF managed bean is created. For this reason we should name our visual web JSF pages following Java class naming conventions.

The first visual web JSF page we add to our project is automatically added to the `<welcome-file-list>` element of the `web.xml` deployment descriptor in our web application. therefore this file will be rendered when navigating to the application's root context.

Now we can click **Finish** and our new page is generated for us.

Adding User Interface Components to the Page

Now that we have our page, it is time to start adding components to it. The first component we will add is a standard grid panel. This component can be found in the palette window under the **Woodstock Layout** header.

We need to drop our grid panel into the **Navigator** window, right inside the **form1** component.

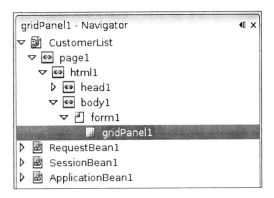

This grid panel component will be used to lay out other components in the page. In this page we wish to have all components in a single column, therefore there is no need to set the `columns` property of the grid panel, since its default value is `1`.

Now we need to add a static text component, which can be found in the palette under **Woodstock Basic**, to the grid panel.

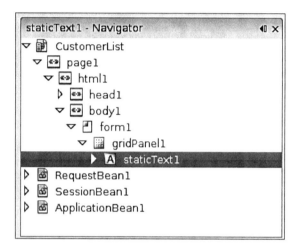

At this point we need to set a few properties in our static text component. To set its text property to the appropriate value we simply need to right-click on the component in the **Navigator** window and select **Edit Text**. at The text field component in the design window will become editable, the value we want for this components is **Customer Management**.

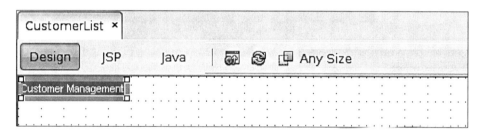

Since we want this static text field to act as a header for the page, we need to modify it's style so that the text is displayed with a bigger font. The easiest way to do this is to click on the ellipsis (...) next to the **style** property in the **Properties** window.

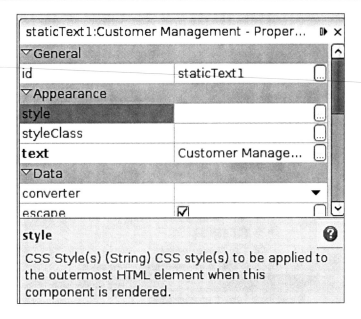

Then set the font size to **large**.

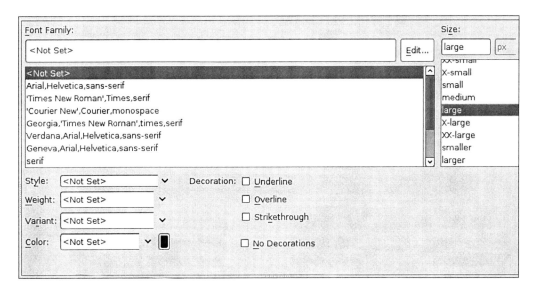

Next we need to add a table component (found under **Woodstock Basic**) and a group panel (found under **Woodstock Layout**) to the grid panel, then add two button components (under **Woodstock Basic**) to the layout panel, then set the button labels to `Delete Selected` and `Add New` (button labels can be edited by right-clicking on the button and selecting **Edit Button Text**).

After following the steps described in the previous paragraph, our **Navigator** window should look like this:

And the design window should look like this:

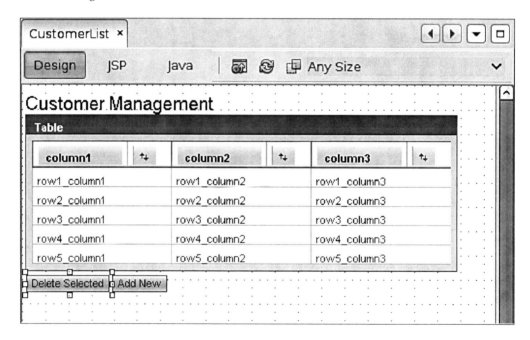

Now what we need to do is display all customers in the database in the table. The woodstock table component has the concept of **data providers**; data providers provide data for the table to populate itself. There are several data providers available; the easiest one to use in visual web JSF is the **Object Array Data Provider**, since we can simply graphically bind an object array property to a table, and an object array data provider with all the appropriate values is generated in the code automatically.

 Consult `http://developers.sun.com/docs/jscreator/apis/` `dataprovider/index.html` for more information about the different data providers.

The `CustomerFacade` session bean we generated when implementing the data access layer of our application contains a method named `findAll()` that returns all customers in the database, this method returns the customers as a `List`. In order for us to be able to take advantage of NetBeans visual web JSF functionality, we need to convert the generated values into an array of `Customer` objects. It is a good idea to keep these objects in the session, that way they can be reused across HTTP requests. Therefore we will add a method to the generated `SessionBean1` managed bean to invoke the `findAll()` method, convert the returned list into an array of customers, and return this array. The following code listing illustrates the necessary modifications to `SessionBean1.java`.

```
package com.ensode.customermanagement.managedbean;

//imports omitted for brevity

public class SessionBean1 extends AbstractSessionBean {

    @EJB
    private CustomerFacadeLocal customerDAO;
    private Customer[] customerArray;

    //Other methods omitted for brevity

    public Customer[] getCustomerArray() {
        List<Customer> customerList = customerDAO.findAll();

        if (customerList != null) {
            customerArray =
            customerList.toArray(new Customer[0]);
        } else {
            customerArray = null;
        }
        return customerArray;
    }
}
```

The first thing we did was to add an instance variable of type CustomerFacadeLocal and decorate it with the @EJB annotation. CustomerFacadeLocal is the local interface for the CustomerFacade stateless session bean we generated in the previous section. The @EJB annotation allows an instance of a class of type CustomerFacadeLocal to be injected into our managed bean at runtime, freeing us from having to do a JNDI lookup to initialize this variable.

Next we added a private instance variable that will hold the array of customer objects, which will be used to populate the table. Then we implemented a getter method for this variable.

The java.util.List interface provides a method to convert the list to an array. This method takes a single parameter which is an array of the type we wish the returned array to have. We are taking advantage of this method to simplify the conversion from the list returned by the findAll() method in the session bean to an array of Customer objects.

Populating the Table

At this point we are ready to bind our array of customers to the table. In order to do this, we simply need to right-click on the table in either the design window or the navigator window and select **Bind to Data**. In the resulting window, we then need to select the **customerArray** property in the drop-down box labeled **Get Data From.**

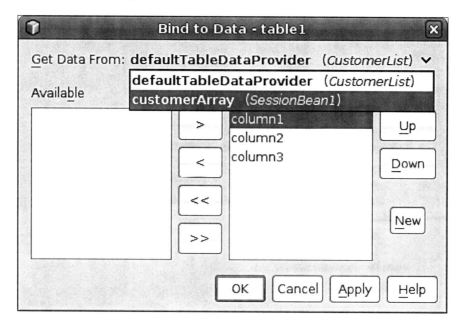

By default, all properties in the `Customer` class are added to the **Selected** list. Properties in this list are shown in each row in the table. For our example, we only want to display the `firstName`, `middleName`, `lastName`, and `email` properties, therefore we need to remove all but these properties from the **Selected** list. After organizing the properties by selecting them and clicking the **Up** and **Down** buttons as appropriate, we should have only the desired properties in the selected window and in the correct order.

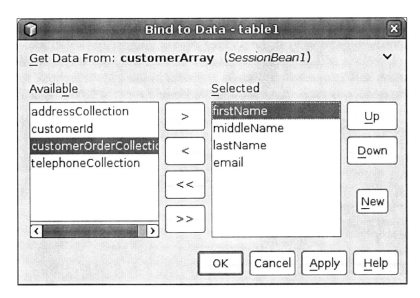

After clicking **OK**, we can see that our table has changed in the design window. The property names are shown as column headers, and the placeholder text **abc** is shown as a dummy value representing the dynamic data that will be shown in each cell.

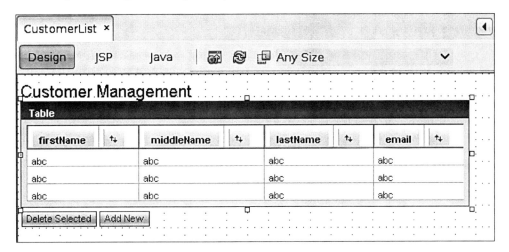

We should change each column header to a more user friendly value. We can do this by selecting each **tableColumn** component in the **Navigator** window, then modifying its **headerText** property in the **Properties** window. Similarly, we can change the table title by selecting the table component in the **Navigator** window and modifying its **title** property.

Testing Our Application

At this point, we are ready to test the functionality we have implemented so far. We can execute our application by right-clicking on our enterprise project and selecting **Run**. The application will be deployed and a web browser window pointing to it's root context will be opened. If there is any data in the CUSTOMER table it will be shown in the table, otherwise the message **No items found** will be displayed.

Adding Missing Functionality

Now that we are confident that our table is displaying the correct data, we need to make some additional modifications to our application; for starters the buttons at the bottom of the table are not yet functional. Additionally, we need to add a column containing checkboxes so that one or more rows can be selected, and another column containing a button to edit the data on a particular row.

The first thing we will do is to add a new column left of the **First Name** column to hold checkboxes. In order to do this, we need to drag a **Table Column** component, found under **Woodstock Basic**, from the palette to the **Navigator** window, right under the **tableRowGroup1** component. Then we need to delete the static text component that is automatically added to the new column, and delete the value of the **headerText** property in the **Properties** window. We then need to add a **Checkbox** component from the **Woodstock Basic** section of the palette to our new column, then delete the value of its **label** property in the **Properties** window. After following all these steps, our design window should look like this:

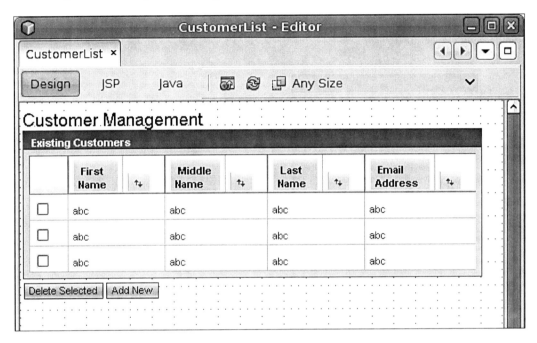

Now that we have the checkboxes, we need to add a new column right of the **Email Address** column, delete the value of its **headerText** property, then add a **Button** component to it and change its **text** property to **Update**. Our design window should look like this:

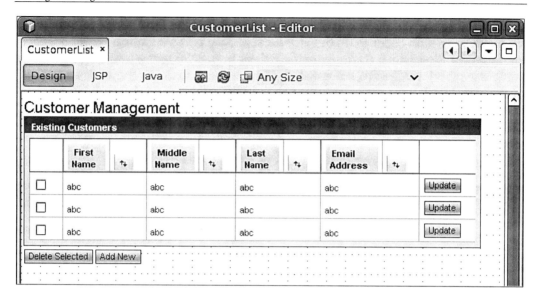

Now that we have all the necessary components in our page, we need to add some logic to our code so that the checkboxes and buttons work as expected. By clicking on the **JSP** tag in our page we can examine the generated markup for our table.

```
<webuijsf:table augmentTitle="false" id="table1" title="Existing
Customers" width="400">
  <webuijsf:tableRowGroup
      id="tableRowGroup1" rows="5"
      sourceData="#{SessionBean1.customerArray}"
      sourceVar="currentRow">
    <webuijsf:tableColumn id="tableColumn5" width="200" >
      <webuijsf:checkbox id="checkbox1"/>
    </webuijsf:tableColumn>
    <webuijsf:tableColumn headerText="First Name"
        id="tableColumn1" sort="firstName">
      <webuijsf:staticText id="staticText2"
          text="#{currentRow.value['firstName']}"/>
    </webuijsf:tableColumn>
    <webuijsf:tableColumn headerText="Middle Name"
        id="tableColumn2" sort="middleName">
      <webuijsf:staticText id="staticText3"
          text="#{currentRow.value['middleName']}"/>
    </webuijsf:tableColumn>
    <webuijsf:tableColumn headerText="Last Name"
        id="tableColumn3" sort="lastName">
      <webuijsf:staticText id="staticText4"
```

```
          text="#{currentRow.value['lastName']}"/>
      </webuijsf:tableColumn>
      <webuijsf:tableColumn headerText="Email Address"
          id="tableColumn4" sort="email">
        <webuijsf:staticText id="staticText5"
            text="#{currentRow.value['email']}"/>
      </webuijsf:tableColumn>
      <webuijsf:tableColumn id="tableColumn6" width="200">
        <webuijsf:button id="button1" text="Update"/>
      </webuijsf:tableColumn>
    </webuijsf:tableRowGroup>
  </webuijsf:table>
```

As we can see, the `<webuijsf:table>` tag has a nested `<webuijsf:rowGroup>`
tag; this tag is used to control the rows in our table. Notice that the `sourceVar`
attribute of `<webuijsf:rowGroup>` is automatically set to `currentRow`. Rows in a
table are generated dynamically from a data provider (in our case, we are using
the `customerArray` property of the `SessionBean1` managed bean). While iterating
through the elements in the data provider, the current element is stored in this
variable (`currentRow`). We need to use this attribute in order to obtain the selected
elements in the table.

In order to keep track of, which rows are selected in our table, we need to create an
instance of `com.sun.webui.jsf.event.TableSelectPhaseListener`. This class has
two methods, `getSelected()` and `setSelected()`, that we need to use in order to
keep track of which rows are selected. Since we are using checkboxes to select rows,
we need to link the `selected` attribute of the checkbox to these methods. In order to
do this, we need to add two methods to our managed bean.

```
    public void setSelected(Boolean selected) {
      RowKey rowKey = (RowKey) getValue("#{currentRow.tableRow}");

      if (rowKey != null) {
        tableSelectPhaseListener.setSelected(rowKey, selected);
      }
    }
```

All managed beans generated in a visual web JSF project extend `com.sun.rave.web.`
`ui.appbase.FacesBean`, either directly or by extending one of its subclasses. This
class contains a convenience method called `getValue()`. This method takes a `String`
containing a **Unified Expression Language** (UEL) expression, and returns the object
to which the expression is bound.

Recall that `currentRow` is the value of the `sourceVar` attribute of the `<webuijsf:tableRowGroup>` tag in our table. The value of this attribute is used to get a reference to the current row in the table as it is generated dynamically from a data provider. The UEL expression `#{currentRow}` resolves to an instance of `com.sun.data.provider.impl.TableRowDataProvider`. This class has a `getTableRow()` method that returns an instance of `com.sun.data.provider.RowKey`. In the above method, we are invoking this method by using the dot notation of the Unified Expression Language.

Once we have a reference to the `RowKey` object for the current row, we need to pass it to the `setSelected()` method of our `TableSelectPhaseListener` instance, since it uniquely identifies the current row. The second parameter we pass to this method is the `Boolean` value that our method receives as a parameter, which indicates if the current row is selected or not.

Now that we have implemented the logic to set the selected property of each checkbox in the table, we need to implement the logic to obtain the value of this property, which needs to be done, of course, in a getter method.

```
public Boolean getSelected() {
    RowKey rowKey = (RowKey) getValue("#{currentRow.tableRow}");

    return
        (Boolean) tableSelectPhaseListener.getSelected(rowKey);
}
```

In this method we simply obtain the `RowKey` instance for the current row the same way we did in the setter method, then invoke the `getSelected()` method on our `TableSelectPhaseListener` instance, passing the `RowKey` instance as an argument, then we return the return value of this method invocation.

By implementing `setSelected()` and `getSelected()` methods in our managed bean, we have actually added a property to our managed bean. We need to bind this property to the `selected` property of our checkbox so that our methods are invoked automatically when the page is rendered. We can do this by right-clicking on the checkbox either on the design or the **Navigator** window, then selecting **Property Bindings**....

At this point we need to select the **selected** property from the **Select bindable property** list, then select the **selected** property of the **CustomerList** managed bean in the **Select binding target** list.

The `selected` attribute of the checkbox component simply indicates if the checkbox is selected, that way it can be rendered checked or unchecked in the page as appropriate, but it doesn't set the actual selected value that is sent to the server on form submission. For this purpose, we need to use the `selectedValue` attribute of the checkbox tag.

The value we would like each checkbox in the table to have is the index of the object whose data is being displayed in its row. The RowKey class has a getRowId() method that returns a numeric String object representing the index of the current row, which happens to coincide with the index of the current object in the array. Therefore all we need to do is obtain the RowKey for each row, and return the value of its getRowId() method:

```
public String getSelectedValue() {
  RowKey rowKey = (RowKey) getValue("#{currentRow.tableRow}");
  if (rowKey != null) {
    return rowKey.getRowId();
  } else {
    return null;
  }
}
```

Now we have created a read only property in our managed bean, we need to bind it to the selectedValue attribute of our checkbox. This can be done by following a very similar procedure to the one we used for its selected property. We need to right-click on the checkbox, select **Property Bindings...**, then click on either the **Advanced** or **All checkbox**, then select the **selectedValue** bindable property and the selected property of the **CustomerList** managed bean as the binding target.

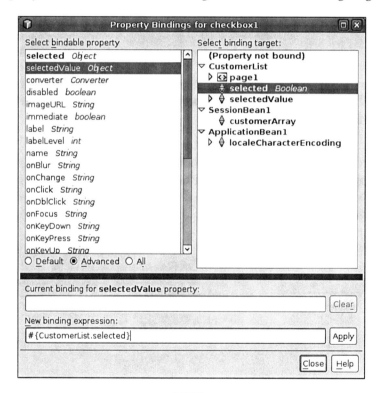

In addition to the checkbox, the `tableRowGroup` component in our table also needs to be aware of what rows are selected. We can accomplish this by binding it's `selected` attribute to the **selected** property of our managed bean.

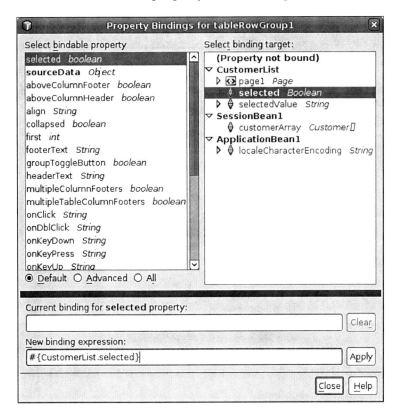

Additionally, the column containing the checkboxes needs to be aware of the component id of the component used to select a row (the checkbox in our example). For this we need to set the value of it's `selectId` attribute to match the value of the `id` attribute of the checkbox.

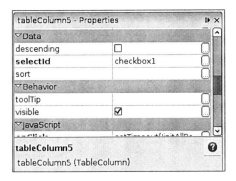

The visual web table component automatically highlights any selected rows; typically its status is updated after a server request that results in navigation to the page containing the table. In order to have the table component refresh itself and highlight any selected rows when a checkbox is clicked, we need to invoke a JavaScript function provided by the Woodstock JSF components; the name of this function is `initAllRows()`. We will write our own JavaScript function that will invoke the `initAllRows()` function.

To do this, we need to drag a **Script** component from the **Advanced** section of the palette to the **Head** component in the **Navigator** window.

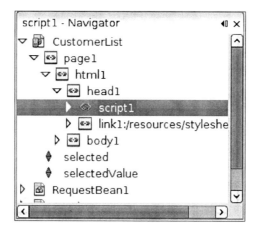

Now we need to click on the **JSP** tab and add a JavaScript function to the tag.

```
<webuijsf:head id="head1">
  <webuijsf:script id="script1">
  function initAllTableRows() {
  document.getElementById("form1:table1").initAllRows();
  }
  </webuijsf:script>
  <webuijsf:link id="link1" url="/resources/stylesheet.css"/>
</webuijsf:head>
```

We named our JavaScript function `initAllTableRows()`. It obtains a reference to the `table` element in the page's **Document Object Model (DOM)**, then invokes the Woodstock provided `initAllRows()` JavaScript function on it. After adding our function, we need to invoke it whenever the row containing the checkboxes is clicked; this can be done by adding the appropriate value to the column's `onClick` attribute. This can be done graphically from the **Properties** window or by directly editing the page markup.

```
<webuijsf:tableColumn id="tableColumn5"
    onClick="setTimeout('initAllTableRows()', 0)"
    selectId="checkbox1" width="200">
  <webuijsf:checkbox id="checkbox1"
      selected="#{CustomerList.selected}"
      selectedValue="#{CustomerList.selected}"/>
</webuijsf:tableColumn>
```

Notice, we wrapped the invocation of our JavaScript function in a call to the
setTimeout() JavaScript function. The reason we need to do this is to force the
call to run in a separate thread. If we invoke our function directly, we run the risk
of having our application become unresponsive, as the method invocation may be
invoked after invoking other methods in the main JavaScript thread.

At this point, we have implemented all the logic necessary to select one or more rows
in the table, we implemented this functionality so that we can delete the selected
rows from the database.

The first thing we need to do is to create a data input page. This would be a simple
and straightforward page with text fields to enter a user's first name, middle name,
last name, and email address. After dropping all the components in the page and
adding the labels as appropriate, our page would look something like this:

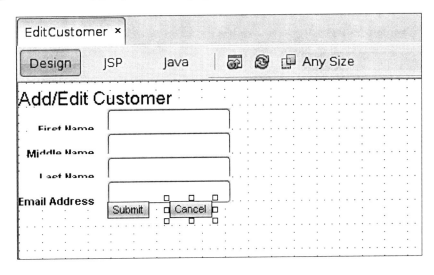

 When using the label attribute of text fields in adjacent rows, the labels
don't render properly in the **Design** window, however they do render
properly when the page is displayed in the browser.

After adding all the necessary components to the page, we need to bind each text field to a property in the `Customer` JPA entity. In order to do this, we need to add this entity as a managed bean. We need to open `faces-config.xml`, click on the **XML** tag, then right-click on the file and select **JavaServer Faces | Add Managed Bean...**.

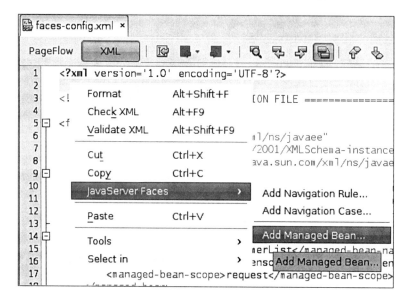

We need to enter a name for the new managed bean, select or type the fully qualified name of the managed bean class, and select a scope for the new managed bean.

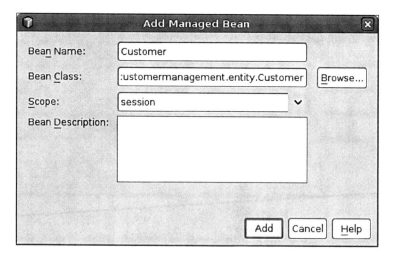

Once we have added the managed bean to the project, we need to bind the input fields in the data entry page to the appropriate properties in the bean. Since we added this bean manually to `faces-config.xml` it does not show up on the **Property Bindings** window when we right-click on the components on the **Design** or **Navigation** windows, therefore we need to add the bindings "by hand" by editing the JSP markup for our page.

```
<webuijsf:textField id="textField1" label="First Name "
    text="#{Customer.firstName}"/>
<webuijsf:textField id="textField2" label="Middle Name "
    text="#{Customer.middleName}"/>
<webuijsf:textField id="textField3" label="Last Name "
    text="#{Customer.lastName}"/>
<webuijsf:textField id="textField4" label="Email Address "
    text="#{Customer.email}"/>
```

 NetBeans code completion works when adding property bindings, after entering #{, hitting *Ctrl+Space* will show a list of all managed beans in the project. Ditto after typing the dot after the managed bean name.

Once we have created the bindings for the text fields, we need to add some logic to be executed when the **Save** or **Cancel** buttons are clicked.

Since we will be persisting `Customer` objects to the database, we need to use the `CustomerFacade` session bean. Therefore we need to add an instance variable of type `CustomerFacadeLocal` to the `EditCustomer` managed bean corresponding to our page.

```
@EJB
private CustomerFacadeLocal customerDAO;
```

The `@EJB` annotation is used so that the class is injected at runtime, freeing us from doing a JNDI lookup to locate it.

Double-clicking on the **Save** button in the **Design** window results in an action listener method being created for this button. We need to replace the body of this method to include our logic.

```
public String saveButton_action() {
    Customer customer = (Customer) getValue("#{Customer}");

    if (customer.getCustomerId() == null) {
        customerDAO.create(customer);
```

```
    } else {
        customerDAO.edit(customer);
    }

    return "success";
}
```

The first thing we do in this method is to obtain the current session scoped instance of the `Customer` managed bean by invoking `getValue()` (this method is inherited from `com.sun.rave.web.ui.appbase.FacesBean`). This method will be used both for updating an existing customer and for inserting a new customer to the database, therefore we need to check the value of its `customerId` property. If it is `null`, it means we are dealing with a new customer, therefore we need to insert it by invoking the `create()` method on the `CustomerFacade` session bean, otherwise we need to invoke its `merge()` method, which will update the corresponding row in the database. Finally we need to return a `String` to be used in the appropriate navigation rule in `faces-config.xml`.

At this point we are ready to implement the logic to be executed when the **Cancel** button is pressed, double-clicking on this button in the **Design** window automatically generates the action listener method.

```
public String cancelButton_action() {
    return "cancel";
}
```

All we need to do in this method is simply return a `String`, which will be used to navigate back to the **Customer Management** page when this button is pressed.

Now that we have a fully functional edit page, we need to add the remaining functionality to the Customer List page.

Double-clicking on the **Add New** button in the **Design** window results in the action listener method for this button being generated.

```
public String addNewButton_action() {
    setValue("#{sessionScope.Customer}", new Customer());
    return "addNew";
}
```

In this method we simply initialize the customer managed bean to a new instance of our `Customer` class and return a `String` to be used for page navigation.

The action listener method for the **Update** button can be generated by double-clicking on it.

```
public String updateButton_action() {
    RowKey rowKey = tableRowGroup1.getRowKey();
    Customer[] customerArray =
        getSessionBean1().getCustomerArray();
    Customer selectedCustomer =
        customerArray[Integer.parseInt(rowKey.getRowId())];

    setValue("#{sessionScope.Customer}",
        selectedCustomer);

    return "editCustomer";
}
```

In this method we need to find for which row the **Update** button was pressed, therefore we need to reference the `TableRowGroup` instance corresponding to the `<webuijsf:tableRowGroup>` tag in our page. The simplest way to bind the tag to an instance variable of the appropriate type in our managed bean is to click on the **tableRowGroup1** component in the **Navigator** window and select **Add Binding Attribute**.

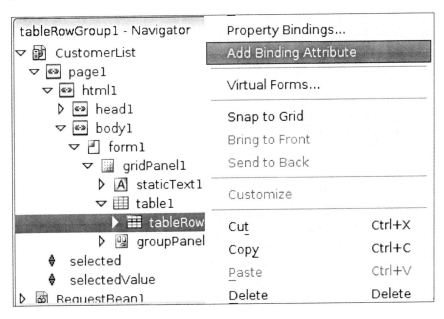

This will result in the appropriate instance variable and corresponding getter and setter methods being generated in our managed bean, as well as the `binding` attribute being added to the `<webuijsf:tableRowGroup>` tag. We can now use the generated `TableRowGroup` instance to obtain the row that was clicked on. Invoking the `getRowKey()` method on `TableRowGroup` returns an instance of `com.sun.data.provider.RowKey`. The returned `RowKey` instance corresponds to the row that was clicked on. By invoking its `getRowId()` method we can obtain a `String` representation of the index for the row that was clicked, which happens to correspond to the index of the corresponding `Customer` object in the `customerArray` property in the `SessionBean1` managed bean. Therefore by converting the returned value to an `int` we can obtain the appropriate `Customer` object.

Once we have obtained the appropriate `Customer` object from the customer array, we need to set it as the session scoped customer managed bean. We do this by invoking `setValue()` with the appropriate UEL expression as the first parameter and the `Customer` instance as the second parameter. The reason we are doing this is so the Edit page can get a hold of it, display its data, and update the database when its **Save** button is pressed.

As can be seen in the code previous, we need to explicitly specify that we want the `Customer` object in the session scope. If no scope is specified, `setValue()` by default will attach it to the request.

Now that we have implemented the logic to add and update customer data, we need to implement the logic to delete customers from the database. Double-clicking on the **Delete Selected** button generates its corresponding action listener method.

```java
public String deleteButton_action() {
  if (tableRowGroup1.getSelectedRowsCount() > 0) {
    RowKey[] selectedRowKeys =
        tableRowGroup1.getSelectedRowKeys();
    Customer[] customerArray =
        getSessionBean1().getCustomerArray();

    for (RowKey rowKey : selectedRowKeys) {
      customerDAO.remove(
          customerArray[Integer.parseInt(rowKey.getRowId())]);
    }
  }
  return null;
}
```

Once again in this method we need to use the `TableRowGroup` instance we created for the update logic. In this case we need to invoke its `getSelectedRowKeys()` method, which returns an array of `RowKey` objects corresponding to all the rows that are selected in the table.

In our method, we iterate through the selected `RowKey` objects, and delete each corresponding `Customer` object from the database by invoking the `remove()` method on the `CustomerFacade` session bean, and passing said object as a parameter.

Defining Navigation Rules

At this point we have implemented the logic to be performed when each and every button in our pages is clicked. Now all we need to do is to define navigation rules. This can be done graphically by opening `faces-config.xml`, clicking on the **PageFlow** tab, then connecting both pages and entering the corresponding return values for each action listener method to each connector as appropriate.

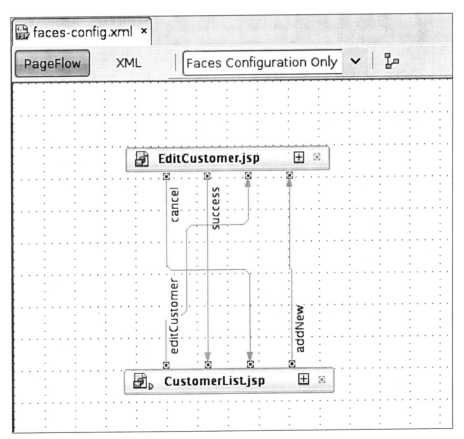

Testing the Completed Application

We now have finished developing our application, in order to test it we simply need to right-click on our enterprise project and select **Run**. At this point the application will be deployed and a browser window will open displaying the page containing the table. All data in the CUSTOMER database table is displayed in the table.

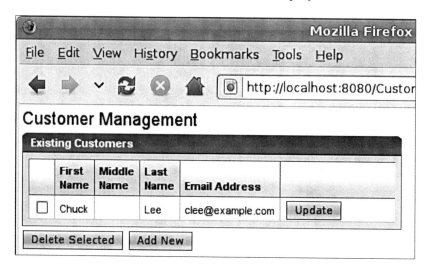

By clicking on the **Add New** button we navigate to the data entry page.

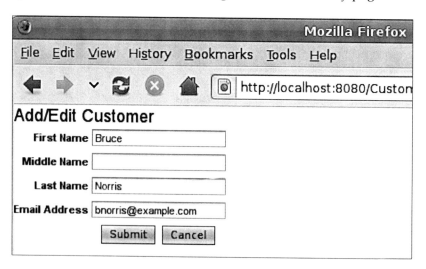

After entering some data and clicking on the **Submit** button, we navigate back to the **Customer Management** page and see the newly inserted row displayed on the table.

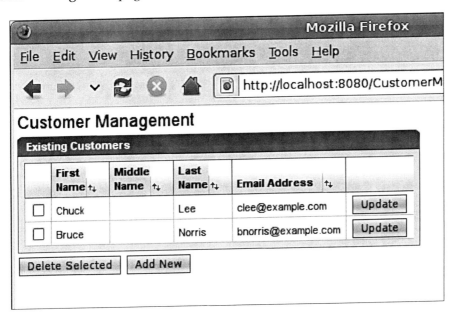

Clicking on the **Update** button for a row allows us to edit existing data.

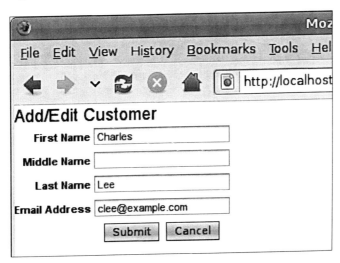

After modifying some of the data in the page and clicking **Submit**, we can see the updated data in the table.

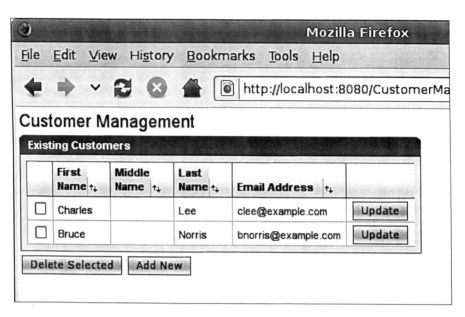

Clicking on one or more checkboxes results in the selected rows being highlighted.

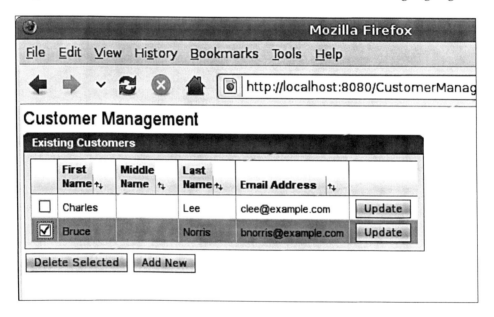

Finally, clicking **Delete Selected** results in the selected rows being deleted from the database.

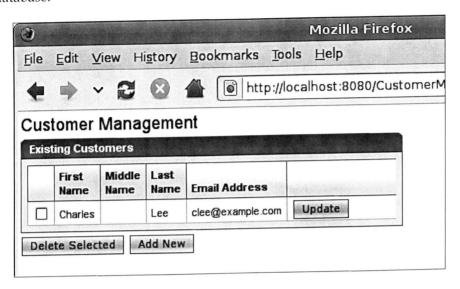

At this point we have verified all functionality in our application works as expected.

Summary

In this chapter we looked at how several of the technologies discussed in the book can be used together to create an enterprise application. We covered how to create **Java Persistence API (JPA)** entity beans by simply generating them from existing tables in the database.

Additionally, we saw how the Data Access Object (DAO) design pattern can be implemented by generating stateless session beans from existing JPA entities in our project. Session beans are a good choice when writing DAO logic with JPA since we can take advantage of EJB transactions without having to manually write any transaction handling code.

We also saw how to create a JSF application visually by taking advantage of NetBean's Visual Web JSF functionality. In our example we took a close look at the visual web table component, and how to write code to maintain its state on the server side. We also saw how NetBeans can generate JSF action listener methods by simply double-clicking on a component that fires an action event, such as the visual web button component.

Debugging Enterprise Applications with the NetBeans Debugger

Debuggers help us test and debug applications. NetBeans includes a debugger that can help us seamlessly debug all of our Java applications, including enterprise applications. In this appendix we will cover the NetBeans debugger, highlighting features that make our lives as Java EE developers easier.

Debugging Enterprise Applications

Typically debugging enterprise Java EE applications is somewhat a complicated process, and our application server needs to be started in "debug mode". The procedure for doing this is different depending on the application server, but typically involves passing some command line parameters to the shell script or executable that starts the application server. Our code must also be compiled with debugging enabled. This is usually done either setting a parameter on the IDE or passing some arguments to the `javac` executable. Also, our debugger must be "attached" to the application server so that it can see the code running in a separate JVM.

Thankfully, all of the steps described in the previous paragraph are automated when using NetBeans with the bundled GlassFish application server. When using this combination, all we need to do is open our Enterprise Application Project then right-click on it and select **Debug**. At this point the application server is started in debug mode (or restarted in debug mode if it was already running in standard mode), the application is deployed and the debugger is automatically attached to the application server.

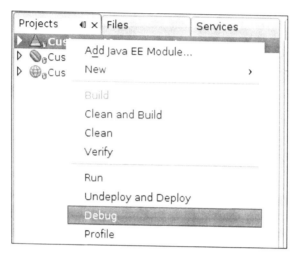

We will use the application we developed in Chapter 10 to illustrate NetBeans debugging capabilities. In order to illustrate such capabilities, we will make one slight modification to the application in order for it to break under certain circumstances. Recall that all JPA entities were generated for that application. When generating JPA entities with NetBeans, we either need to set the primary key explicitly when inserting a new row in the database, or we need to set automatic primary key generation using the @GeneratedValue annotation. In our example we used the second approach. In order to "force" our application to break when inserting new rows, we will remove this annotation from the Customer JPA entity.

After clicking the **Add New** button in our application, entering some data and clicking the **Save** button, we are now greeted with the following page.

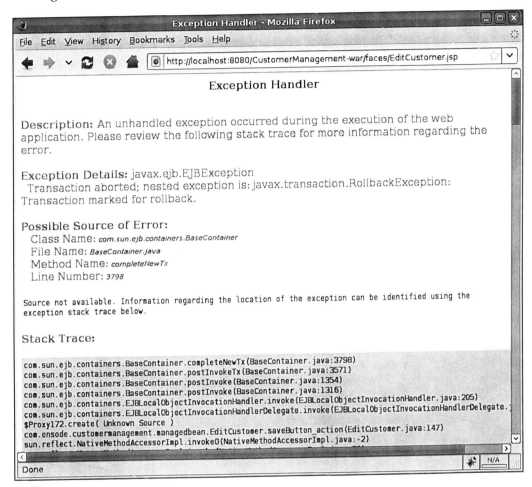

Looking closely at the **Stack Trace** displayed on the above page, we can see the following line:

com.ensode.customermanagement.managedbean.EditCustomer.saveButton_action(EditCustomer.java:147)

The above line is telling us that the exception occurred on line 147 of `EditCustomer.java`, therefore we need to pause our application's execution just before that line is executed, so that we can inspect the values of all relevant variables at that point.

One central feature of debuggers is the ability to pause execution of the application being debugged by adding **breakpoints** to it. When a line of code where a breakpoint has been placed is about to be executed, the application pauses, allowing us to inspect the values of all instance and method scoped variables in the class where the breakpoint was placed. In NetBeans, placing a breakpoint in a line is very simple; all we need to do is click on the left margin of the source editor right next to the line where the breakpoint will be added. At this point the line will be highlighted in red plus a red square icon will be placed in the left margin.

To make the left margin display line numbers, we need to right-click on it and click on the checkbox labeled **Show Line Numbers**.

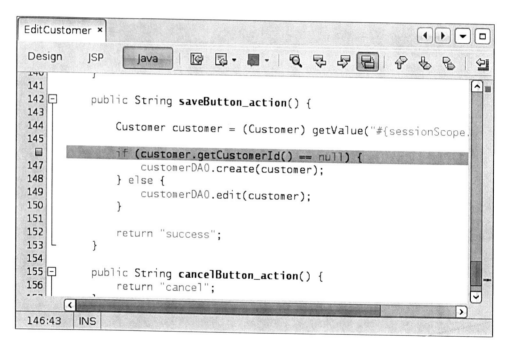

At this point we are ready to debug our application, which we can do by simply right-clicking on our project and selecting **Debug**. Doing this causes our application to be deployed and executed as in debug mode.

We need to test our application as usual in order to get to the point where it is failing. In our example we would simply click on the **Add New** button in the Customer list page, then enter some data for a new customer and click on the **Submit** button. At this point the line containing the breakpoint will be reached, and our application execution will be paused.

Looking at the editor, we will see that the line containing the breakpoint is now highlighted in green, plus an arrow has been placed on the left side margin.

These changes indicate the current line in the execution path. Once the execution has been paused, we can execute the code line-by-line in order to pinpoint exactly where the problem is happening. There are two ways we can execute each line: we can either **step over** the line, or **step into** it. The difference being when we step over, we will not go "into" any method calls, simply going "over" the line; when we step into, we actually navigate inside any method calls that are being invoked in the current line.

In our example, stepping into the current line would take us to the getCustomerId() method of the Customer class, which we are certain works correctly. Therefore the most appropriate course of action is to step over the current line.

In NetBeans, we can step over the current line by pressing *F8* or clicking on the 🖼 icon. Doing so will take us to the next line to be executed in the current file, which will be highlighted in green, and an arrow will be placed next to it in the left margin.

At this point we haven't reached the failure point of our application yet, and it seems unlikely that the problem will be in the current file. Therefore we need to step into the current line to navigate to the code in the create() method of the customerDAO object. In NetBeans, we step into code by clicking on the 🖼 icon or pressing *F7*.

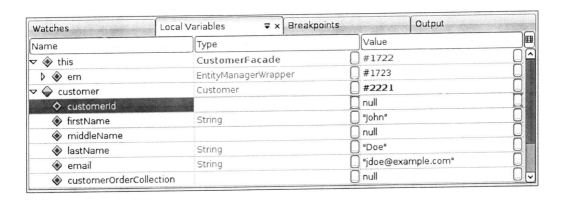

```
14 ┌ /**
15 │  *
16 │  * @author heffel
17 └  */
18    @Stateless
19    public class CustomerFacade implements CustomerFacadeLocal {
20        @PersistenceContext
21        private EntityManager em;
22
  ┌─      public void create(Customer customer) {
⇨              em.persist(customer);
25 └      }
26
  ┌─      public void edit(Customer customer) {
28            em.merge(customer);
29 └      }
30
```

```
24:1    INS
```

Since there is only one executable line in this method, we know that stepping over this line will cause the exception. We can inspect any local variables in the current class and method by looking at the **Local Variables** window.

 The **Local Variables** window can be opened by going to **Window | Debugging | Local Variables** or by pressing *Alt+Shift+1* on windows and Linux systems, and *Ctrl+Shift+1* on Mac OS X systems.

Name	Type	Value
▽ ◈ this	CustomerFacade	#1722
▷ ◈ em	EntityManagerWrapper	#1723
▽ ◆ customer	Customer	#2221
◇ customerId		null
◈ firstName	String	"John"
◈ middleName		null
◈ lastName	String	"Doe"
◈ email	String	"jdoe@example.com"
◈ customerOrderCollection		null

Watches   Local Variables   Breakpoints   Output

By expanding the node corresponding to our `customer` object, we can see the values of all of its properties. At this point we should notice that the `customerId` property is `null`, which results in the code attempting to insert a new row with a null primary key. We have discovered the problem. Now that the problem is known, fixing the code is trivial. In our example, the easiest way to fix it is to add the `@GeneratedValue` annotation to the `customerId` property of our entity bean.

Summary

In this appendix we covered how to debug enterprise applications using NetBeans. We saw how NetBeans makes debugging remote applications deployed to an application server as simple as debugging standard Java applications.

We also saw how we can add breakpoints to pause execution of our applications and either step into or step over each line.

Additionally we saw how we can inspect the values of all variables in scope by looking at the **Local Variables** window.

B

Identifying Performance Issues with NetBeans Profiler

Sometimes we run into performance problems in some of our applications. At times, identifying the code to be optimized may be trivial, but sometimes it is not easy. Profilers are tools that can help us pinpoint performance problems in our code. NetBeans comes with a very good profiler that we can use with our Java EE applications.

Profiling Our Application

All we need to do in order to profile our application is right-click on it in the **Projects** window and select **Profile**.

Before we can profile an application, we need to calibrate the NetBeans profiler by going to **Profile | Advanced Commands | Run Profiler Calibration**.

The first time we attempt to profile our application, the following dialog will pop-up:

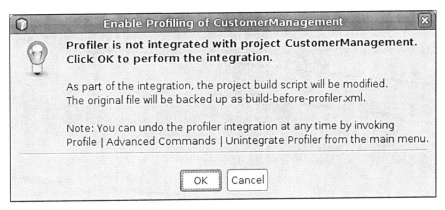

After clicking **OK**, NetBeans will make some changes to the project's build script to allow profiling our application, then the following dialog will pop-up:

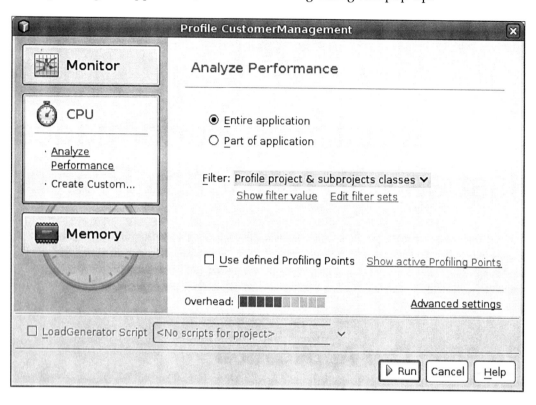

As we can see, there are several aspects of our application we can profile, such as memory allocation and CPU usage. One of the most useful features of the NetBeans profiler is the ability to report how long each method invocation in our application is taking. This information is provided when we profile CPU usage.

In order to start profiling, we simply click on the **Run** button. At this point the application server will start in profiling mode, and our application will be deployed and executed. After a few seconds the **Profiler** control panel will open.

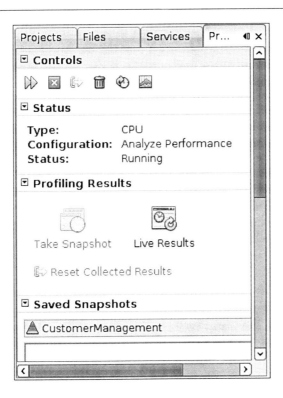

We can see how long each method is taking and how many times each method has been executed by simply clicking on the **Live Results** button.

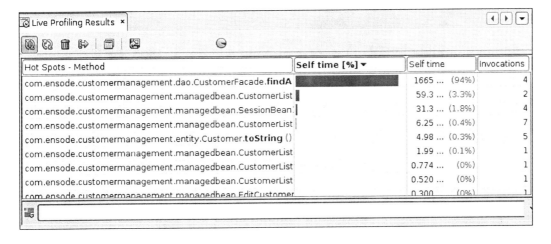

The **Live Profiling Results** window displays every method invocation, with the percentage of total time in the application that the method is using, the number of milliseconds the method takes to complete. It also shows how many times each method has been invoked.

As we can see, the NetBeans profiler can be very helpful in pinpointing areas of our application that are having performance problems, allowing us to easily identify these areas so that we can better focus our performance optimization efforts.

At this point we can take a snapshot so that we can compare performance of the application after we modify it in the future. We can take a snapshot by simply clicking on the icon labeled **Take Snapshot** in the **Profiler** window.

Taking a snapshot will result in a new tab being opened, displaying exactly the same information we saw in the **Live Profiling Results** window. We can save the snapshot by simply going to **File | Save**, or by using the usual keyboard shortcut, just like we save any other file.

At this point we will see our snapshot listed in the **Saved Snapshots** section of the **Profiler** window.

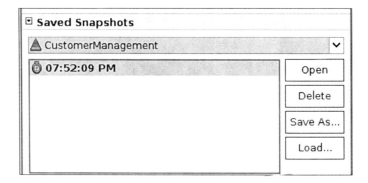

Although knowing how long each method in our application is taking to complete is very valuable information, it is by no means the only information we can obtain from the NetBeans profiler. We can see how much memory our application is using by simply opening the **VM Telemetry Overview** window by clicking on the ▨ icon on the Profiling control panel.

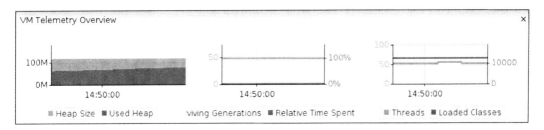

The graph on the left shows (in red) the total amount of heap allocated in our application's Java Virtual Machine, additionally, it shows the total amount of heap used by our application (in purple).

The graph in the middle is useful for detecting "memory leaks". (Java has garbage collection, therefore, in theory, memory leaks are impossible, however if we keep references to objects that are no longer needed, they are never garbage collected, therefore in practice a memory leak is possible.) The purple line in the middle graph indicates the amount of time the JVM spends doing garbage collection. The red line indicates "Surviving Generations". A generation is a set of objects that were created within two garbage collection intervals. A "Surviving Generation" is a generation that survived one or more garbage collections. We can force our application to garbage collect by clicking on the 🗑 icon in the Profiling control panel. If the graph indicates a high number of surviving generations between garbage collections, we might have a memory leak in our application.

The graph on the right of the **VM Telemetry Overview** window indicates the number of active threads and the number of loaded classes in our application.

Summary

The NetBeans profiler is a very valuable tool in identifying performance problems in our applications. It provides several useful tools to aid us in identifying poorly performing code, as well as allowing us to easily monitor memory usage and object allocation in our applications. More information about the NetBeans profiler can be found at http://profiler.netbeans.org/.

Index

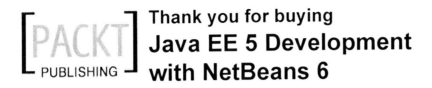

Thank you for buying
Java EE 5 Development
with NetBeans 6

About Packt Publishing

Packt, pronounced 'packed', published its first book "*Mastering phpMyAdmin for Effective MySQL Management*" in April 2004 and subsequently continued to specialize in publishing highly focused books on specific technologies and solutions.

Our books and publications share the experiences of your fellow IT professionals in adapting and customizing today's systems, applications, and frameworks. Our solution based books give you the knowledge and power to customize the software and technologies you're using to get the job done. Packt books are more specific and less general than the IT books you have seen in the past. Our unique business model allows us to bring you more focused information, giving you more of what you need to know, and less of what you don't.

Packt is a modern, yet unique publishing company, which focuses on producing quality, cutting-edge books for communities of developers, administrators, and newbies alike. For more information, please visit our website: www.packtpub.com.

Writing for Packt

We welcome all inquiries from people who are interested in authoring. Book proposals should be sent to author@packtpub.com. If your book idea is still at an early stage and you would like to discuss it first before writing a formal book proposal, contact us; one of our commissioning editors will get in touch with you.

We're not just looking for published authors; if you have strong technical skills but no writing experience, our experienced editors can help you develop a writing career, or simply get some additional reward for your expertise.

Java EE 5 Development using GlassFish Application Serv

ISBN: 978-1-847192-60-8   Paperback: 400 pages

The complete guide to installing and configuring the GlassFish Application Server and developing Java EE 5 applications to be deployed to this server

1. Concise guide covering all major aspects of Java EE 5 development

2. Uses the enterprise open-source GlassFish application server

3. Explains GlassFish installation and configuration

4. Covers all major Java EE 5 APIs

EJB 3 Developer Guide

ISBN: 978-1-847195-60-9   Paperback: 259 pages

A Practical Guide for developers and architects to the Enterprise Java Beans Standard

1. A rapid introduction to the features of EJB 3

2. EJB 3 features explored concisely with accompanying code examples

3. Easily enhance Java applications with new, improved Enterprise Java Beans

Please check **www.PacktPub.com** for information on our titles

JDBC 4.0 and Oracle JDeveloper for J2EE Development

ISBN: 978-1-847194-30-5   Paperback: 431 pages

A J2EE developer's guide to using Oracle JDeveloper's integrated database features to build data-driven applications

1. Develop your Java applications using JDBC and Oracle JDeveloper

2. Explore the new features of JDBC 4.0

3. Use JDBC and the data tools in Oracle JDeveloper

4. Configure JDBC with various application servers

5. Build data-driven applications quickly and easily

Service Oriented Architecture with Java

ISBN: 978-1-847193-21-6   Paperback: 192 pages

Using SOA and web services to build powerful Java applications

1. Build effective SOA applications with Java Web Services

2. Quick reference guide with best-practice design examples

3. Understand SOA concepts from core with examples

4. Design scalable inter-enterprise communication

Please check **www.PacktPub.com** for information on our titles

Printed in the United Kingdom by
Lightning Source UK Ltd., Milton Keynes
138848UK00001B/67/P